Information at War

Information at War

Journalism, Disinformation, and Modern Warfare

Philip Seib

polity

First published in 2021 by Polity Press

Polity Press
65 Bridge Street
Cambridge CB2 1UR, UK

Polity Press
101 Station Landing
Suite 300
Medford, MA 02155, USA

ISBN-13: 978-1-5095-4856-9
ISBN-13: 978-1-5095-4857-6 (pb)

A catalogue record for this book is available from the British Library.
Library of Congress Cataloging-in-Publication Data
Names: Seib, Philip M., 1949- author.
Title: Information at war : journalism, disinformation, and modern warfare / Philip Seib.
Description: Cambridge, UK ; Medford, MA : : Polity Press, 2021. | Includes bibliographical references and index. | Summary: "A smart, wide-ranging introduction to the role of information in warfare from WWI to Russiagate"-- Provided by publisher.
Identifiers: LCCN 2020047011 (print) | LCCN 2020047012 (ebook) | ISBN 9781509548569 (hardback) | ISBN 9781509548576 (paperback) | ISBN 9781509548583 (epub)
Subjects: LCSH: Mass media and war. | War in mass media. | Information warfare. | War--Press coverage. | Disinformation. | Propaganda--Technological innovations.
Classification: LCC P96.W35 S45 2021 (print) | LCC P96.W35 (ebook) | DDC 070.4/333--dc23
LC record available at https://lccn.loc.gov/2020047011
LC ebook record available at https://lccn.loc.gov/2020047012

Typeset in 10.5 on 12 Sabon
by Fakenham Prepress Solutions, Fakenham, Norfolk NR21 8NL
Printed and bound by CPI Group (UK) Ltd, Croydon, CR0 4YY

For further information on Polity, visit our website:
politybooks.com

A great part of the information obtained in war is contradictory, a still greater part is false, and by far the greatest part is of doubtful character.

Carl von Clausewitz, *On War*

Contents

Preface and Acknowledgments   ix

Introduction   1
1   Living-Room Wars   16
2   Competing for Information Control   42
3   War Information Expands   68
4   Social Media Go to War   94
5   Russia and New Dimensions of Information at War   115
6   From Media Manipulation to Media Literacy   151
7   Where We've Been, Where We're Going   172

Notes   188
Selected Bibliography   212
Index   215

Preface and Acknowledgments

I have been writing about media and war for several decades, focusing mostly on 20th- and early 21st-century conflicts. "Media" in that context meant mostly traditional print and broadcast journalism, and cases such as the Vietnam War and Iraq War provided plenty to write about.

Then came the media explosion: regional and global satellite television channels that could sail above many of the world's borders, and the internet-based information venues that made obsolete the notion of the "audience" as merely a passive recipient of information. Within the span of a few years, many of the nearly 8 billion people on the planet had access not just to unprecedented quantities of journalism, but also information about health, education, making a living, and other essential topics (with some cat videos added to the mix).

The democratization of the information process has had profound effects. When George Floyd was killed on a Minneapolis street in May 2020, how did we find out about it? A bystander captured the horrific episode on a cellphone camera, and within a short time the video could be seen by much of the world. When Bashar al-Assad murdered his own people with chemical weapons, how did we learn it had happened? Some brave Syrians filmed and described events and posted the information online. Again, the world became a witness.

Information is powerful, and if it is accurate and meaningful, the more the better; the public benefits. But the new information venues also lend themselves to manipulation, including governments' efforts to destabilize other nations' political systems. Such weaponization of information requires countermeasures that depend on the public understanding the components of media literacy. Meanwhile, militaries are finding that information can be a valuable supplement to conventional weaponry, making their own efforts more effective and undermining adversaries' willingness to fight.

These are complex and vital matters. This book is designed to stimulate thinking about the past, present, and future of information at war.

Acknowledgments

Several of my students at the University of Southern California (USC) served as my research assistants during the writing of this book: Adriana Robakowski, Felix Bartos, and Fatime Uruci. They worked hard, and I thank them all. Also at USC, I have consistently been supported by Annenberg School Dean Willow Bay and Journalism School Director Gordon Stables.

Others who helped include another USC student, Christopher Cheshire, who provided some bibliographic material, and an international array who read parts of the manuscript and supplied comments and specialized material: Mariami Khatiashvili, Barbora Maronkova, Di Wu, and Mohamed Zayani. They all have my gratitude.

Polity Books is once again a wonderful partner. Publisher Louise Knight and her assistant Inès Boxman are quick and thorough in all editorial matters, and they are consistently a pleasure to work with. I also thank the two anonymous reviewers whom Polity asked to read my draft manuscript. Their suggestions were most helpful.

Much of my writing took place amidst the Covid-19 pandemic and social isolation. I was buoyed by the friendship of Anita Yagjian. Special thanks to Machiavelli (Mac) Seib, my canine companion and editorial assistant, who helped me retain a bit of sanity by requiring frequent trips outdoors.

Introduction

Rage – Goddess, sing the rage of Peleus's son Achilles,
murderous, doomed, that cost the Achaeans countless losses,
hurtling down to the House of Death so many sturdy souls,
great fighters' souls, but made their bodies carrion,
feasts for the dogs and birds,
and the will of Zeus was moving toward its end.
Begin, Muse, when the two first broke and clashed,
Agamemnon lord of men and brilliant Achilles.

Homer, *The Iliad*[1]

Before social media, there were bards. They provided information about war to scattered listeners as they traveled the countryside and recited their stories of warriors and gods to audiences enthralled by tales of bloody daring. In Homer's case, his vivid reporting about the siege of Troy was delivered about four centuries after the events he described, a concept that may be hard to grasp by those of us accustomed to real-time bulletins from today's battlefields.

The *Iliad* has through the years been an anchor in the history of conflict. Like many tales of war, it is both horrifying and rousing. The *Iliad* dates to roughly 3,000 years ago, but its depictions of combat are not too far removed from the grittiest reporting from Syria, Somalia, Afghanistan, and other places dominated by contemporary warriors' rage.

People throughout the world today may be distant in time and space from most conflicts, but instead of depending on the occasional bard's visit to learn about a war hundreds of years after it was fought, we can now get information about war quickly and constantly. Our televisions and mobile devices can bring us war as it is being fought. We stare at the wine-dark blood of a distant battlefield for a few moments and then casually move on to more information from more sources about more topics.

Information at war is sometimes history. Without Homer's words, what would we know about the Trojan War? Spearheads and chunks of pottery from a spot in today's Turkey are information of a sort, but such artifacts do not stir the spirit as words do. And today, words need not stand alone; they arrive supplemented by sounds and images from the battleground.

We will see that information at war has many functions, memorializing wars of the past and shaping wars of the present. As was the case on the plains of Troy, rage still begets more rage, and fighters' souls continue to hurtle down to the House of Death. Warfare's carnage belongs to no single epoch. As in Homer's time, there are today plenty of wars. Inflicting death and destruction for purportedly noble reasons remains a persistent trait of humankind.

"Information" can appear in varied forms. In this book, one mutation of information that will receive considerable attention is *disinformation*, which has been defined by UNESCO as "information that is false and deliberately created to harm a person, social group, organization, or country." This is different from *misinformation*, which is "information that is false but not created with the intention of causing harm," and it may be disseminated in the belief that is true. Another category is *mal-information*, that is "based on reality, but is used to inflict harm," such as true information that violates someone's privacy without a public interest justification.[2] (The work of gossip columnists and paparazzi may be included in this category.) Disinformation has long been used by governments as a weaponized form of communication that is a tool of warfare. Today's technologies make this more pervasive and more effective.

Some other terms used in this book are these:

- "troll": communicator, human or mechanical, of inflammatory material designed to provoke or harass;
- "bot": performs automated tasks, such as high-speed, high-volume retweeting or attacks on a computer network;
- "deepfake": video and speech combination for which a computer has learned appearance and speech patterns of the targeted

subject. (If you see a realistic online video of Barack Obama endorsing Donald Trump, you may assume it is a deepfake.)

Another principal focus of this book is war journalism. With so much recent emphasis on disinformation as a way to affect public opinion, the importance of the news media is sometimes overlooked. When considering information at war, a holistic approach is needed. Despite efforts in numerous countries to undermine the credibility of journalists – through tactics that include labeling their work "fake news" and in some places imprisoning them (or worse)[3] – much of the global public still uses news coverage as an important element in shaping opinions about wars near and far.

Among the constituencies of conflict are those who fight wars, those who use their power to bring about and manage armed conflict, those who disseminate information about wars, and those who consume that information. This book examines slices of their shared stories, beginning in the mid twentieth century, when the rise of radio, and its bards such as Murrow and Shirer and Sevareid, marked the start of the era in which broadcasting brought timely information that helped redefine publics' perceptions of the nature and costs of war.[4]

War's evolution has been shaped by shifts in geopolitics and by advances in technology. In scattered combat zones, states fight among themselves, against non-states (such as Al Qaeda), and sometimes against their own people (the Syrian War that began in 2011 being one example). As for the tools of war, we have moved from the longbow to the ballistic missile, and in the information universe from the messenger racing on horseback to the satellites and cellphones that reach billions.

Information at war has always been a weapon in itself – generating anger, sorrow, determination, and other facets of mass psychology that can influence the outcomes of conflict. As we will see, in the twenty-first century roles for information have become truly integral, rather than merely supplemental, parts of warfare.

Information can now circle the globe in moments, and few boundaries can stop it.

More significant than the gadgets of communication technology are the ways in which global publics have been able to use information tools to understand and affect the course of conflict. They have become more than spectators. Billions of people have devices that allow them not only to watch warriors in action, but also to tell potentially vast audiences what they themselves are seeing and add their own comments (some accurate, some not) to the flow of war-related information. Individual combatants themselves sometimes describe their views.[5] Distances between fighters, professional information providers, and the public continue to shrink, while the ranks of those who share information have expanded dramatically. Twitter and its kin have become, in some cases, instruments of war.

Intensified scrutiny, both objective and biased, changes the ways in which wars are conducted. No conflict is detached from politics, and information helps tighten the connection. Information can alter the level of accountability of those who authorize and pay for wars, as well as the responsibilities of those who do the fighting. Those who decide to wage war must be able to influence – if not wholly control – information.

Henry Kissinger wrote that what has great significance in world affairs "is not only the number of people with access to information; it is, even more importantly, how they analyze it. Since the mass of information available tends to exceed the capacity to evaluate it, a gap has opened up between information and knowledge and, even beyond that, between knowledge and wisdom."[6] Ideally, thoughtful consideration of information at war will help to close that gap.

One slice of this book's overall topic is "media and war," which has been the subject of many studies that focus on a relationship that is in some ways symbiotic but usually maintains some level of separation between its two elements. "Media" in such analyses is usually equated with *news* media, and the journalism of war is a rich field that continues to produce important examinations of how wars are fought and managed. Especially in democracies, independently gathered and reported news content has long been a factor in how wars are perceived. Journalists' depictions of a particular victory or defeat can influence public opinion and shape the course of a war. The accuracy or inaccuracy of that reporting may have profound effect on policy. This was the case during the 1968 Tet offensive in Vietnam, among other instances. That coverage and other reporting from the Vietnam War (addressed in chapter 1) has seen, over the years, its accuracy challenged,[7] and it has clearly contributed to increasingly adversarial dealings between press and government. This dynamic tension fosters an environment in which the motives and even the patriotism of the protagonists have been called into question. When carried to extreme levels, such vilification may not only affect war-making but also jostle the foundations of civil society.

Fast and easy access to information through social media and other venues has changed the role of gatekeepers – traditionally the news organizations through which information has long been channeled and filtered on its way to the public. The universe of information providers is much larger today, and it keeps growing, which means the concept of "information hegemony" is increasingly obsolete. This increased number of information sources sometimes contributes to a "clash of emotions," which can shape a political environment in ways that affect whether or how a war is fought.[8]

This has led to non-journalistic media influencing warfighting in new ways. Even governments that have long controlled the information that reaches the public have learned that they can be circumvented with increasing frequency. Censors can be eluded, and firewalls can be scaled – not always, but frequently enough to broaden the range of voices making themselves heard about war.[9]

In this volume, perhaps more significant than conventional issues related to news media performance during war is the weaponization of information itself. We have moved into an era beyond news media monopolization of information about armed conflict. "Information" in this context has, to an unprecedented degree, become much more than "news" as we have traditionally known it, and it is affecting warfare in ways that continue to evolve at a brisk pace. Because information has become so easy to gather – or to invent – and disseminate, state and non-state actors can wield it to stir anger, sabotage elections, and soften or stiffen the resolve of citizens who are too often treated as mere pawns in politics and conflict.

Can information start a war? Not on its own, but it certainly can influence the likelihood of one. When the Hearst and Pulitzer newspapers in the United States were screaming for war against Spain in 1898, they affected the American political environment and nudged, if not pushed, President William McKinley toward war.[10] Today, an individual or group putting inflammatory material on social media can help cause civil disorder, and perhaps – in combination with other factors – incite pro-war sentiment.

Information conveyed through popular culture also can affect attitudes about war.[11] *Mrs. Miniver*, a British film (based on a best-selling novel) released in 1942, showed audiences in the United Kingdom and elsewhere how heroically resolute the British people were, even in the face of heavy bombing and the evacuation from Dunkirk. German propaganda minister Joseph Goebbels noted its effectiveness, saying, "There is not a single angry word spoken against Germany; nevertheless, the anti-German tendency is perfectly accomplished."[12] The Germans themselves knew the value of cinematic propaganda, as exemplified by films such as Leni Riefenstahl's *Triumph of the Will*. Through the Second World War, the Cold War, and beyond, fictive and documentary films have been, to varying degrees, persuasive in how publics view specific conflicts and war generally. A detailed examination of this topic is outside the scope of this book, but it is an intriguing field for exploration.

Information's credibility has long been affected by the venues through which it is presented, but these venues are now so plentiful that information consumers may lack the knowledge needed to distinguish among sources and weigh their relative credibility as they decide what to believe. Online content competes with the media forms to which we grew accustomed during earlier decades. YouTube rivals television; websites and the likes of Facebook and Twitter vie with print; text messaging and email supersede face-to-face conversation and provide incessant updates about events. The speed and variety of providers have few limits, and members of the public dip into various offerings with a click or a tap that unleashes a river of information that washes over them.

This book is about relationships among primary contributors to information at war, including the public, which must be defined broadly. Some members of the public watch war as if it was a spectator sport; the television or cellphone screen does not drip the blood of combat onto the living-room carpet, and escaping a war zone is merely a matter of switching channels or clicking on another app. Others might have much more at stake: those who are themselves caught up in war, including the noncombatants who become "collateral damage" (an obscenely cold-blooded term) as war's fury touches their lives. Some of these may choose to be "citizen journalists" themselves, tweeting, blogging, or otherwise presenting information about the rage of warriors and the damage they inflict.

Information tools available to the public are also used increasingly by conflicts' actors themselves. Within recent years, we have seen inflammatory – and often false – information deployed within targeted populations as part of long- or short-term provocation leading toward military action, as was the case with Russia's 2014 invasion of Ukraine.[13] Joining the ranks of conflict-related communicators are "trolls," "bots," and other mechanical and human spreaders of tales that are designed to disrupt. "Deepfakes," for instance, can look and sound so real that they can mislead even those who consider themselves to be savvy information consumers.

Distorted information has long been used for military advantage. To some extent, this could be offset by influential mainstream information providers with the skill and wherewithal to verify and, if needed, correct misleading material. In recent decades, these have included trusted print publications as well as many of the foundational news broadcasts on radio and television, their ranks expanded by global and regional cable and satellite news networks. Today, however, that policing role has shriveled due to the ease with which global publics can obtain information directly from an always-growing universe of sources, some of which have negligible allegiance to truth.

We are in a transitional period during which individuals are learning (at varied speeds) how to navigate the sea of information. Which information providers offer safe harbors with reliably accurate content? Which ones are actually whirlpools that lure audiences with appealingly angry messages? How can the public distinguish among them? What level of media literacy is essential in the information era?[14]

War is always with us in one way or another. Information can change the course of war, and war can change the role of information. The persistence of conflict and the relentless flow of information ensure that information at war will long continue to be part of our lives.

This book proceeds roughly chronologically.

During war, as at other times, information can make the remote seem proximate. The first true "living-room war" was a function of radio, and one of the most distinctive voices early in the era of electronic media was a young man born near Polecat Creek, North Carolina – Edward R. Murrow. As we see in chapter 1, "Living-Room Wars," Murrow told many of his stories of war from the battle zone in real time, which captivated their audience and heightened their impact. His voice came into American living-rooms from across the Atlantic in 1940 as Great Britain was enduring intense German bombing, and his reports helped to chip away at the isolationism that was strongly influencing US politics. His work and that of other journalists provided President Franklin D. Roosevelt with room to maneuver as he sought to help keep Britain afloat in its fight against Nazi Germany.

War being brought into the living-room also had great effect two decades later, when television had been established as a principal news provider. By 1960, nearly 90 percent of American households had a television set,[15] and seeing as well as hearing about war on a continuing basis would sharpen public perceptions about the nature of conflict. As portrayed by some in the news media, the costs of the fighting in Southeast Asia and the apparent endlessness of that war fueled Americans' growing doubts about the necessity of such a conflict.

While television coverage was capturing attention, journalists working in other media were also wielding increasing influence. Certain print journalists made clear that they were not "on the team" in terms of shaping their reporting to conform to government officials' wishful thinking. Correspondents such as David Halberstam of the *New York Times* aggressively challenged the purported wisdom of "the best and the brightest" policymakers.[16] Such print reporters' diligence, coupled with the dramatic force of television, reshaped the balance of power between news media and government in wartime. With increased amounts of vivid information available to them, more and more Americans had grounds for doubting, and then opposing, the war policies of their elected leaders.

Television's rise also contributed to greater emphasis on the *optics* of war. In itself, this was nothing new. From the armor of Achilles gleaming in front of the walls of Troy to the giant missiles in parades through Red Square (and, more recently, Pyongyang), the appearance of military might has affected fighters' and publics' attitudes about their prospects in conflict. When news media deliver consistently pessimistic appraisals supported by grim visual evidence, a government (at least in a democracy) must devote ever greater effort to sustain popular backing for a war. This may include attempts to counteract the effects of information that the government deems to be an obstacle to achieving its goals in the conflict. That might be done in a number of ways, such as by interfering with collection and dissemination of information perceived to be unhelpful, and by the government producing its own information to offset unsupportive content.

Information has value only if it is credible. During wartime, government and news media may engage in a struggle for primacy in credibility, and the viability of the war effort may be shaped by the outcome. Newer information providers – including individuals – are now part of the mix. Sometimes their content offers valuable perspective on events, but sometimes their material may be politicized to the point of being fraudulent. This makes careful appraisal of information's validity more important among information consumers who find such decisions complicated by the sheer volume of information flowing toward them.

As chapter 2, "Competing for Information Control," illustrates, when governments recognize unhelpful political repercussions of news coverage of conflict, they might resort to simple obstruction, such as taking advantage of complex logistics to delay reports from the battleground. During the Falklands War between Great Britain and Argentina in 1982, the British Ministry of Defence controlled the transmission of news from the remote location of the fighting.[17] During the 1991 Persian Gulf War, the US Department of Defense kept war-zone journalists on a tight leash, impeding their reporting. This involved supervising reporters' interviews and delaying communication of reports.[18]

Some of these constraints were a matter of political convenience rather than military necessity, but journalists themselves were coming to recognize that technology-enabled advances in real-time reporting could prove problematic. In the 1991 Gulf War, television networks and even local television stations could use satellite transmission to report live to their audiences during the fighting. Enemy militaries could tap into these broadcasts and learn, for example, about the efficacy of their artillery and missile attacks. Military officials and news executives knew they had to address this, preferably in a joint effort. There *would* be some degree of censorship, and news organizations had to determine how much of it they would impose on themselves rather than leaving that decision solely to the military.[19]

Such realization led, a decade later, to the cooperative venture of embedding about 700 American and international journalists with US military units during the early stages of the Iraq War that began in 2003. The embed process was designed cooperatively by the Defense Department and representatives from the news media, and technology was a factor in the Pentagon's rulemaking. Military commanders knew that satellite broadcasting capability had expanded significantly since the 1991 Gulf War, with gear that was more portable and affordable, and so journalists would have greater ability to escape constraints and report on their own. Beyond that, the military wanted to influence news content without appearing to be doing so. Making journalists beholden for access (and personal safety) was a way to accomplish that. For their part, news organizations wanted to bring their audiences timely, exciting, "up close" reporting from the frontlines. The arrangements that were agreed upon were far from perfect, but they more or less served the interests of both parties.[20]

The military units in which journalists were embedded found themselves with their mission expanded in a nontraditional way. Fighting the Iraqi enemy was the principal task, but some soldiers' frontline responsibilities now included feeding, housing, and safeguarding a coterie of journalists. Most of these journalists had never served in the military and had received only brief training in matters such as first aid and dealing with a chemical weapons attack. Despite their occasional bravado, these men and women were amateurs among warfighting professionals, and they had to be treated with care by their hosts.[21]

The military wanted to facilitate news gathering that would show US efforts in the most favorable light to ensure continued popular support from the American public. With the 9/11 attacks of 2001 still very much on the public's and journalists' minds, some news organizations decided that putting a patriotic spin on their coverage would appeal to news consumers (and advertisers).[22] Mutually beneficial coexistence between combat operations and journalism was becoming a more integral element of military and journalistic doctrine.

Nevertheless, with the Vietnam War still a frequently cited precedent, the government and news media continue at times to wrestle for control of the information flow. As journalists know, the boundaries between "military necessity" and "political expedience" can sometimes be hard to discern when it comes to withholding information or making it available to the public.

Chapter 3, "War Information Expands," considers the broadened scope of war-related information-gathering. While wars keep being fought and journalists keep covering them, use of new information technologies has extended well beyond the professionals to whom it had long been limited. Perhaps the most revolutionary new tool is the cellphone camera. With it, unseen wars can be brought into the vision of governments and publics, and they can decide whether this information merits intervention in response. Today we can look into the past and ask, "What if ...?" about previous wars. What if Tutsis in Rwanda in 1994 had been able to show the world their country's genocide in progress? Would foreign governments have responded more promptly? A half-century before that, what if the Holocaust had been documented as it happened? Would the Allied powers have altered their strategy and made liberating the Nazi concentration camps a higher priority?

The list of such questions is virtually endless. The device so many of us carry in our pockets today may not have been available to alter events and save lives in the past, but it might do so today. Along with other tools, it is used by "citizen journalists" who have little or no formal journalism training but gather and disseminate descriptions and images of events that take place in front of them. Established news organizations see them as assets. The BBC, for instance, may ask witnesses to terrorist attacks and other such occurrences to provide photos, video, and general information that can be included in news reports.[23] Sometimes a deluge of responses is the result. At first glance, this may seem to be a valuable expansion of the flow of news. But vetting can be difficult; once the door is opened, fraudulent photos, videos, and text might come racing through. This means news organizations must pay particular attention to the accuracy of material from citizen journalists. Errors may be deliberate or accidental, but they should not be presented to the public.[24]

Nevertheless, citizen journalists' work can have great value. Syrians reporting from their hometowns during the war that began in 2011 have bravely provided coverage from places that conventional news organizations cannot (or dare not) reach. Rulers such as Syrian President Bashar al-Assad are finding it more difficult to slaughter their opponents without the rest of the world learning about it. How the world will respond to atrocities documented in real time remains open to question, but perhaps this new dimension of information availability will somewhat alter the calculations of bloodletting.

"Slaughter" is not too strong a word to describe what happens in a war, and not just to combatants. Civilian casualties and the destruction of homes, schools, hospitals, and much else tend to receive only secondary attention; they are the detritus of war. But some in the news media and those working for humanitarian organizations are determined that the world should know about this aspect of the costs of war. Cold objectivity sometimes is set aside in favor of a "journalism of attachment" that tells the truth about wartime savagery as it affects individuals.[25]

In chapter 4, "Social Media Go to War," examples of social media's effects on conflict are reviewed. More sophisticated than citizen journalists are the information arms of nations' militaries. They battle each other on social media, making their respective cases to near and distant audiences. Given that so many media venues are now global in reach, the contest over worldwide public opinion accompanies even conflicts in which the physical battlefield is small and isolated. Such has been the case between the Israel Defense Forces (IDF) and the Hamas fighters of Gaza. In terms of basic military power, this is a mismatch; the IDF possess much more firepower and other war-fighting technology than their Palestinian opponents do. In an all-out conventional confrontation, the IDF would certainly prevail. But political factors somewhat limit Israel's combat options, and on the information battleground social media can serve Hamas as a kind of political equalizer if users possess the skills needed to produce attention-getting content.

The IDF–Hamas conflict is relatively transparent for those who want to watch the two sides make their cases in an online debate in which they are armed with words and images. But make no mistake – people still die while the barrages of information fly back and forth.

Non-state actors such as terrorist groups have also found that social media offer congenial platforms for their information purposes. Islamic State, Al Qaeda, and others have relied on online tools for recruiting, fundraising, and delivering a mix of threats and self-promotion, as well as for on-the-ground combat coordination. They use traditional news releases, in several languages, to tout their latest bloody accomplishments, and although mainstream media organizations can deny these extremist groups access to the public through their own venues, wholly excluding tech-smart users from social media is difficult. When Twitter sought to purge Islamic State messaging, it closed down more than 100,000 accounts in just one month, but it was far from certain that this effort had been as comprehensive as intended, and many of these accounts may have been swiftly reconstituted, either on Twitter or in "darker" recesses of the internet. Dealing with terrorist information initiatives will become more important if Islamic State concentrates on a virtual, rather than physical, caliphate, and if groups such as Boko Haram and Al Shabaab become more adept in their online efforts.[26]

Gatekeepers have always been present in one form or another to govern information flows. In some cases, such as in China, these are government censors who rigidly oversee content before it can reach the public. In countries where information freedom is respected, newspaper editors, television producers, and other media professionals make decisions about newsworthiness based on criteria ranging from basic moral values to commercial interests such as keeping advertisers happy.

These gatekeepers were particularly influential when the media universe was more finite. Fifty years ago in the United States, consumers of television news had only three national channels to choose from, and newspapers served only limited geographic areas. Today, in much of the world, there is no such thing as local, or even national, news in terms of limitations on distribution to an audience. Even many small community newspapers rely on their websites to deliver their product, and so people anywhere in the world with internet access may read about town council doings and school lunch menus. On a grander scale, online news and satellite television are largely unconstrained by national borders. Citizens of most nations can read, listen, or watch how news media in other countries cover their own and others' homelands. Governments that don't want this coverage to reach their populations must struggle mightily to choke off incoming material that they find uncongenial.

Although gatekeepers still make decisions about newsworthiness and appropriateness of content of their own products, much of the information universe today is populated not by traditional providers but rather by websites, videos, and text content carried by the likes of Twitter, Facebook, Weibo, QQ, YouTube, and many others. For the most part (with the exception of extreme content, such as child pornography, that government regulators or communication companies themselves ban), the material that citizens around the world see on social media passes through limited or no review processes. Most gateways for information are wide open, and damaging material might not be flagged except *post facto*. Artificial intelligence systems that rely on screening algorithms are useful, but not foolproof.[27]

Is the result of this openness information democracy or information anarchy? Probably some of both. For refugees in Congo wanting to tell their story to the world, having direct access to global publics is invaluable. For the workers in a Russian troll farm using false information to provoke conflict in a foreign country, their access is similarly vital.

Chapter 5, "Russia and New Dimensions of Information at War," analyzes disinformation. This kind of war-by-influence has existed for many years. In 1940 and 1941, while Edward Murrow was broadcasting from London about the plight of the British under attack by Nazi Germany, British agents operating in New York City were producing information – much of it false – designed to push America toward entering the war.[28]

Their efforts pale by comparison with those orchestrated today by the Kremlin, which has made information warfare a principal element in its military doctrine while it relies on troll factories and other content generators to disseminate largely false information that serves the purposes of Russian foreign policy.[29] The key to their efforts is volume, with hundreds of trolls producing thousands of online messages every day.

Measuring the effects of contemporary political information warfare is still a developing science, but it is reasonable to assume that Russian disinformation efforts had at least some impact on the 2016 US presidential election and the 2016 British "Brexit" referendum. Further, such self-serving information tactics can be used to influence public attitudes about kinetic measures such as Russia's invasion of Ukraine in 2014.[30]

Just as major militaries have had to expand their expertise beyond grand battlefield scenarios and adjust to the demands of combatting insurgencies and terrorists, so too must they develop strategies to address the exigencies of information-centric conflict. For now, Vladimir Putin's Kremlin and Islamic State stand out as having relied heavily on information-enhanced tactics, but they will almost certainly be joined by others. The United States has responded, targeting terrorists' online recruitment efforts and, in November 2018, launching a preemptive electronic attack on a Russian troll farm to prevent possible disruption of that month's US congressional elections.[31]

Nevertheless, it is more than likely that state and non-state actors will continue to develop their information war capabilities. The Putin government has shown – in Ukraine, the Baltic States, and elsewhere – that it is committed to mastering the human–machine combination of hybrid warfare that relies heavily on information tactics. In addition to using information in armed conflict, Russia vigorously uses information to disrupt political processes within rival countries, such as the United States, as well as in Europe. One question this book addresses is whether such activity can reach a point at which it constitutes "war," even if no bullets are fired. NATO has adopted a policy that expands the definition of "attack" beyond conventional armed conflict and now includes cyberattacks. Individual nations might soon do the same.[32]

Chapter 6, "From Media Manipulation to Media Literacy," examines cases related to information at war in the Middle East, Afghanistan, and elsewhere, and addresses how the flow of information can shape public attitudes about those who fight. This chapter also considers how publics around the world might adjust to the threats posed by information warfare. On their own and through broad-based education programs, citizens need to enhance their media literacy. They must know when to greet information with skepticism, and they must understand how to go about verifying news and other material, particularly online content delivered from unfamiliar sources. Truth is a powerful weapon to be used against malign information, and the public must become far more proficient at wielding that weapon.

Anticipatory information at war is present even when armed conflict is unlikely. Disinformation about the Covid-19 virus, vaccinating children against measles and other illnesses, and similar topics can be used to foster uncertainty and disunity among publics of nations that are considered long-term adversaries. Probing and softening a country's resolve are parts of the long game of information at war – laying a foundation for possible future conflicts.

Chapter 7, "Where We've Been, Where We're Going," pulls together elements from past and present and considers what might lie ahead. Shakespeare wrote "What is past is prologue," and another way to say that is "Nothing is new." The preceding chapters presented numerous examples of how information has been used in war, and these instances provide some guidance about what the future might hold.

This final chapter also focuses on the giant looming over the future of information at war: China. This material appears near the end of the book because dealing with China and its information-oriented "three warfares" strategy will be so crucial to the future of so many aspects of global affairs moving forward in the twenty-first century. This will be the next great challenge for those who address issues related to information at war.

A note about the focus of this book: many of the examples cited relate to American journalistic and military issues, although there are substantial explorations of topics grounded in experiences of the United Kingdom, Russia, China, Ukraine, Finland, the Baltic States, Middle Eastern countries, and numerous others. The author, being an American and having written much about US media and foreign policy, is trying to make the best use of his expertise and is certainly not trying to understate the significance of the military and information-related histories of any other nation.

What would Homer have thought about all this? How would he have told his audiences about our contemporary manifestations of rage – wars with many weapons, including information? I refer to Homer's work in several places in this book because I consider him to be a prime ancestor of those who gather and disseminate information at war.

In his book *Why Homer Matters*, Adam Nicolson stated: "Homer knows about the reality of suffering but never thinks of a world without conflict ... . We might long for peace, but we live in war."[33] Civilization will always be plagued by conflict of one kind or another, including those that use words and images as well as bullets. Information at war will be part of that.

1

Living-Room Wars

Information matters. How most people shape their attitudes about a war – support or opposition – is determined largely by the information they receive about the particular conflict, as well as by information they have acquired over time about wars of the past and international affairs generally. Whether their perspective on the conflict primarily reflects sadness or anger or jubilation or nonchalance, whether they decide to turn away or desire to learn more, their response might depend on the vividness, thoroughness, and eloquence with which the information that they receive is presented.

Once individuals have digested information and developed a position on the war (varying in firmness from person to person), they might want to do something about what they have learned. If they choose to act, they must decide what that should entail. The information might stir passionate support or opposition, which could lead citizens into the streets to demonstrate their feelings. Or it could shape how they will vote in the next election. The range of options is wide. Once received, information does not simply vanish; it lingers in the mind, with effects of variable significance over time.[1]

Sources of information are diverse. The news media and governments shape messages according to their own interests and standards. Additional contributors might include family, friends, neighbors, co-workers, and others who populate one's social milieu.[2] Conversations at the dinner table, over the backyard fence, or at the workplace water cooler are building blocks of opinion, as are an individual's religious and ethical beliefs and life experiences. Depending on its quality and source, information can make war real even to those physically distant from the fighting. It can perhaps motivate them to learn more and decide about taking particular action.

A nation's collective experience of war can affect receptivity to information about conflict. For many Americans, more than the citizens of any other major power, war is something of an abstraction, a remote phenomenon that has rarely touched the homeland. With a few exceptions – such as the 9/11 attacks in 2001 – the last time a foreign adversary brought combat to the American mainland was during the War of 1812. In terms of casualties, the most devastating conflict for Americans was their own civil war, which ended in 1865.

Many other countries have not been as fortunate in escaping war and the suffering that accompanies it. The following events took place less than a century ago, all within a short span of time: the rape of Nanking, the London Blitz, the battle of Stalingrad, the Holocaust, and the obliteration of Hiroshima and Nagasaki. They are among the countless examples of humankind's capacity to destroy. Beyond the "big" wars that have occupied the world's stage, episodes of intra-state conflict, genocide, ethnic cleansing, and terrorism have taken place with such frequency that they sometimes escape the world's attention. That should not happen. When governments and publics fail to acknowledge and respond to any such bloodletting, the moral fabric of humanity is damaged. News media, civil society institutions, and even individuals have responsibilities as sentinels of conscience.[3] Disseminating information, whether by a global television network or in an individual's tweet, can be effective in stirring consideration of the moral and practical implications of conflict.

War is a sad, inescapable reality. Its persistence as a societal phenomenon underscores the need to devise better ways to prevent conflict or bring it to a quick end. Such responsiveness depends in part on information flowing sufficiently swiftly and broadly for it to stir the scruples of states and their citizens. In 1938, British Prime Minister Neville Chamberlain abandoned Czechoslovakia to Nazi Germany rather than intervene in what he called "a quarrel in a faraway country between people of whom we know nothing."[4] Today, more than at any previous time, the technology-enabled availability of information ensures that there should be no people "of whom we know nothing" and whom we abandon. Even if people are living in remote villages of Sudan or Myanmar, information about them – perhaps even appeals coming online directly from them – can promptly reach much of the world.

The way information is delivered to its audience is crucial. Eloquent words always have power, but perhaps not as much as when they are accompanied by sound or images. The impact of information also depends in part on the context in which the information is received. What makes information memorable? What aspects of it stir people? What elements of information open pathways to taking action and influencing policy?

This book will take us up to the present day ... and then look beyond. But to begin, it is important to consider several past cases of the relationship between information and war.

Murrow in London

"This is London." With those words, CBS correspondent Edward R. Murrow began his reports from the British capital in 1940 and 1941. London was under the aerial siege, known simply as "the Blitz." Determined to batter England's defenses prior to launching a cross-Channel invasion, Adolf Hitler's Luftwaffe massed as many as 1,000 aircraft on a single raid over London and other cities. The Blitz resulted in approximately 43,000 British civilians killed and another 139,000 wounded.

Beginning in September 1940, the relentlessness of the Blitz accentuated its impact – attacks night after night for two months. Afterward, there was more bombing, less predictable in its timing but no less ferocious, that continued until May 1941. Later in the war, there would be still more attacks on London, including by the Germans' devastating V-1 flying bombs and V-2 rockets in 1944 and early 1945.

But the Blitz during the early years of the war was the real test of Britain's ability to survive. The breadth of the devastation was stunning. During the first six weeks of the Blitz, 16,000 London houses were destroyed, 60,000 were seriously damaged, and 300,000 people needed temporary housing. One Londoner in six was homeless at some point during the nine months of the Blitz.[5] The world had never seen anything like this massive use of air power against civilians.

For many Americans, "It has nothing to do with us" was a prevailing sentiment as the Blitz began. The United States had bailed out European allies during the Great War less than 30 years earlier and most Americans had little interest in again sending their soldiers across the ocean. Let the Europeans clean up their own mess. Many Americans were merely spectators, intent on keeping their distance.

Radio, however, narrowed that distance. Murrow was determined that his countrymen must not ignore battered Britain, because if

Britain fell, the United States would inevitably have to face Hitler on its own. He brought the war into their living-rooms with vivid and sometimes poetic descriptions of what was going on around him. He reflected Londoners' scorn for the enemy; the bombing, he said, "makes headlines, kills people, and smashes property, but it doesn't win wars ... . Things will have to get much worse before anyone here is likely to consider it too much to bear."[6] Londoners' toughness was a theme that ran through many of Murrow's broadcasts. He said: "I've seen some horrible sights in this city during these days and nights, but not once have I heard man, woman, or child suggest that Britain should throw in her hand. These people are angry."[7]

Virtually all of Murrow's reports gave his listeners a sense of what it was like to be in the midst of the Blitz. In one broadcast, he spoke of what he had seen during "several hours of observation from a rooftop" while the bombing was under way, and in another he said: "The air raid is still on. I shall speak rather softly, because three or four people are sleeping on mattresses on the floor of this studio." He told of the resolve of firefighters, police officers, railroad workers, and others who combed rubble for the dead and the still-living, and dealt with unexploded bombs. "Military medals," said Murrow, "are getting rather meaningless in this war. So many acts of heroism are being performed by men who were just doing their daily job."[8]

He also noted little things. He described the "rainbow bending over the battered and smoking East End just when the 'all-clear' sounded." He told of standing in front of a smashed grocery store and hearing a dripping inside. He investigated and found that "two cans of peaches had been drilled clean through by flying glass and the juice was dripping down onto the floor." And in the background, there were symbols of resilience and continuity: "The tolling of Big Ben can be heard in the intervals of the gunfire." He was trying, he said, to give a sense of "the life in London these days – the courage of the people; the flash and roar of the guns rolling down streets where much of the history of the English-speaking world has been made." But, he added, "These things must be experienced to be understood."[9]

For those not physically present during the attacks, receiving information was a way to "experience" the Blitz. Connecting information and experience can be done through vivid storytelling. Murrow convinced British authorities to allow him to broadcast live while the bombing was going on. He painted word pictures while the war provided the background soundtrack: "Four searchlights reach up, disappear in the light of a three-quarter moon ... . Just overhead now the burst of the anti-aircraft fire ... The searchlights now are

feeling almost directly overhead. Now you'll hear two bursts a little
nearer in a moment. There they are! That hard stony sound." The
next night: "I'm standing again tonight on a rooftop looking out
over London, feeling rather large and lonesome ... . As I look out
across the miles and miles of rooftops and chimney pots, some of
those dirty-gray fronts of the buildings look almost snow white in the
moonlight here tonight." He saw a rooftop spotter and said, "There
are hundreds and hundreds of men like that standing on rooftops in
London tonight watching for fire bombs, waiting to see what comes
out of this steel-blue sky."[10]

That kind of reporting underscored a difference between broadcast
and print. Although a newspaper or magazine reporter could
eloquently write about this same scene, there was special dramatic
power about the mix of voice and background sounds – sirens, explosions – arriving in faraway homes. The impact of this was heightened
by its novelty; the world had not yet become accustomed to real-time
news delivering the sounds of major stories as a matter of course.
(Not many years later, video would be wedded to these sounds,
enhancing impact even more.) For the American audience, secure in
its isolated cocoon, these reports stirred imagination and, perhaps,
conscience.

The domestic political backdrop of Murrow's reports was a
contest between strong isolationist sentiment and President Franklin
Roosevelt's recognition that Britain would not survive without
American help. But FDR's primary concern as the Blitz began was
his own reelection in November 1940. He was seeking an unprecedented third term and faced an unconventional Republican opponent
in Wendell Willkie, a one-time Democrat who was not wholly
persuaded by the isolationist mantra of the Republican leadership.
Robert Sherwood observed that Willkie's relatively moderate foreign
policy stance "tended to remove the isolationist–interventionist issue
from the campaign (at least until the final days)."[11] In those final
days, opinion polls showed that Willkie – increasingly aggressive in
labeling Roosevelt a warmonger – had cut into the president's lead
in the race. Several days before the election, Roosevelt tried to put
the issue to rest in a Boston speech: "I shall say it again and again:
your boys are not going to be sent into any foreign wars." (This
pledge included a typical FDR sleight of hand. As he told his aide
Sam Rosenman, "If somebody attacks us, then it isn't a foreign war,
is it?"[12])

While the nominees for president mostly avoided debating the case
for providing substantial aid to Britain, Murrow continued to deliver
the war to American living-rooms. So did his CBS colleagues in

London. Eric Sevareid observed in one of his reports: "London fights down her fears every night, takes her blows and gets up again every morning. You feel yourself an embattled member of this embattled corps. The attraction of courage is irresistible."[13]

These were the mixed messages Americans were receiving. From the presidential candidates, rhetoric about how much more committed to peace each was; while from Murrow and his colleagues more dramatic – and perhaps more believable – reports that clearly, if implicitly, endorsed the British cause.

On Election Day, Roosevelt won 449 electoral votes to Willkie's 82, although the popular vote margin of just 5 million votes was FDR's smallest in his three presidential campaigns. Post-election opinion analysis, however, bolstered Roosevelt's foreign policy position. A survey found that 11 percent of Roosevelt voters backed him because of the international situation, while only 2 percent of Willkie's supporters backed him because of his promise to keep America out of the war.[14]

Freed from campaign pressures, Roosevelt no longer had as much need to zig-zag in foreign affairs. American public opinion was steadily coming more into line with the president's pro-British views. A Gallup survey in May 1941 asked if the United States should continue to aid Britain even at the risk of being drawn into the war, and 77 percent said yes. By a slight but consistent majority, Americans also approved using the US Navy to guard convoys sailing to Britain.[15]

Roosevelt's actions reflected his precise sense of what was politically possible – how far and how fast the public and Congress would allow him to go. Beginning in May 1941, the Gallup Poll asked, "So far as you personally are concerned, do you think President Roosevelt has gone too far in his policies of helping Britain, not far enough, or about right?" Commenting on the responses to that question, polling expert Hadley Cantril cited "the almost uncanny way in which the president was able to balance public opinion around his policies." Despite the steady increase in US aid to Britain after May 1941, said Cantril, "the proportion of people who thought the President had gone too far, about right, and not far enough remained fairly constant." ("Too far" and "not enough" each had held at about 20 percent, and "about right" at around 50 percent.)[16]

Americans also increasingly believed that Britain was holding its own against Germany. Cantril noted the close relationship between the willingness to help Britain and the expectation of an eventual British victory. "We do not like to bet on a loser," wrote Cantril, "even if he is a friend." He also observed that, although isolationism was far from extinct, it was on the wane. Public figures such as Charles Lindbergh and Joseph P. Kennedy who had said that Britain was doomed to defeat saw support for their position begin to wither. By mid-1941, the interventionists had become more fervent than the isolationists. Cantril observed that interventionism had grown stronger because "most of us were simply convinced that it was to our own self-interest to defeat the Nazis ... Our extensive news services and mass media of communication won our confidence and kept us so well informed that we became increasingly alert to the implications events and courses of action had for our self-interest."[17]

By November 1941, belief in the inevitability of the United States going to war seemed to have taken hold. Among the public, the dominant question was "When will we fight?" Polls found that more than 80 percent of Americans expected war with Germany, and close to 70 percent anticipated war with Japan. About 70 percent said that it was more important to see Germany defeated than to stay out of the war, and approximately the same number said that if America's political and military leaders thought the only way to stop Germany was to go to war, then it should be done.[18]

How much of the shift in US public opinion was attributable to Roosevelt, Murrow, or any information in particular is difficult to know; survey research at the time was not as detailed as it later became. For that matter, the importance of any one type of information delivery was also difficult to measure consistently. But, as A. M. Sperber observed, Murrow's broadcasts "were becoming a national listening habit, as essential, in millions of homes, as the evening meal."[19]

Radio delivered the messages of Murrow, Roosevelt, and many others – journalists, politicians, entertainers, and more – into America's living-rooms. Hearing these voices, rather than reading their words or learning about them second-hand, increased their impact and credibility.

Probably the most important foreign visitor to American living-rooms during this time was Britain's prime minister, Winston Churchill. The rumbling rhetoric of his broadcast speeches captured the attention of even those Americans not ready to commit to his cause. Eleanor Roosevelt later said his speeches "were a tonic for us here in the United States as well as to his own people."[20] Churchill understood how dependent Britain was on American help and thus on Franklin Roosevelt's goodwill, which was in turn dependent on the political temperature of the American voter. Churchill's recognition of this was a factor in his appointing his close aide, Brendan Bracken, in July 1941 to run Britain's Ministry of Information. Bracken was knowledgeable about US politics and American journalism. He well understood the reason for Churchill putting him in this post; he promptly told the Ministry's American Division that its job was to "draw the Americans into the war."[21] When prominent American journalists and news executives such as *Washington Post* publisher Eugene Meyer came to London, they were assiduously courted by Bracken and often invited to 10 Downing Street for a drink with Churchill.[22]

At this time, radio was still something of a novelty; in the United States it was just in its second decade as a mass medium, but its reach was growing rapidly. In 1921, 60,000 American homes had radios and there were 30 radio stations in the country. By 1940, there would be radios in more than 29 million US homes (out of a total 35 million households) tuned in to 814 stations.[23] Perhaps most important, it was a national venue. Across the country, radio networks' listeners could hear the same news bulletin at the same time, which was unprecedented. Today, the entire nation (and much of the rest of the world) can tune in to broadcasts that are "going live." This is now the standard, not the exception, and it changes how we regard events ranging from a football game to a battlefield firefight.[24]

The novelty of a particular technology should not, however, overshadow the importance of the content it delivers. Staying with Murrow and Roosevelt as examples, their presentations of information were anything but prosaic. The power was in the words, not solely the medium. Consider these excerpts from FDR's fireside chat of December 29, 1940:

> If Great Britain goes down, the Axis powers will control the continents of Europe, Asia, Africa, Austral-Asia, and the high seas. And they will be in a position to bring enormous military and naval resources against this hemisphere. It is no exaggeration to say that all of us in all the Americas would be living at the point of a gun – a gun loaded with explosive bullets, economic as well as military. We should enter upon a new and terrible era in which the whole world, our hemisphere included, would be run by threats of brute force ... The people of Europe who are defending themselves do not ask us to do their fighting. They ask us for the implements of war, the planes, the tanks, the guns, the freighters which will enable them to fight for their liberty and for our security. Emphatically, we must get these weapons to them, get them to them in sufficient volume and quickly enough so that we and our children will be saved the agony and suffering of war which others have had to endure ... We must be the great arsenal of democracy. For us this is an emergency as serious as war itself. We must apply ourselves to our task with the same resolution, the same

sense of urgency, the same spirit of patriotism and sacrifice as we
would show were we at war.[25]

When reading this on a page today, Roosevelt's words still have
power, but not as much as when they came directly from the White
House into living-rooms, forging a connection between the country's
president and its citizens.

For his part, Murrow was working toward the same end: to
present the view from Britain and push Americans toward realizing
the importance of providing the British with the tools they needed to
continue the fight. His colleague Eric Sevareid later wrote: "Murrow
was not trying to 'sell' the British cause to America; he was trying to
explain the universal human cause of men who were showing a noble
face to the world. In so doing he made the British and their behavior
human and thus compelling to his countrymen at home."[26] Excerpts
from Murrow's broadcasts illustrate this:

> [After visiting an air raid shelter at 3:30 a.m.] How long these people
> will stand up to this sort of thing I don't know, but tonight they're
> magnificent. I've seen them, talked with them, and I know.
> [About Londoners] They've become more human, less reserved;
> more talkative and less formal. There's almost a small-town atmos-
> phere about the place ... There's been a drawing together.
> [Watching a German air attack] The fires up the river had turned
> the moon blood red. The smoke had drifted down until it formed a
> canopy over the Thames; the guns were working all around us, the
> bursts looking like fireflies in a southern summer night ... Huge pear-
> shaped bursts of flame would rise up into the smoke and disappear.
> The world was upside down.[27]

Murrow knew that the most effective way to present news is by
wrapping issues into stories of people with whom the audience could
empathize. When his sonorous voice came into American living-
rooms from London's streets or the CBS studio there, the information
he provided – forceful, but not overtly political – was about the
British people and how they managed in their transformed world.
Murrow later reflected on the challenges he and his colleagues faced:
"In reporting this new kind of warfare we have tried to prevent our
own prejudices and loyalties from coming between you and the information which it was our duty to impart. We may not always have
succeeded. An individual who can entirely avoid being influenced
by the atmosphere in which he works might not even be a good
reporter."[28]

As Murrow's observation indicates, he and other pro-interventionist journalists had to walk an ethical tightrope: reporting in a straight-forward way about a topic that stirred mixed feelings within the news audience, while still recognizing that they were being "influenced by the atmosphere" in which they worked. Being physically distant from his audience may have limited Murrow's understanding of the power of his broadcasts, but those watching the trends in American public opinion recognized the effect of his words.

Librarian of Congress Archibald MacLeish, speaking at a New York dinner in Murrow's honor just a few days before the Pearl Harbor attack, addressed the historic significance of Murrow's voice spanning an ocean:

> You destroyed the superstition of distance and time ... You destroyed in the minds of many men and women in this country the superstition that what is done beyond three thousand miles of water is not really done at all; the ignorant superstition that violence and lies and murder on another continent are not violence and lies and murder here ... It was not in London really that you spoke. It was in the back kitchens and the front living-rooms and the moving automobiles and the hotdog stands and the observation cars of another country that your voice was truly speaking. And what you did was this: You made real and urgent and present to the men and women of those comfortable rooms, those safe enclosures, what these men and women had not known was present there or real. You burned the city of London in our houses and we felt the flames that burned it. You laid the dead of London at our doors and we knew the dead were our dead – were all men's dead – were mankind's dead – and ours.[29]

Such was – and is – the power of information. A new technology – radio – had enhanced information's effects, just as television would do when it arrived some years later. This occurred most strikingly during the Vietnam War (or, as it is known by many Vietnamese, "the American War").

The Early Stages of the Vietnam War: John F. Kennedy and "Managing Information

One of the most enduring myths about the Vietnam War is related to information: "The news media lost the war." According to this notion, negative and inaccurate news reporting about the conflict so poisoned American public opinion that it became politically impos-sible for the government to pursue the fighting with the patience and aggressiveness needed to win.[30]

Granted, information provided by the news media helped to fuel dissatisfaction with the conduct of the war, especially during the presidencies of Lyndon Johnson and Richard Nixon. But journalists were mostly following a path that was charted by government policy-makers and that led into the much-discussed "quagmire" in which the US war effort foundered. Clark Clifford, who succeeded Robert McNamara as Secretary of Defense during Johnson's final year in office, later wrote:

> The press made errors in reporting, as it does in every war, but the bulk of the reporting from the war zone reflected the official position. Contrary to right-wing revisionism, reporters and the antiwar movement did not defeat America in Vietnam. Our policy failed because it was based on false premises and false promises. Had the results in Vietnam approached, even remotely, what Washington and Saigon had publicly predicted for many years, the American people would have continued to support their government.[31]

Much of the analysis of news media performance during the Vietnam years has focused on coverage of the Tet offensive in early 1968, which will be addressed later in this chapter. But the government–press relationship, which had been relatively cozy during World War II, was changing earlier than Tet, notably during the presidency of John F. Kennedy.

Two episodes not related to Vietnam set the stage for later tensions. Both centered on Cuba: the Bay of Pigs invasion in April 1961 and the Missile Crisis of October 1962. In each instance, the flow of information to the public was significantly limited by behind-the-scenes agreements between the White House and leading news organizations.

Trying to maintain secrecy about the upcoming American-sponsored invasion of Cuba, the White House pressured the *New York Times* and several other publications to withhold, or at least modify, stories before the invasion date, lest they tip off Fidel Castro's regime about the coming attack. They agreed and did so. Nevertheless, the invasion was a disaster; almost all of the 1,400 US-backed anti-Castro Cubans were killed or captured as they went ashore at the Bay of Pigs on Cuba's southern coast.

Although Kennedy had orchestrated the pressure campaign to limit coverage, he later told *Times* managing editor Turner Catledge, "Maybe if you had printed more about the operation you would have saved us from a colossal mistake." Catledge later observed: "On the one hand he condemned us for printing too much, and in the next breath he condemned us for printing too little. He wanted it both ways, and he did not change my view that the newspapers, not the government, must decide what news is fit to print."[32]

As we will see, journalists deferring to the White House is not uncommon when "national security" is cited. Those in the higher echelons of government often seem to believe that "We know more and we know better than you do," with "you" encompassing not just the news media but the broader public as well. Sometimes the officials are correct; the breadth of their information sources – which may include the intelligence community and others not available to the press or the public – might give them enhanced perspective on events of the moment. But a government's access to information does not, in itself, always lead to wisdom, and journalists generally agree that they should resist pressure even when it is dressed up as an appeal to patriotism.

Compared to the Bay of Pigs situation, the 1962 Missile Crisis was a very different matter, as the stakes involved were so enormous. At issue was not an invasion of Cuba by a ragtag military unit, but rather a real danger of nuclear war between the United States and the Soviet Union because of the placement of Soviet missiles in Cuba. Alerted by aerial reconnaissance photos, Kennedy had decided to impose a naval quarantine on Cuba as part of a strategy to force the Kremlin to remove the missiles. "Quarantine" meant a blockade, which under international law constitutes an act of war and, in this case, could easily have led to a confrontation between American and Soviet naval vessels. The United States was poised to launch airstrikes and an invasion force if the missiles were left in place, and US bombers armed with nuclear weapons were ready to attack the Soviet Union. Kennedy planned to address the American people and the rest of the world on Monday evening, October 22, and he was counting on the Soviet leadership not knowing beforehand about the American response to the crisis.

So, when Kennedy learned that the *New York Times* and *Washington Post* were prepared to run stories about the quarantine and US troop movements before the speech, the President asked *Times* publisher Orvil Dryfoos and *Post* publisher Philip Graham not to print information that would give the Kremlin time to issue its own ultimatum before Kennedy's address. Graham quickly agreed, but the *Times* moved more slowly. Washington bureau chief James Reston called the president and, citing the agreement by the *Times* the previous year to withhold information about the Bay of Pigs, asked: "If we hold out on our readers now, are we going to be in a war against the Russians before we print another edition? Some of us wonder whether you are asking for secrecy until after the shooting has begun." In response, Kennedy promised, "There will be no bloodshed before I explain this very serious situation to the American people."[33]

With that, the *Times* agreed, and it published only a vague report about "an air of crisis" in Washington. Kennedy gave his speech, which included this frightening message: "It shall be the policy of this nation to regard any nuclear missile launched from Cuba against any nation in the Western hemisphere as an attack by the Soviet Union on the United States requiring a full retaliatory response upon the Soviet Union."[34] After an exceptionally tense six days, Soviet Premier Nikita Khrushchev declared (after the United States had secretly agreed to remove its nuclear missiles from Turkey) that the missile sites in Cuba would be dismantled. The crisis was over.

These two Cuban crises illustrate how the news media operated as a gatekeeper determining what information reaches the public. As a matter of Constitutional law, news organizations could not be *ordered* to withhold information, but shared perceptions of national interest sometimes fostered *de facto* partnership. The public's "right to know" became secondary to what news executives, in collaboration with the government, defined as a "need to know." Between the government and the leading news organizations, a chokehold could be applied to the flow of information. Government officials and journalists could negotiate among themselves the timing for the public being able to learn important facts about a particular situation.

In 1962, was the withholding of information a proper role for the news media? During the Missile Crisis, the public was left in the dark, albeit briefly, but the exigencies of the situation may have dictated news organizations' restraint as being in the public's interest. According to Graham Allison, when the missiles in Cuba were first discovered, Kennedy's national security adviser McGeorge Bundy told the president that they probably had a week before the news leaked. Kennedy took six days to formulate his response and "noted afterward that if he had been forced to make his decision in the first 48 hours, he would have chosen the air strike rather than the naval blockade – something that could have led to nuclear war."[35]

From the perspective of those at the White House, this collaboration between the press and the government was a good thing, as diplomacy had time to work and defuse the situation. But the gatekeeper role cited here has changed considerably in recent years. With the presence of expanded broadcast outlets and the arrival of social media, there are now so many information "gates" that they cannot be controlled by a few media executives. Today, rather than

having Kennedy's seven days to devise a plan, the time during which
secrecy could be maintained would probably be closer to seven hours.
If Twitter, YouTube, and other such venues had existed in October
1962, they would almost certainly have been filled with individuals'
reports about troop movements in Florida, leaks from people in
government supporting and opposing the administration's proposed
measures, disinformation from the Soviets, and other content – some
of it accurate and some of it not. With social media available, it
would be relatively easy to circumvent any limitation on information,
no matter how high-minded the intent. The president would have
faced a far more demanding timetable for deciding what to do.

Even in the early 1960s, the government's reliance on "national
security" as a rationale for discouraging journalistic enterprise was
wearing thin as a new, aggressive corps of correspondents made their
presence felt. In their work during the initial years of the American
presence in Vietnam, a number of these journalists reflected a more
adversarial approach to covering their country's military operations and a more confrontational attitude toward policymakers. In
many ways, this was a contest for control of information, with news
professionals rejecting the notion that they should be merely conduits
for government-generated material and be deferential when the
government wanted information altered or suppressed. They increasingly embraced their independence in their role as the principal
providers of information to the public.

Among the most notable of these journalists was David Halberstam
of the *New York Times*. Halberstam was not yet 30 years old when
he arrived in Vietnam in mid-1962, and he soon became frustrated
by what he considered stonewalling and false information from US
officials – civilian and military – in the country. So, he went off on
his own. He wrote to an editor at the *Times*: "There are no briefings
to attend, no easy way of coverage. The only way to get a story here
is to walk through the swamps and climb the mountains and ride
the helicopters into battle. I have been shot at innumerable times."[36]

Halberstam saw it as a holy mission to tell his readers what was
really going on in a war that, as yet, was receiving little attention
from the American public and from most American news organizations. As his colleague William Prochnau later wrote, Halberstam
understood journalism's innate power:

> As the media grew more influential in American life, it became more
> common among journalists, still is among some, to disingenuously
> diminish themselves – we have no power, we send out no armies, we

raise no taxes, we only carry messages. Halberstam had no tolerance
for such humbuggery. The press had power, the power to create images
and myths, to tilt history, to drive large forces.[37]

But journalists could not wield that power without encountering
pushback. The government had ample power of its own and was
willing to use it on occasion to undermine press coverage. An
example of this occurred in August 1963, when Halberstam sent a
story to the *Times* about South Vietnamese government attacks on
Buddhist activists. Halberstam reported that Ngo Dinh Nhu, the
brother and chief adviser of Vietnam's President Ngo Dinh Diem
(who was supported by the United States), ordered the attacks by
secret police and special forces under his command, presumably with
President Diem's approval. President Diem denied this, claiming that
the Vietnamese army, some of whose leaders were his political rivals,
had carried out the attacks without his backing.

The White House and State Department defended their man
Diem, denying the allegations in Halberstam's reporting and telling
Times editors that Halberstam had it wrong. Under pressure from
the administration, editors at the *Times* could not decide whom to
believe. The result, in William Prochnau's words, was "one of the
most bizarre front pages in the history of the *New York Times* ... In
effect, the world's most influential newspaper told its readers to flip
a coin."[38] The front page of the *Times* on August 23, 1963 carried
the headline, "Two Versions of the Crisis in Vietnam: One Lays Plot
to Nhu, Other to Army." Beneath the headline, in two side-by-side
columns, were Halberstam's story from Saigon and one from Tad
Szulc of the *Times*'s Washington bureau, who had to rely more heavily
on administration sources. Each story directly contradicted the other.

Amidst the confusion that surrounded so much of the Vietnam
War, this episode was far from being earthshaking, but it illustrated
the evolving dynamics of the government–press relationship. At
this time, the byword for the government was not to "censor" or
"control" the news flow, but rather to "manage" it.[39] That euphemism
did not mask the growing anger that some in the Kennedy administration (including the president himself) felt toward journalists who
they believed were undermining the American public's support for
their anti-communist efforts in Vietnam. This led to putting pressure
on reporters and their editors to conform to the administration's
worldview.

The president became angry enough to ask the CIA to review four
months of Halberstam's articles. The intelligence agency's report
stated:

A review indicates that he is by and large accurate in terms of the facts that he includes in his articles. The conclusions he draws from his facts plus the emphasis of his reporting, however, tend to call his objectivity into question. In his almost invariably pessimistic reports, Halberstam makes liberal use of phrases "some Americans," "informed Vietnamese," or "lower (or higher) ranking Americans," etc. Such sourcing is impossible to refute ... optimistic sources are almost never quoted by Mr. Halberstam.[40]

Soon thereafter, Kennedy tried – unsuccessfully – to get *Times* publisher Arthur O. Sulzberger to reassign Halberstam, moving him out of Vietnam.[41]

Some journalists responded to the administration's anger with anger of their own. Halberstam used military vernacular: "What began as sniping turned into an orchestrated attack. It became a full-fledged war with more fronts than Vietnam. We were getting cannon fire from a different direction every day: the Pentagon regiment, the White House regiment, the embassy regiment, the press regiment, the right-wing regiment – and all of it feeding the regiments from our own offices."[42]

Halberstam's last point is important because it underscores the fact that "the press" is not monolithic. Among those in the profession, and even within a single news organization, different points of view sometimes collide. During the early years of the Vietnam War, journalists such as Marguerite Higgins and Joseph Alsop endorsed the American war strategy and were not shy about criticizing fellow correspondents.

A lesson Kennedy learned painfully during his brief presidency was that the American chief executive is far more constrained than he would like to be when it comes to prolonged armed conflict. Only rarely can an administration count on continued public support for going to war. This happened after the Pearl Harbor attack in 1941, when the United States declared war on Japan, Germany, and Italy, and after the 2001 terrorist attacks, when the United States invaded Afghanistan. But even in those cases, it soon became obvious that a war waged by a democracy can be politically precarious for the government in charge. There may be an initial surge of patriotic fervor, but support for a conflict is likely to diminish as casualties mount and negative economic consequences are felt.[43] Delivering information to the public during this process may become something of a competition between government and news media, with each seeking to be considered the more credible provider.

Kennedy apparently did not fully appreciate how problematic this process could be. As news reports from Vietnam took on a more critical tone, Kennedy ordered that a new press policy be implemented in Saigon. Richard Reeves wrote:

> [Kennedy] wanted "maximum feasible cooperation and guidance" for correspondents, with the goal of directing them away from "undesirable" situations and stories. The President was trying to keep bad news from Americans, but the real effect of keeping the press away from unpleasantness was that he himself might be the last to know what was happening in Southeast Asia if he depended only on official reports.[44]

Even presidents' actions are grounded in the information they receive. As Reeves points out, reducing press access to information can prove self-defeating, limiting the breadth of the picture the president has of a situation about which he must make decisions. But in the hothouse of politics, what is perceived as "bad press" is often considered intolerable.

Part of Kennedy's concern with news coverage was based on his recognition that the American role in Vietnam was rightly susceptible to criticism and legal challenge. In a private conversation, he told *Newsweek*'s Benjamin Bradlee, a personal friend and later editor of the *Washington Post*: "The trouble is, we are violating the Geneva agreement. Not as much as the North Vietnamese are, but we're violating it. Whatever we have to do, we have to do in some kind of secrecy, and there's a lot of danger in that."[45] (As an illustration of how journalists can become too close to the powerful, Bradlee did not write about this conversation until years after Kennedy's death.)

How much did government obfuscation and news media criticism matter to public opinion about the conduct of the war during the Kennedy years? Not much. At that point in the war, the public was paying limited attention to even the most critical news coverage, and the war had not become the politically existential menace that Kennedy's successor, Lyndon Johnson, found it to be. The war simply did not yet resonate, certainly not to the degree that civil rights and other domestic issues did. The cost in American casualties was nowhere near the peak it would reach in later years, the economic costs were not yet perceived to be great, and neither news coverage nor public opinion showed signs that the United States might be marching into a future "quagmire." If there was a foreign trouble spot that would capture Americans' interest, it would probably be Berlin, Cuba, or another familiar Cold War testing ground.

During the Kennedy presidency, there was a widening stream of negative information flowing to the public from the elite media, a class that grew to include television news. Two months before he was killed in November 1963, Kennedy appeared on the CBS and NBC nightly newscasts that had just expanded from 15 to 30 minutes (ABC followed in 1968). The evening news became a regular presence in millions of American homes, and Walter Cronkite at CBS and Chet Huntley and David Brinkley of NBC became trusted providers of information in much the way Edward R. Murrow had via radio during World War II. Television reports from the Vietnam War soon became broadcast staples, and the power of the visual made itself felt.

Lyndon Johnson's War, Television's War

During the 1960 presidential campaign, Kennedy had been the first candidate to benefit from television exposure, as "looking presidential" became a new criterion for elective office. His successor, Lyndon Johnson, became the first president to be forced to contend with television's power during a war.

Johnson's long political rise – congressman, senator, vice president, president – had been a product of his mastery of political deal-making and one-on-one negotiating. As Senate majority leader during the 1950s, in the back rooms of Capitol Hill he could count votes and outmaneuver his opponents. When he became president in November 1963, he soon had to face extraneous factors over which he had little control.

Things began well for Johnson's presidency. In 1964, he was elected to a full term in the White House in a landslide that reflected the mood of a nation still grieving after the Kennedy assassination. With him he carried into power overwhelming Democratic majorities in Congress and saw enacted an ambitious domestic policy agenda, including breakthrough civil rights legislation. But, increasingly, he was distracted by the fighting in Vietnam, a conflict from which he was determined not to "cut and run." When Johnson took office, there were about 16,000 US troops in Vietnam. By the time he wrapped up his presidency at the end of 1968, there were 536,000.[46] As of early 1965, 225 Americans had been killed; by the war's end, the number of US dead (including those killed in Cambodia and Laos) was more than 58,000.[47] Although estimates vary widely about the number of North and South Vietnamese combatants and civilians who were killed in the war, the total is almost certainly considerably more than 1 million.[48]

As the troop numbers and casualties increased, Johnson's political support gradually declined. The American public was receiving mixed messages about the war. From the government came upbeat reports about seeing "the light at the end of the tunnel" as the forces of democracy beat down the evil communists. But from many journalists came very different appraisals – lack of combat success for the Americans and their South Vietnamese allies and dramatic reports of a country being torn apart while American soldiers died.

The information flows reaching the American public were different from those during the Kennedy years. News coverage of Vietnam during the early 1960s was limited in terms of news organizations' commitments of money, people, and technology. By the midpoint of the Johnson presidency, however, the television networks were highlighting their coverage from Vietnam and were at least equal to print media in terms of influence.

A basic premise of this book is that if a government wants to wage war, it must control – or at least influence – the information ecosystem. The Johnson administration was ineffective in its efforts to do this, partly because the president and his team did not fully appreciate the ways in which television reporting – however imperfect it might be – altered that environment.

Someone who did understand this was Michael Arlen, television critic of the *New Yorker* magazine. In 1966, noting that 60 percent of Americans were getting their news about Vietnam from television, Arlen watched several weeks of network evening news coverage and came away from his viewing uncertain about the effect it was having on its audience. He saw wounded US soldiers grimacing in pain, helicopters chopping noisily above a jungle canopy, South Vietnamese soldiers firing at distant targets (with unknown results), and other pieces of information indicating inconclusive outcomes on the battlefield. "That's the way it often is with television's reporting of the war," he wrote, "and it's hard to know what to make of it."[49] He also wrote that television's perspective on the war was limited, and so viewers "look at Vietnam, it seems, as a child kneeling in a corridor, his eye to the keyhole, looks at two grownups arguing in a locked room – the aperture of the keyhole small; the figures shadowy, mostly out of sight; the voices indistinct."[50]

Among Arlen's most valuable contributions in his writings about the war were his observations about how information was affected by being delivered by television into American living-rooms. This is particularly important because it addresses how information's impact is shaped by the environment in which it is received.

During World War II, information via radio (from Murrow, FDR, and others) had come into the living-room, but television was not yet a mass medium. Video news was available only in movie theatres as part of newsreels or government-sponsored documentaries. Consider how one watched these visual slices of war. First, going to the movies was something of an occasion; you left your home, bought a ticket, and sat in the dark amidst a large number of people, most of whom you did not know, seeing giants on the screen. This was not everyday reality. What you watched – a conventional film or a newsreel – could make an impression, but when you left the theatre you left behind at least some of the emotional power of the images and went on your way, back to more familiar surroundings.

Watching reports about the Vietnam War on television was quite different. You were at home, in your own living-room, perhaps joined by family members. Watching television news was more a part of your life than going to the movies; maybe you tuned in almost every night. And as the TV screens became larger and correspondents focused. on individual soldiers, faces of the fighters on the screen were close to life-size. Arlen wrote that viewers were watching "real men get shot at, real men (our surrogates, in fact) get killed and wounded."[51] And suppose that as part of the family group watching the evening news was a 17-year-old son – a year away from draft age and looking distressingly similar to the 19-year-old wounded soldier the family had just seen being carried off the Vietnam battlefield.

That has emotional and political impact akin to, and perhaps greater than, the word-pictures delivered by Murrow several decades before. If you are Lyndon Johnson, you need to consider this when you contemplate ways to retain domestic political support for this war you are determined to fight. But Johnson had no television-related precedent on which to base a responsive strategy. In 1968, when he was planning to run for reelection, he found that presidential power could sometimes be overmatched by television power.

Tet

The 1968 Tet offensive is one of the best-known episodes of the Vietnam War. It was covered intensively by American news media and was an important factor in Lyndon Johnson's political demise. It was also, according to critics of the press, an example of how the news media can rush to judgment and deliver information that is fundamentally flawed.

On January 30 and 31, 1968, more than 80,000 North Vietnamese and Viet Cong troops began coordinated attacks in South Vietnam, targeting three-quarters of the country's provincial capitals and most major cities, including the national capital, Saigon.[52] In terms of shock value, the communists were immediately successful. The American military had not anticipated such a sweeping offensive, and the American public was dismayed to find that the consistently upbeat information they had been receiving from its government was clearly wrong. Because so much of the press corps was based in Saigon, initial reports from the fighting were filled with first-hand accounts of the attacks there, including the communists' success (although brief) in breaching the defenses of the US embassy.

Clark Clifford, who had just been confirmed by the Senate as US secretary of defense, later wrote about the deluge of bad news during the next several weeks:

- On February 18, the Pentagon reported the war's highest one-week American casualty toll: 543 killed, 2,547 wounded.
- On February 23, the Selective Service announced it would draft an additional 48,000 men, the second-largest call-up of the war.
- On February 25, General William Westmoreland, commander of the US forces in Vietnam, told the press that he would need even more troops. General Earle Wheeler, chairman of the Joint Chiefs of Staff told the White House that as many as 205,000 more soldiers would be needed.[53]

Other pieces of information also contributed to the appearance of chaos in South Vietnam. A widely seen photograph taken by Eddie Adams of the Associated Press showed South Vietnamese police general Nguyen Ngoc Loan executing a handcuffed Vietcong prisoner, Nguyen Van Lem, on a Saigon street. In another incident, Associated Press correspondent Peter Arnett reported that an American officer said about the fighting in the Mekong River town of Ben Tre, "It became necessary to destroy the town to save it."[54] Herbert Schandler later wrote about this famous quote: "This widely repeated sentence seemed to sum up the irony and the contradictions in the use of American power in Vietnam and caused many to question the purpose of our being there. If we had to destroy our friends in order to save them, was the effort really worthwhile, either for us or for our friends?"[55]

President Johnson understood the precariousness of his military and political positions, and he knew that the "unmanaged" information about Tet was worsening his situation. (The White House and Pentagon began a hunt for the officer whom Arnett had quoted, but Arnett refused to divulge his name and the search was unsuccessful.[56]) Daniel Hallin observed:

For the most part, journalists seem to have interpreted Tet, without consciously making the distinction, for what it *said* rather than what it *did* – as proof, regardless of who won or lost it, that the war was not under control ... . The journalists were inescapably a part of the political process they were reporting. If they said Tet was a political defeat for the administration, they were helping make it so; if they resisted the journalistic instinct to put Tet in that context, they were helping the administration out. Most of them followed that journalistic instinct.[57]

Tet may have been a tipping point at which information from the news media became ascendant, outweighing the government's messaging and reshaping perceptions of the war. Hallin cited the "ideological framing" of the war "as a conflict between a 'Western-backed regime' and 'Communist guerrillas.'"[58] For Americans during the Cold War, such a match-up presented an easy choice, requiring little debate. But Tet introduced factors that complicated the thinking about the war. It was no longer simply a choice between "good" and "bad," but now also required cost–benefit analysis: was this war truly worth fighting? And what information should be relied upon in formulating an answer to that question?

Public opinion was shifting. In November 1967, a Gallup Poll asked respondents if they thought the United States was losing, standing still, or making progress in Vietnam. The answers were 8 percent losing, 33 percent standing still, 50 percent making progress, with 9 percent undecided. Just three months later, in February 1968 (a few weeks after Tet), the responses were 23 percent losing, 38 percent standing still, 33 percent making progress, and 6 percent undecided.[59]

Understandably, many members of the American public may have been uncertain about whom to believe and what to think. The Tet offensive seemed to reflect the "false premises and false promises" that Clark Clifford later cited. The heavy (and sometimes bloody) news coverage of the fighting further undermined Johnson's credibility. For the president, the *coup de grâce* may have been a February 27 CBS News special, "Report from Vietnam by Walter Cronkite," America's most widely known journalist, who was sometimes referred to as "the most trusted man in America." The hour-long broadcast included footage from Cronkite's post-Tet visit to Vietnam and concluded with his commentary from his New York anchor desk. He said, in part: "To say that we are mired in stalemate seems the only realistic, if unsatisfactory conclusion ... . It is increasingly clear to this reporter that the only rational way out then will be to negotiate, not as victors, but as an honorable people who lived up to their pledge to defend democracy, and did the best they could."[60]

Johnson tried to retake control of the information reaching the public. He dispatched his cabinet members to television talk shows and said at a news conference that "the enemy will fail and fail again because we Americans will never yield."[61] But these efforts could not compete effectively with the information coming from the more than 200 American journalists in Vietnam. Under Secretary of the Air Force Townsend Hoopes later wrote that "the scale, virulence, and tenacity of the Tet offensive had all but severed the remaining strands of the Administration's credibility. The President was speaking out forcefully, but his words and their tone struck listeners as more shrill than reassuring; in them one detected a profound inner discomfort and unease, a thrashing about in uncertainty."[62]

In the past – as recently as during the Kennedy years – the government–press dynamic often favored the government because there were limited ways that information could reach the public. The turnaround had taken hold beginning on November 22, 1963 when Kennedy was assassinated. People turned to television to confirm the news of his death and to gather details. The audience continued to grow; according to Nielsen research, 81 percent of the approximately 50 million American homes with a television were tuned in to the President's funeral on November 24.[63] Within the space of a few days, television had established itself as the nation's go-to source for crisis information.

Aside from the sheer number of viewers, this event provided evidence of a media-connected national community. Whether you were in Miami or Seattle, you watched the funeral at the same moment, as it happened. No longer did you need to wait for information to wend its way across the country. Radio had achieved something similar 20 years before, but in 1963 the impact of information was heightened by being able to see the funeral. This created the effect of being at least emotionally present at the ceremonies. Information was becoming more immersive and more personal, and, at a time of national tragedy, information was the country's connective tissue.

Lacking Kennedy's ease in front of the TV cameras, Johnson was on unfamiliar and hostile terrain. His efforts in the weeks following the first Tet attacks were not enough to offset the pessimism that imbued news reports about the Vietnam situation. In a March 31 televised address, Johnson announced a bombing halt and new efforts to have the South Vietnamese do more of the fighting. He concluded his speech by saying, "I shall not seek, and I will not accept, the nomination of my party for another term as your president."

This was from someone who in the election just four years before had won 61 percent of the popular vote, carried 44 states, and won 486 electoral votes (while his Republican opponent, Senator Barry Goldwater, won 52). Had Vietnam – and specifically the Tet offensive – done him in? If so, was the information that contributed to his political downfall accurate?

On the day after his speech from the White House, Johnson spoke to the National Association of Broadcasters and offered his cautionary view of television coverage of war:

> As I sat in my office last evening, waiting to speak, I thought of the many times each week when television brings the war into the American home. No one can say exactly what effect those vivid scenes would have on American opinion. Historians must only guess at the effect that television would have had during earlier conflicts on the future of this nation: during the Korean War, for example, at that time when our forces were pushed back there to Pusan; or World War II, the Battle of the Bulge; or when our men were slugging it out in Europe.[64]

Johnson's point was that graphic depictions of military setbacks – even temporary ones – can undermine the popular support essential in a democracy for those waging war. To an extent, that can be viewed as a self-serving outlook that considered only part of the information situation. Even Johnson's national security adviser Walt Rostow admitted that the administration had failed to present a "clear and persuasive" picture of what was happening in Vietnam, thus ceding information dominance to the news media, whose work Rostow characterized as "generally undistinguished and often biased."[65] Even if Rostow's appraisal was correct, the Johnson administration had lost control of the war narrative and found itself plagued by a "credibility gap."

Further, suppose that the information provided in the news coverage was wrong. Suppose that Tet had actually been a massive setback for the North Vietnamese and Viet Cong forces, but journalists had been so surprised by the breadth and ferocity of the attacks that they assumed the communists were victorious. If the public were to learn about such inaccuracy, would Johnson and his war policy be vindicated? In terms of influence, what would it mean about the role of television and other news media, and how would this affect policy-makers' decisions about information management in the future?

We will later see how a "Vietnam syndrome" – an offspring of the credibility gap of the Johnson years – had significant effect on some future wars. For now, it is useful to consider flaws in the news coverage of the Tet offensive, which many historians today consider to have been a military defeat for the communist forces that were unable to hold territory or spur a popular uprising in the South. They did, however, achieve political success because they were *perceived* as victorious by many journalists. The United States and its allies had previously relied on misleading information to create expectations that could not be fulfilled. The communist forces were able to puncture that balloon.

The principal analyst of Tet news coverage and its impact was Peter Braestrup, who was Saigon bureau chief of the *Washington Post* during Tet. His book, *Big Story*, was published in 1977 in two volumes. In it, he meticulously chronicles events during Tet and how they were covered. Among his conclusions:

> Rarely has contemporary crisis-journalism turned out, in retrospect, to have veered so widely from reality. Essentially, the dominant themes of the words and film from Vietnam (rebroadcast in commentary, editorials, and much political rhetoric at home) added up to a portrait of defeat for the allies. Historians, on the contrary, have concluded that the Tet offensive resulted in a severe military-political setback for Hanoi in the South. To have portrayed such a setback for one side as a defeat for the other – in a major crisis abroad – cannot be counted as a triumph for American journalism.[66]

Valuable lessons about what *not* to do can be found in the flawed news reports. The journalistic errors were partly attributable to mutual distrust between press and government. Even when the government-supplied information was accurate, many journalists were so skeptical that they were inclined to treat it as being misleading. Johnson's failure to understand the breadth of the enlarged information universe is also significant. With the addition of radio and then television, the news media environment had become less forgiving of leaders who did not understand it and respond to its demands. Braestrup wrote of this: "In contrast to John F. Kennedy during the 1962 Cuban missile crisis, or to Franklin D. Roosevelt after Pearl Harbor, [Johnson] started by setting a hesitant tone – which did not go unnoticed in the media. Initially, the President sought to repeat his 1967 public-relations strategy, dominating the media with reassuring statements about Vietnam by subordinates."[67]

Johnson did not recognize that the increase in the number of news venues meant that information would be more difficult to manage.

The information pie now had more slices from which the public could choose. By the late 1960s, it was impossible to dominate the information flow as some of Johnson's predecessors had been able to do. Television, for instance, had already helped to amplify the debate about Vietnam at home, as when NBC in 1966 had televised five hours of testimony by George Kennan, retired diplomat and critic of the Johnson war policy. Kennan told the Senate Foreign Relations Committee and the national television audience that "There is more respect to be won in the opinion of this world by a resolute and courageous liquidation of unsound positions than by the most stubborn pursuit of extravagant or unpromising objectives."[68] That was the kind of message that was now, to Johnson's distress, reaching the American public more consistently.

When Johnson had been, in Robert Caro's words, "master of the Senate," he was largely able to control the political atmosphere in which he worked, including much of the information related to the Senate's business. As president, on a vastly larger playing field, he learned painfully that he did not retain that kind of power, and without it he could not fight "his" war as he wanted to.

The cases examined in this chapter are by no means the only examples of information affecting public support for or opposition to a war. What does emerge, however, from this chapter is evidence that, as information flows become more diverse and pervasive, they are more difficult for political leaders to manage.

Evidence of this can be seen in the fact that the myth that "the press lost the Vietnam War" survives a half-century after it was born. Johnson's abdication has haunted more recent US presidents, and also has served as an object lesson for other governments. The result: consistent, forceful, and increasingly sophisticated efforts to control information at war.

2

Competing for Information Control

Which pieces of war-related information reach various publics for their consideration, and which are kept out of view by governments, news media, and others? What are the criteria for choosing openness or secrecy? What are the ramifications of these choices for the kinetic and political aspects of war?

Information concerning war is often difficult for the public to access. Even in countries where the "public's right to know" is proclaimed, in practice that "right" may be more aspirational than real. For the United States, try to find it enumerated in the Constitution. It is not there, although it is implied in a limited way by the "freedom of the press" and "freedom of speech" clauses of the First Amendment. In the United States and other democracies, there may be statutes that can be considered "freedom of information" laws, but they vary greatly in their breadth and in how (and if) they can be enforced. Granted, even the most democratic of countries has some need of secrets, but an all-too-frequently used rationale citing "national security" provides a convenient veil to obscure the public's vision. A claim of "national security" can take on a life of its own and grow to extreme proportions. It can be used for reasons more about politics than security, and in such instances information may become a hostage, subject to contestation that heightens adversarial tensions between the news media and the government.

The public might not be aware (or even care) that such wrestling matches are under way. The freedom of the press has long been taken for granted, but today it is in significant jeopardy in the United States and elsewhere. Public opinion about the news media has increasingly become polarized along partisan lines, with attitudes likely influenced by harsh rhetoric from politicians – including the US president – who denounce journalists as "enemies of the people" and unflattering reports as "fake news." Results of a Pew Research Center survey conducted in early 2018 reflected this divide. It asked if "media criticism of political leaders keeps them from doing things they shouldn't," and found that 82 percent of Democrats but only 38 percent of Republicans agreed.[1] A related survey in Western Europe, also conducted by Pew in 2018, found that "public views of the news media are divided by populist leanings – more than left–right political positions," and that "those who hold populist views value and trust the news media less."[2] (Discussing 21st-century "populism" is outside the scope of this book, but suffice it to say that in current usage the word has been adopted by or applied to mostly far-right political movements.)

Governments may become frenzied in their efforts to control information, particularly when it is related to military affairs. This could be seen during the final two decades of the twentieth century, as the United Kingdom in the Falkland Islands and the United States in Kuwait went to war. Both governments were intent on avoiding by preemption the kind of political damage that was still perceived to have been caused by news reporting from Vietnam.[3] These two wars were brief, but both lasted sufficiently long for tight information controls to be imposed. These measures may have helped the two governments to achieve short-term political gains, but the ill will generated by their heavy-handed actions related to news reporting led to negotiated reforms that produced somewhat less restricted information availability in conflicts that followed.[4]

Complicating government efforts to restrain movement of information has been the steady advance of communication technology. This fostered faster, broader, and more independent gathering and dissemination of information. During the Falklands and Gulf conflicts, this new technology had limitations, such as its cost and the unwieldiness of some of the equipment it required, but it nevertheless highlighted new challenges that had to be addressed by governments seeking to control information. In the evolution of information at war, these "small wars" were important.

Falklands War 1982

The Falkland Islands (Islas Malvinas) are 8,000 miles from the United Kingdom, but they are home to about 3,200 British subjects (who are greatly outnumbered by their sheep). Ownership of the islands had long been a point of contention between Britain and Argentina before Argentina seized the islands in April 1982. British Prime Minister Margaret Thatcher promptly dispatched a naval task force to reclaim the territory.

Thatcher and the British military kept the Vietnam War in mind as they devised their strategy for controlling information.[5] Robert Harris wrote that "the American experience in Vietnam did as much as anything to shape the way in which the British government handled television during the Falklands crisis ... . The Vietnam analogy was a spectre constantly stalking the Falklands decision-makers and was invoked privately by the military as an object lesson in how not to deal with the media."[6]

The Thatcher government's approach to information control was stated forcefully by Foreign Secretary Francis Pym: "The duty of the government is to help the services win the war. In this sense if information withheld makes it easier to win the war, it should be withheld. There is no such thing as a public right to know information which reduces the possibility of the war being waged successfully."[7] From the Ministry of Defence came a pronouncement only slightly more moderate: "We aimed throughout not to lie. But there were occasions when we did not tell the whole truth and did not correct things that were being misread."[8]

The remote location of the Falklands worked to the advantage of the British information strategy. Journalists could not reach the war zone unless they were taken there by the Royal Navy. The communication technology of the day was still such that, once there, correspondents had no independent means of delivering their reports and had to rely on Ministry of Defence facilities to do so. As a result, information moved with pre-modern slowness. In 1854, during the Crimean War, the Charge of the Light Brigade was described in *The Times* of London 20 days after the battle happened. In 1992, some television reports took 23 days to get from the Falklands to their British audiences, and the average delay between filming and availability for broadcast was 17 days.[9]

Journalists traveling with the Royal Navy task force were told they must adhere to guidelines for "responsible reporting," as defined by the government, and commanding officers had authority to prevent transmission of reports that were judged to be in violation of those guidelines.[10] One shipboard press officer informed reporters, "You must have been told when you left you couldn't report bad news."[11] Journalists were also told by government press officers that their coverage would be "cleared," not "censored," and when, unappreciative of the semantic distinction, reporters tried to state in their stories that the content had been censored, that was disallowed; the word "censored" was censored.[12]

The British government soon paid a price for being so restrictive. British news organizations began using Argentine coverage, including television footage. They also found sources in the US government who were not sympathetic to the British decision to go to war and would quietly provide information about the conflict.[13]

Thatcher herself made clear that she was not interested in even-handed coverage of the war, particularly from the BBC. Speaking in the House of Commons, she said:

> Many people are very concerned indeed that the case for our British forces is not being put over fully and effectively. I understand that there are times when it seems that we and the Argentines are being treated almost as equals and almost on a neutral basis. I understand that there are occasions when some commentators will say that the Argentines did something and then "the British" did something. I can only say that if this is so, it gives offence and causes great emotion among many people.[14]

The prime minister preferred that news organizations use "we" or "our troops," rather than the more neutral "the British." The BBC and some other news organizations clung to semantic objectivity even during the war. Thatcher found support from some in the tabloid press, such as the conservative-leaning *Sun*, which praised her Commons remarks, saying in an editorial, "The Prime Minister did not speak of treason. The *Sun* does not hesitate to use the word."[15]

This kind of nastiness, whether from politicians or from within the news media, raises the stakes in any debate about information availability during wartime. In this instance, the war was brief and ended with a British victory, but even in a democracy such as Britain a poisonous residue may linger to affect other information in other circumstances.

Thatcher mellowed somewhat with the war's successful conclusion, which strengthened her political position. In early 1982, before the Falklands War, her personal approval rating in public opinion polls had been 24 percent. At war's end, her rating had risen to 60 percent approval. Labour Party politician Denis Healey wrote, "Mrs. Thatcher exploited the victory of our forces in the Falklands to create the feeling, both at home and abroad, that Britain was great again; she portrayed herself as the greatest national leader since Churchill, if not since Elizabeth the Virgin Queen."[16] Along similar lines, writing about the Falklands-influenced political milieu in which Thatcher operated, Peter Jenkins wrote: "The psychological need was for a success, a success of some kind, an end to failure and humiliation, to do something well, to win. Nostalgic knee-jerk reaction it may have been, vainglorious posturing in a post-imperial world of Super Powers, but it made people feel better, not worse."[17]

In the war's aftermath, British newspaper editor Charles Wintour observed that the government considered information to be a political commodity to which the public was not automatically entitled. He wrote that:

> the hidden attitudes of many people in authority toward the media have been exposed. They think the public should be told as little as possible. They don't object to deception on matters both large and small. They dislike reporters. And they prefer that ruling circles should be left to run the state without being bothered by troublesome disclosures and unpleasant truths. In fact, some of them don't really care much for democracy either.[18]

Similar concern was voiced by another British journalist, Sir Ian Trethowan, who wrote that politicians' restrictive approach to wartime information dissemination "showed an alarming lack of confidence in the emotional sturdiness of the public on whose behalf they claim to govern."[19]

As will be seen in the following analysis of another brief conflict, little impetus is needed for governments to move toward information controls in wartime; it is an almost instinctive reaction. Keeping the public well informed about a war undertaken in its name sometimes tends to be treated more as a nuisance than as a constructive obligation.

Gulf War 1990–1991

In August 1990, Iraq's army rolled into its small, oil-rich neighbor Kuwait and quickly seized control of the country. This invasion was a clear violation of sovereignty as well as being a threat to the stability of the region and the global oil economy. President George H. W. Bush was determined that "this shall not stand," and he began to build a coalition of Arab and other militaries to liberate Kuwait. Iraq's ruler, Saddam Hussein, likewise began preparing for a full-scale war.

Before going to war, Bush, who was facing a reelection campaign in 1992, needed to win the support of Congress and the American public, both of which displayed limited enthusiasm for the venture. Recognizing that he lacked the rhetorical flair of his predecessor Ronald Reagan,[20] Bush knew that he would need to build his case by selectively providing information that would push public opinion in the direction he wanted it to go.

Opinion surveys indicated that Americans were ambivalent about how the administration should respond to the Iraqi invasion. When the trumpets sound, public opinion rallies, but only to a certain extent. A *Washington Post* – ABC News poll found that 74 percent of respondents supported Bush's decision to send troops to the region with hopes that this show of force would convince Iraq to withdraw from Kuwait. But 68 percent opposed actually invading Iraq to drive its troops out of Kuwait.[21]

Bush knew that a strategy of strength without sacrifice (meaning threat without follow-up) was unlikely to suffice, and so he needed to prepare Americans for war and the expected costs in lives and money. The Pentagon's initial tactics in dealing with the news media were part of this preparation. Information about the upcoming war was focused on the US troops who were being deployed. Lawrence Grossman, who had been president of NBC News (until 1988), wrote: "The war build-up story was pictured largely in terms of personal vignettes and human-interest features. The amount of coverage was overwhelming and people could not seem to get enough of it."[22] Bolstering the administration's efforts was a public relations campaign orchestrated by the PR firm Hill and Knowlton, which had been hired by Citizens for a Free Kuwait to make the case for war. Supposedly a group of concerned individuals acting privately, Citizens for a Free Kuwait had a $12 million budget, $11.8 million of which came from the Kuwaiti government in exile.[23] Opponents of the looming war were not able to match this kind of lobbying effort.

Unlike Lyndon Johnson during *his* war, President Bush, Secretary of Defense Dick Cheney, and Joint Chiefs Chairman General Colin Powell not only understood the importance of controlling the narrative – especially as it was presented by television – but also knew how to do so. News organizations, however, did not seem to fully understand the domestic political significance of what they emphasized in their coverage. General Powell observed, "Once you've got all the forces moving and everything's being taken care of by the commanders, turn your attention to television because you can win the battle [but] lose the war if you don't handle the story right."[24]

This dynamic tension illustrated how the military may under-stand the news media better than the news media understand the military. In a postwar report, the Gannett Foundation stated that the news media's approach to the war was "without much planning or reflection and certainly with little historical perspective on the role of the press in wartime. At the same time, the military had made studious preparations for dealing with the press in this war, far beyond whatever had been done before."[25]

For the Pentagon, "handling the story right," as Powell prescribed, involved taking advantage of an important change in one way that information was reaching the public: the rise of Cable News Network, CNN. Founded in 1980 as television's first 24-hour global news channel, CNN was a perfect venue for a continuing news story that elicited great public interest. When the war began on January 16, 1991, CNN delivered live audio reports from Baghdad as the Iraqi capital was being attacked from the air by the American-led coalition. (Live video was not available that night.) This was the first time that the world could witness the beginning of a war in real time.

CNN's war coverage soon surpassed the big three broadcast networks in audience ratings. People wanted information about the war and wanted to access it on *their* schedules, not merely when news organizations decided to give it to them. For many, the morning newspaper and the evening newscast were no longer sufficient. If someone wanted to check on what was happening in the war at 2:00 pm or 2:00 am, she or he could do so by turning on CNN.

Of course, a 24-hour news channel needs lots of content, and that is where the Pentagon saw a great opportunity. One example: traditionally, an hour-long news briefing by the Defense Department would be taped and edited down to a few minutes at most for the standard 30-minute network newscast. But CNN had plenty of airtime to fill and would carry it live – meaning unedited – and then perhaps repeat it later in the day. The Defense Department also made available its footage from smart-bomb nose cameras that reduced battlefield destruction to videogame bloodlessness. Such content was always available from helpful Pentagon press officers. An all-news channel was a beast that needed to be fed, and the Pentagon was happy to provide the groceries.[26]

Another important change was the growing capability of US local broadcast news stations in covering international stories such as war. Local television outlets were eager to tell the stories of hometown soldiers, and they could purchase chunks of satellite time for reporting from the coalition staging areas in Saudi Arabia. The Pentagon offered local journalists (print as well as broadcast) free transportation from the United States to the war zone. Once there, the reporters were given access to service personnel from their locales, although this access was closely supervised by military public affairs officers. Meanwhile, Department of Defense press officers were also closely reading news stories to identify individual reporters' special interests and to screen out correspondents likely to produce negative coverage.[27]

The audience for war news eagerly consumed reports from the combat zone. *Newsweek* magazine saw its sales increase 90 percent, and the *Los Angeles Times* printed 200,000 extra copies of the daily paper.[28] From a political standpoint, this enlarged audience represented both peril and opportunity. During the Vietnam War, government officials saw their control of the information that reached the public decreasing as the war proceeded and individual journalists and their news organizations asserted their independence. By the time of the Gulf War, the mindset of the Bush administration – particularly within the Pentagon – was that this would not happen again. The result: rules strictly limiting journalists' freedom to report from the war zone. Documents outlining the Pentagon's public information policy included these points:

- "News media representatives will be escorted at all times. Repeat, at all times."
- Reporters could operate only in pools – small groups that went to places and talked with personnel selected by the escorting public affairs officers.
- The public would receive news stories that concluded with the phrase "Reports reviewed by military censors." This was the first time this had happened since World War II.[29]

News organizations had been outmaneuvered by the Pentagon's planners and had little time to protest because the ground war lasted only 100 hours before the Iraqis asked for a ceasefire. The resulting coverage gave news consumers a largely sanitized picture of war. ABC's Ted Koppel observed, "I'm not sure the public's interest is served by seeing what seems to have been such a painless war, when 50,000 to 100,000 people may have died on the other side."[30] *Newsweek*'s media critic Jonathan Alter stated: "The sad truth is that we 'covered' the war but we didn't report the war. There was very little independent journalism until the last hours of the conflict. Pool coverage is not journalism – it's something else. I'm not quite sure what it is, but I wouldn't call it journalism."[31] Correspondents, particularly those providing real-time coverage, became stars of their own manufactured dramas, sometimes donning gas masks and offering first-person accounts of the rumors and conjecture they had come across. Johanna Neuman wrote that television viewers "could not so much see war as they could observe news gathering in the war zone."[32]

This was fostered to some extent by the news media themselves. As Marcy Darnovsky observed:

> One of the major themes of media coverage during the 1991 Gulf War was itself media coverage of the Gulf War. Denunciations and defenses of the media's performance abounded in every genre of television and radio show and in every sort of newspaper and magazine. Stories about Pentagon press censorship and public approval of it, about fan clubs for a CNN reporter and the slickness of the networks' graphics, about Saddam Hussein's television strategy – all of these "angles" provided grist for the saturation coverage of the war.[33]

Among the challenges to truly covering the war were those related to censorship of real-time information. "Censorship" is considered by many in the news business to be abhorrent as a concept, but the realities of war and the sensitivity of battlefield information require occasional modification of reflexive opposition to governments' information controls. Even as vigorous a champion of the free flow of news as Edward R. Murrow had said in 1941: "I should be unwilling to broadcast from a nation at war without any censorship at all. The responsibility for human lives would be too great. It is impossible for the layman to know on all occasions just what piece of information, even a small detail, may cause the loss of a proud ship or a company of brave men."[34]

Murrow understood that the German military listened to his broadcasts to help to determine the effects of their bombing of Britain. Take Murrow's experience and move it forward 50 years and you find a similar situation with the televising of Iraqi missile strikes on Israel in January 1991. Live television pictures, which could be seen by the Iraqi military, showed smoke rising from where the missiles hit in Tel Aviv and elsewhere.[35] For the Israelis, there was no choice but to impose some censorship to prevent such news coverage from inadvertently serving as open source intelligence for the Iraqis. News organizations in the combat zone recognized the legitimacy of Israeli authorities' concerns (and also had no choice but to conform to the Israeli censors' rules).

At some point, however, censorship moves from military necessity to political expediency. Such was the case when the Bush administration in early 1991 declared the US Air Force base in Dover, Delaware – site of the military mortuary that would be used for

Americans killed in the war – to be off limits to news photographers. The Pentagon argued that this was to protect the privacy of the families of those killed in action, but a case can be made that the real reason was that Bush and his advisers did not want the public to be reminded on a daily basis, if the war were to go badly, of the true cost of war, exemplified by rows of flag-draped coffins being unloaded from aircraft. (The policy at the Dover base was not rescinded until 2009.)[36]

Whenever information is censored, the public is being deprived of knowledge. Sometimes this concerns matters about which there is no "*need* to know," and which involve true security issues. Sometimes, however, it is about topics that ought to be reported to the public but that the government wants to hide for political reasons. Censorship may be justified, as in the case of an in-progress intelligence or military operation that requires secrecy. Governments, however, deserve careful oversight because, as in the Dover case, it is easy to drift into tightening control of the information flow for reasons unrelated to operational security. One of the challenges in sustaining such oversight is being able to encourage the public to care about the dangers of rampant censorship. Without manifestations of public (as well as news media) objections to such maneuvering, governments may proceed unchecked as they shrink the amount of information available to their citizens.

The military understandably desires to avoid having combat objectives compromised by promiscuous disclosure of sensitive information. The public, meanwhile, deserves to possess enough information so it can make judgments about whether to support a war carried out in its name. In a democracy, trade-offs are inevitable.

Information Channels as Wartime Diplomatic Tools

Prior to the January 1991 air offensive against Iraq that was the prologue to the Gulf War's Operation Desert Storm, Saddam Hussein's government gave CNN permission to use in Baghdad a special kind of satellite telephone that was independent of Iraqi communication facilities. Only CNN had received this permission, which allowed them to broadcast live audio reports when the bombing of Baghdad began. Competitor networks were cut off after a few minutes when the Baghdad telephone-exchange building was hit during the attack, and these other news organizations found themselves needing to rely on the CNN reporting.[37]

Why did the Iraqis allow CNN to operate with such relative

freedom? Not primarily because they wanted to see how CNN was reporting the war, but rather because Saddam Hussein wanted to ensure that he had a means of *sending* information to the world, especially to the White House and the Pentagon, as well as to global publics. If, for example, during the early bombardment of Baghdad he had wanted to propose a ceasefire (which he didn't), the fastest way to do so would have been to arrange a live CNN interview – which the network would be eager to schedule – and say whatever he wanted, knowing that the broadcast would be monitored by the American and other coalition governments. The Iraqis also understood that they could influence live and taped reporting from Baghdad by controlling access to locations and people, such as areas damaged by US bombing and victims of the attacks.

Believing himself to be adept at media manipulation, Saddam Hussein thought he could shape worldwide (and particularly Arab) public opinion by having such a forum for information that he controlled. For its part, CNN understood that it was being used in this way, but the network saw the commercial, as well as journalistic, advantages of its information monopoly. CNN told its viewers that the coverage they were seeing had been supervised by Iraqi censors, but the public was hungry enough for unique coverage that concerns about such controls were mostly set aside. The Iraqis' information tactics often achieved what their government desired.

It turned out, of course, that information could not match firepower. From the bombing of Baghdad to the coalition ground forces destroying much of the Iraqi army, the Gulf War was a disaster for Saddam Hussein, although he survived to rule for more than another decade.

The Gulf War broadcast coverage was in some ways a televised descendant of Edward R. Murrow's London Blitz reporting a half-century earlier. It brought real-time war to global audiences, and it marked the further evolution of the relationship between war-making and information. This was largely a result of technological developments, CNN's "four-wire" satellite phone being just one of these. On another level, it also illustrated the lopsided nature of information management, with the Bush-orchestrated coalition able to push its version of events and its justification for its military action through global media venues. According to Douglas Kellner, "the mainstream media became a conduit for Bush administration and Pentagon policies and rarely allowed criticism of its actions, disinformation, and mishaps during the war. Television served primarily as a propaganda apparatus for the multinational forces arrayed against the

Iraqis and as a cheerleader for their every victory."[38] A harsh, but not inaccurate, judgment.

After 100 hours of combat, President Bush announced a ceasefire. For the American forces that were the spearhead of the coalition, the casualties were relatively light: of the 219 US deaths (212 men and 7 women), 154 were killed in battle and 65 died from non-battle causes; 35 of the battle deaths were a result of friendly fire.[39] Iraqi deaths were difficult to calculate; estimates range from 20,000 to 100,000.[40]

More wars lay ahead.

Embedded War

From the post-Korean-War years until the Gulf War, the US government's true "control" of conflict-related information had occurred only in brief episodes, such as during the military interventions in Grenada in 1983 and Panama in 1989. For the most part, as was the case during the Vietnam War, information streams from the government and news media may have competed against each other, but only rarely – and briefly – were they controlled by one party to the significant disadvantage of the other. They coexisted in a democratically anarchic environment.

The government-imposed controls during the Gulf War changed that dramatically, and after the war concluded in January 1991, news organizations knew that they needed to decide how to move forward. Legal action was not a satisfactory solution, because a case related to ensuring better journalistic access to the battlefield, if adjudicated after the Gulf War had concluded, would require the court to speculate about a situation that might or might not exist in a future war. Thus, a Gulf War-related lawsuit that was brought by news organizations was dismissed by a US District Court judge, who wrote that "prudence dictates that a final determination of the important Constitutional issues at stake be left for another day when the controversy is more sharply focused."[41]

So, just as military planners had developed a post-Vietnam information strategy, news professionals and other defenders of information freedom now had to plan for the next war – which would surely happen – and reassert the importance of freely accessing and disseminating information without excessive government interference. For their part, the Pentagon's public affairs specialists knew they would need to contend with new, technology-enhanced assertiveness on the part of journalists. The expensive and cumbersome

tools of information gathering that were relied upon during the
Gulf War era were evolving in ways that enhanced news media
independence. During the early 1990s, the satellite transmission
equipment a news organization would need to report live from a war
zone would have cost about $100,000. By 2003, the price tag was
a more affordable $20,000,[42] and heading downward. Further, the
equipment had shrunk, in some cases from truck-size to briefcase-
size. The press corps in the Iraq War, which began in 2003, could
deliver news while being more mobile and thus more independent
than in most previous conflicts.

Military planners recognized that this transformation would
challenge their ability to control – or even influence – the information
reaching global audiences.[43] After the 2001 terrorist attacks on the
United States and the resulting invasion of Afghanistan, the George
W. Bush administration began devising a plan to terminate the regime
of Iraq's Saddam Hussein. As a war to accomplish this became inevitable (perhaps it had long been inevitable), information management
was a crucial part of the US strategy.

There was never much doubt about the *military* outcome of
the initial stages of the war; the Iraqi military, if it did not possess
weapons of mass destruction, was at least as inferior to US forces
in 2003 as it had been in 1991, and would not be able to defeat the
Americans as they rolled toward Baghdad. But the *political* outcome
was far less certain, especially if it turned out that the American
rationale for going to war proved flawed. Similarly, because the
Iraq invasion planning was taking place little more than a year after
the 9/11 attacks, the administration assumed – rightly – that the
domestic public could be convinced to support the war, at least for
the presumably brief time it would take for US forces to accomplish
their mission. But significant constituencies within the *global* public
– especially in the Arab world – could be expected to be hostile to
a new American-instigated conflict. Careful management of information would be needed.

Support, even from the American public, was not left to chance.
The Bush administration forcefully made its case for war with a
sophisticated strategy designed to overwhelm potentially critical news
media and other naysayers. The US government's case was based on
"evidence" that Iraq was preparing weapons of mass destruction
(WMDs)[44] – chemical, biological, and nuclear – that could be used
against Americans and others. Administration officials characterized
(at least by implication) challenges to such allegations as unpatriotic
and dangerous.

To its lasting discredit, the American journalistic establishment failed to provide an appropriately thorough examination of the inconsistent administration rationale, instead mostly presenting the government's case as gospel. From August 2002 until the beginning of the war in March 2003, the *Washington Post* ran "more than 140 front-page stories that focused heavily on administration rhetoric against Iraq. Some examples: 'Cheney Says Iraqi Strike Is Justified'; 'War Cabinet Argues for Iraq Attack'; 'Bush Tells United Nations It Must Stand Up to Hussein or U.S. Will'; 'Bush Cites Urgent Iraqi Threat'; 'Bush Tells Troops: Prepare for War.'"[45] The *Post*'s Karen DeYoung commented in 2004:

> If there's something I would do differently – and it's always easy in hindsight – the top of the story would say, "We're going to war, we're going to war against evil." But later down it would say, "But some people are questioning it." The caution and the questioning was buried underneath the drumbeat ... The hugeness of the war preparation story tended to drown out a lot of that stuff.[46]

"Drowning out" cautionary stories often happened when reports that contradicted the administration's conventional wisdom were placed inside the newspaper, not on page 1, where they would get far more attention. One story by *Post* reporter Walter Pincus challenged government assertions: "Despite the Bush administration's claims [about WMDs], U.S. intelligence agencies have been unable to give Congress or the Pentagon specific information about the amounts of banned weapons or where they are hidden, according to administration officials and members of Congress," raising questions "about whether administration officials have exaggerated intelligence." Despite Pincus and others arguing with editors about the importance of this story, it ended up on page A17.[47]

A 2004 analysis of the *New York Times*'s pre-war coverage by that newspaper's Public Editor offered criticisms similar to those about the *Post*:

> Some of *The Times*'s coverage in the months leading up to the invasion of Iraq was credulous; much of it was inappropriately italicized by lavish front-page display and heavy-breathing headlines; and several fine articles by David Johnston, James Risen and others that provided perspective or challenged information in the faulty stories were played as quietly as a lullaby. Especially notable among these was Risen's "C.I.A. Aides Feel Pressure in Preparing Iraqi Reports," which was completed several days before the invasion and unaccountably held for a week. It didn't appear until three days after the war's start, and even then was interred on Page B10 ... . War requires an extra standard of

care, not a lesser one. But in *The Times's* W.M.D. coverage, readers
encountered some rather breathless stories built on unsubstantiated
"revelations" that, in many instances, were the anonymity-cloaked
assertions of people with vested interests. *Times* reporters broke many
stories before and after the war – but when the stories themselves later
broke apart, in many instances *Times* readers never found out.[48]

The *Washington Post* and the *New York Times* were by no means
the only news organizations whose pre-war coverage merits criticism.
Network television newscasts, such as those offered by Fox News,
tended to dress up reports with martial music and garish on-screen
artwork that seemed to reinforce the notion that waging war against
Iraq was unquestionably a valorous and essential task.

But the news media are not supposed to be cheerleaders. One of
their roles is to take a contrarian position and introduce skepticism
when any one side in a controversial matter – especially if that is
a powerful government's side – is rolling forward unobstructed. In
2002–3, getting to war was too easy, largely because information
was manipulated to help to achieve a political goal, and that manipulation was not adequately challenged. Some news organizations
– including, notably, Knight Ridder / McClatchy – investigated rather
than saluted, but these were in the minority.

In moving toward war, the Bush administration had a political
advantage that had not existed since December 1941, when the
Japanese attack on Pearl Harbor united Americans in willingness to
go to war. In the aftermath of the 2001 terrorist attacks, there was
minimal domestic opposition to the initial US invasion of Afghanistan
in pursuit of Al Qaeda. Devising a rationale for invading Iraq,
however, required more creativity. In part, the pro-war strategy was
this: when in doubt, wrap policy in the nation's flag and denounce
opponents of that policy as being unpatriotic.[49]

Journalists may fear being characterized as opponents of a war,
particularly when the public seems supportive of the government.
Longtime CBS News anchor Dan Rather told an interviewer, "There
was a fear in every newsroom in America, a fear of losing your job ...
the fear of being stuck with some label, unpatriotic or otherwise."[50]
Veteran journalist Andrew Meldrum stated, "The media appeared to
be afraid of being called unpatriotic, when its national duty was to
question if it was wise to send American troops to Iraq."[51] *New York
Times* columnist Paul Krugman wrote in February 2003 that "U.S.
media outlets – operating in an environment in which anyone who
questioned the administration's foreign policy is accused of being
unpatriotic – have taken it as their assignment to sell the war, not to

present a mix of information that might call the justification of the war into question."[52]

Worth noting is that what was attacked as "unpatriotic" in 2002 and early 2003 was likely to be seen as "good journalism" by 2008, when the Iraq War was widely considered by Americans to be a bloody mess from which the United States should extricate itself. (Similarly, pejorative labels attaching to critical reporting about the Vietnam War in 1965 had turned positive by 1968 as opposition to the war grew.) It can be argued that news organizations should not be deterred by name-calling and should just do their jobs. But the news business is a business, dependent on revenue from news consumers and advertisers. News executives, like politicians, read the opinion polls, recognizing that their organizations' financial viability depends not solely on the quality of their product but also on their audiences' goodwill, which can diminish rapidly if charges of being unpatriotic during wartime are believed.

Once combat operations began, the struggle for control of information continued. The Pentagon planned to influence news coverage as thoroughly as possible – not as overtly as during the 1991 war, but with enough "guidance" to shape the public's perceptions of events in Iraq. And so the Department of Defense agreed to provide approximately 700 slots for journalists (about 100 of whom would be from non-US news organizations) who would be "embedded" with the invading force.

According to the Pentagon, these journalists would have "minimally restrictive access to U.S. air, ground, and naval forces," and they would "live, work, and travel" with the military units to which they were assigned. The reason for this approach, as stated by the Pentagon, was this: "Our ultimate strategic success in bringing peace and security to this region will come in our long-term commitment to supporting our democratic ideals. We need to tell the factual story – good or bad – before others seed the media with disinformation and distortions." The audience was understood to be not just Americans, but also "the public in allied countries whose opinion can affect the durability of our coalition, and publics in countries where we conduct operations, whose perceptions of us can affect the cost and duration of our involvement."[53]

The practicalities of gathering information in a war zone were reflected in the caveat that a unit commander could restrict transmission of information in "a combat/hostile environment," particularly if the journalists' work-product referred to specific numbers of troops and plans for upcoming operations. These were common-sense matters that most journalists did not find problematic, although some news organizations – mainly the larger ones – assigned some of their journalists to the embed program and others as "unilaterals" who operated in the combat zone with less Pentagon supervision but at greater personal risk.

The Pentagon's preference was made clear in its policy toward the unilaterals, of whom there were about 1,800 – more than twice as many as were embedded. When some of these journalists were kept from entering Iraq, Department of Defense spokesperson Bryan Whitman (one of the architects of the embedding plan) said: "We are going to control the battle space. Reporters who are not embedded are going to be treated like any other civilian."[54] In other words, the access and physical protection the military provided to the embedded journalists would not be extended to the unilaterals.

Pentagon spokespersons were fond of touting their support for "a free press in a free society" as motivation for the new system, but they also had learned during the recent fighting in Afghanistan that enemies there, primarily the Taliban, were increasingly adept at staging scenes of physical destruction and civilian casualties and blaming them falsely on the Americans. (It should be noted that some such scenes *were* actually the result of US military action.) The Pentagon feared that Saddam Hussein might try to do the same thing in Iraq, and so it wanted news media presence on the battle-field "to do third-person objective reporting that we knew would ... illuminate lies and exaggerations."[55]

This and related concerns were not unique to this conflict. Reports about nonexistent "massacres" and similar events had fueled the propaganda of warring nations for centuries. What was new was the relative ease with which state and non-state actors could deliver such information to global audiences. If, for instance, Al Jazeera or another regional news organization arrived at the scene and produced a report based on what the Taliban claimed had occurred, that story could race through worldwide television and online venues before governments could respond. In such circumstances, it was easy to create a presumption of guilt about a party to the conflict. The increasing emphasis on the speed with which news would be reported sometimes superseded traditional journalistic verification procedures. Since the Iraq War, information delivery has accelerated even more, and – as we will see – the numbers, motivations, and diversity of those who participate in this process have grown exponentially.

Gradually, information was assuming a more central role in warfare, not as a new phenomenon but as one with expanding reach and influence that affected military and related political strategies. From the Pentagon's perspective, increasing the news media's dependence on the military through embedding appeared to be an effective means of limiting the unrestrained Halberstam-like coverage that, 40 years earlier, had purportedly undermined the American public's support for the war in Vietnam and contributed to the American defeat. Myths have a lengthy shelf-life.

For the time being, the Pentagon seemed content with the embedding approach as a means of addressing the political aspects of waging war. Few of the journalists had any military experience of their own, and this made them particularly susceptible to "guidance" from the troops they covered and lived with. Many of the stories from Iraq mixed human interest with battlefield action, and they meshed well with many Americans' post-9/11 patriotism. Much of the early news coverage supported a narrative of intrepid young American troops defending their country from allies of the 9/11 attackers.

When the fighting appears to be going well for one side, the audience on that side tends to be happy with the news coverage, although opinion can shift quickly. During the first days of the Iraq War (March 20–22, 2003) as US forces successfully began their advance toward Baghdad, 80 percent of the respondents in a Pew Research Center survey rated the coverage as "excellent" or "good." By early April, that rating was holding at 74 percent, although 39 percent said the war was receiving too much attention at the expense of other issues, particularly those related to the economy.[56]

Despite the popularity of the early war coverage, there were concerns among some journalists that the "shock and awe" pyrotechnics so embraced by the Pentagon were too dominant in the reporting, obscuring topics such as how a conquered Iraq was to be governed and what the war's long-term effects in the Middle East might be. Jack Fuller, president of Tribune Publishing Co., said that the television coverage during the first weeks of the war had been "utterly riveting," but that it also "demonstrated that there is a difference between seeing and understanding."[57]

One aspect of information at war is creating an intimidation factor for strategic reasons. Global audiences seeing – even if not fully understanding – news portrayals of the unstoppable American sweep toward Baghdad could serve this purpose. As was the case with the "100-hour war" in the Gulf in 1991, the United States was putting its ferocious capabilities on full display, implicitly warning other mid-level nations about America's formidable military prowess. (Major powers such as China and Russia presumably also took heed, even if they were not intimidated, and evaluated the US tactics and weaponry.)

Of course, the Iraq War soon deteriorated into a horrific fiasco. The principal reason stated by the United States for going to war – Iraq's possession of weapons of mass destruction – proved to be untrue. The notion that post-Saddam Iraq would treat American forces as "liberators" and then quickly and easily evolve into a model democracy was soon seen to be ludicrous. Casualties mounted as the war dragged on. According to Brown University's Watson Institute, by 2018 the number of Iraqi civilians killed by direct violence since the US invasion was more than 182,000, with several hundred thousand more estimated to have been killed in other violence related to the war.[58] As for active combatants, from March 2003 through April 2015, 4,489 American troops and 3,481 US military contractors were killed, along with 319 other allied soldiers, and 12,000 Iraqi soldiers and police.[59] Some surveys report much higher numbers.[60]

Initially, the George W. Bush administration proved itself adept at drowning out bad news and criticism about the Iraq War with its own version of events. In an America still traumatized by the 9/11 attacks, invoking the "war on terror" proved a political panacea, at least for a while. Semantics were policed: the treatment of prisoners by US troops at Iraq's Abu Ghraib prison was not "torture"; the fighting among Iraqi factions was not a "civil war." When the news media used such terminology or other language the administration did not like, government officials pushed back with their own messaging delivered through supportive news venues.[61]

Such cases are good examples of the different approaches to using information at war. When a government is intent on building and sustaining support among domestic constituencies, "information" may be based on something less than objectivity. In the run-up to the Iraq War, reinforcing fears about Saddam Hussein's possession of weapons of mass destruction was accomplished by reciting clever, memorable phrases, such as, "If we wait to find the smoking gun, it might appear in the form of a mushroom cloud." The president, vice president, national security adviser, and others in the administration recited this as their mantra.

This illustration is relevant to larger issues related to information at war because "war" should be defined broadly, including pre- and post-combat periods that are integral elements of a conflict. The Murrow example discussed in chapter 1 was concerned with information relevant to America's decisions about its level of engagement in a war to which it was not a party. The circumstances were quite different in 2002–3; the 9/11 attacks had left much of the American public in a far more bellicose frame of mind than had been the case in 1940 and part of 1941, when US isolationist opinion was still strong (although declining). The Iraq War was also very different from the 2001 invasion of Afghanistan, which required virtually no preliminary information efforts, because the Bush administration faced no significant pushback as it quickly began its pursuit of Al Qaeda, the perpetrator of the 9/11 attacks.

Making this more complicated is the fact that what may be considered a "war of necessity" – as arguably was the case initially with Afghanistan – can become a "war of choice." Richard Haass, among others, advanced the argument that the prolonged US combat role in Afghanistan constituted such a transformation of the conflict.[62] When that change occurs, the role of information is also changing in numerous ways: news coverage of government policy gradually becomes more adversarial; government information efforts face greater challenges about their credibility; and public opinion tends to slide away from the reflexive "rally 'round the flag" attitude as information consumers become more receptive to material that is critical of the conduct of the war.

While the fighting in Afghanistan and Iraq continued, changes rooted in communication technology were occurring that would further alter the balance of information power between governments and publics. Internet access was expanding, providing channels for streams of information from an unprecedented array of sources. Social media, in particular, were proving (even in their infancy) to be equalizers in the contest for information control. Dramatic evidence of this evolution would be seen during events in the second decade of the new century, but these were foreshadowed by the presence of important new players.

The traditional providers of wartime information had been the government and conventional news organizations. Then, the bloggers arrived. These were individual soldiers and civilians who used the internet to tell their own versions of events in the war zone. The first days of the Iraq invasion marked the debut of "L. T. Smash," a US military officer who filed reports such as this: "Saddam fired a couple of those Scuds that he doesn't have at me this afternoon. He missed." "Smash's" website quickly attracted 6,000 visitors a day – minuscule by more recent standards but still an important sign of a new class of information provider and a new willingness of at least some members of the news audience to sample the work of those providers.[63] Writing in the *Washington Post*, Howard Kurtz characterized these blogs as "idiosyncratic, passionate, and often profane, with the sort of intimacy and attitude that are all but impossible in newspapers and on television."[64]

The Department of Defense was of two minds about this. Some officials there saw blogging as a way to better connect American service members with the public and thus increase support for the military's mission. Others disliked some soldier-bloggers' criticism of military policy and feared that blogging could be used by enemy propagandists and undermine military discipline. *New York Times* reporter James Dao wrote that "the debate reflects a broader clash of cultures: between the anarchic, unfiltered, bottom-up nature of the Web and the hierarchical, tightly controlled, top-down tradition of the military."[65]

One US Army enlisted man in Iraq, Chris Missick, presented his view of the issue in his blog:

> Never before has a war been so immediately documented, never before have sentiments from the front scurried their way to the home front with such ease and precision. Here I sit, in the desert, staring daily at the electric fence, the deep trenches and the concertina wire that separates the border of Iraq and Kuwait, and write home and upload my daily reflections and opinions on the war and my circumstances here, as well as some of the pictures I have taken along the way. It is amazing, and empowering, and yet the question remains, should I as a lower enlisted soldier have such power to express my opinion and broadcast to the world a singular soldier's point of view? To those outside the uniform who have never lived the military life, the question may seem absurd, and yet, as an example of what exists even in the small following of readers I have here, the implications of thought expressed by soldiers daily could be explosive.[66]

Pentagon officials may have considered blogs such as Missick's to be competing with their official versions of events on the battlefield, but the news media also had to adjust to the presence of these authentic voices that told stories often far grittier than those provided by correspondents who observed the war but did not do the fighting themselves. As for the public, would military blogs ("miliblogs") supplement or replace other information sources? And when a soldier used his cellphone camera in Iraq's Abu Ghraib prison to record incidents of torture by American soldiers, how would people around the world react to this information, which without those photos might not have been discovered by journalists or made public by the Pentagon?

The information universe was becoming more crowded, and that process would soon accelerate.

The 2011 Arab Uprisings

During the 2011 Arab uprisings (sometimes referred to as the "Arab spring"), levels of violence varied greatly. In Tunisia, where it all began, the president quickly opted for exile, the military refused to fire on protestors, and Tunisians set about building their future. At the other end of the spectrum was Syria, where President Bashar al-Assad promptly made clear that even mild protest – such as teenagers painting anti-regime graffiti on walls – would be met by brute force. Syria plunged into a multi-party civil war and, as of this writing in mid-2020, the blood continues to flow.

Some of the impetus for the uprisings was provided by information, which poured through the region with unprecedented speed and reach. Even if, with the exception of Syria, the uprisings were not "wars" in the conventional sense, they provide important lessons about information's power to affect political outcomes in high-stakes circumstances that are in some ways similar to armed conflict.

A primary issue was the "ownership" of information. In Egypt, for instance, the government ordered the dominant state-run news media to suppress reports about the Tunisian upheaval, fearing – correctly, as it turned out – that such information could act as a political virus, infecting Egyptians with a similar desire for regime change. This government tactic had been used for decades with considerable success in the Middle East and elsewhere. But that was before the era of satellite television, and in 2011 many Egyptians were not satisfied with the turgid reporting of government-controlled channels and were instead turning to Qatar-based Al Jazeera and other regional and international satellite networks for news. Al Jazeera was providing ample coverage of events in Tunisia, and there was little the Egyptian government could do about it.

Although internet access was still limited in many Arab countries, satellite television was widely available, as could be seen in the thousands of satellite dishes on rooftops in cities such as Cairo. In Tunisia, for example, broadband penetration was just 24 percent, but television's reach was 93 percent.[67] The satellite dish was a new instrument of popular empowerment.

Social media also were important, and the Egyptian uprising was sometimes called "the Twitter revolution" or "the Facebook revolution." But those labels are not really accurate, for a number of reasons. For one thing, they impose a Western construct on uprisings that belonged to the people who went into the streets to protest. Journalist Richard Engel said that at the root of the uprisings were "people's dignity, people's pride. People are not able to feed their families."[68]

The "Al Jazeera effect" is worth noting because, in the first decades since the channel's founding in 1996, it had a transformative effect in much of the Arab world. The issue for Al Jazeera was not merely providing information that its audience could not get elsewhere. Global news channels such as the BBC and CNN were watched avidly by those wanting news undiluted by their own governments' views. But Al Jazeera offered news about Arabs from Arab journalists, so Arab viewers could see the events that affected them through their own eyes. The biases that appeared in the Al Jazeera reporting were not those of a condescending West, but rather were those widely shared among those in the Arab audience. Al Jazeera first made its mark in 2000 during the Second Intifada, with coverage that was far more passionate and pro-Palestinian than was available from non-Arab news organizations. During the next several years, with the post-9/11 arrival of a huge American military force in the region, Al Jazeera's coverage was relied upon for its Arab perspective on the fighting.

By 2011, Al Jazeera was sharing a more crowded Arab media universe with the likes of the Saudi-backed and more conservative Al Arabiya, as well as with many more localized news and religious channels. The numerous Arab media outlets changed the political context in which regimes such as that of Egypt's President Hosni Mubarak found themselves contending with loud and angry voices.

Also worth noting is the organizational foundation of the 2011 Egyptian demonstrations: although they surprised many world leaders and publics, they were not spontaneous and were not overseen by neophytes empowered by new media tools that they were just then learning to use. Many organizers of the Egyptian protests had been working for at least several years with groups supporting industrial workers and anti-regime groups, honing the skills needed for information-age activism.[69]

Nevertheless, the ability to use internet-based media to share information widely and quickly (and usually safely) was important in 2011 and, as we shall see, its significance in conflict has increased in the years since. Writing in 2011, Clay Shirky asked: "Do social media allow insurgents to adopt new strategies? ... Digital networks have acted as a massive positive supply shock to the cost and spread of information, to the ease and range of public speech by citizens, and to the speed and scale of group coordination."[70]

One word in Shirky's observation worth particular notice is

"insurgents." There are benign insurgencies of those seeking peaceful social change, but we will soon see that some modern insurgencies prove to be a particularly nasty species of conflict that relies heavily on information manipulation.

The basic tool for much of this is the cellphone. As of 2019, there were approximately 5 billion cell- (or "mobile") phone users in the world, roughly 63 percent of the global population.[71] Studies by the Pew Research Center found that in 11 "emerging economy" countries,[72] public opinion was divided about cellphones' usefulness. They provide access to information but also are seen to be causing harm by spreading misinformation.[73]

For organizers of political protests or insurgent warfare, the cellphone provides timely connections among individuals and groups. Its camera lets its users become quasi-journalists, sending images to far-flung audiences. And unless a government is desperate enough to shut down the internet, which could have severe economic repercussions for a country, this information flow is difficult to stop.

The use of cellphones and internet venues in Egypt and elsewhere during the 2011 Arab uprisings demonstrated the significance of technology-based information empowerment. But did proponents of expanded democracy "win"? Despite initial optimism, was the "Arab spring" just a prelude to a particularly harsh Arab winter? In summer 2013, Egypt's experiment came to a brutal end. In Syria, meanwhile, an even worse situation was ripping the country apart.

Syria

As events in Syria, beginning in 2011, have underscored, the extent of information's power depends on numerous factors. It can, for instance, have considerable effect when a political vacuum exists, such as when inept or irresolute rulers do not design effective information strategies of their own to counter those of their opponents. But when information runs into ruthlessly unleashed brute force, it is likely to be overmatched.

This was the case in Syria, as President Bashar al-Assad's regime responded to initially peaceful protests with guns, tanks, and aircraft … and with terror and torture. Further, Assad and his advisers did not view even the most negative information – such as critical coverage by Al Jazeera and videos posted on YouTube by regime opponents – as an existential threat, although it was enough of a problem to deserve heartless suppression. Hostile information could be dealt with. This government in this war had confidence in the supremacy of its violence.

As the Syrian War dragged on year after year, it became ever bloodier, with participants including Islamic State, Russia, Turkish Kurds, and, to a lesser extent, the United States. Estimates of the number of dead vary, but 500,000 is a widely accepted figure (which, as of this writing in early 2020, continues to grow).[74] Approximately 6 million refugees have fled Syria, and more than 6 million others have been displaced within the country.[75] (Those numbers also continue to grow.) The population of Syria was about 17 million in 2019, down from approximately 23 million in 2012.[76]

About two-thirds of Syrian homes had satellite dishes that allowed access – although often surreptitious – to foreign news channels. The content of many of them was harshly critical of the Assad regime. In the face of overwhelming force, however, the average Syrian could do little with this information. Further, the Syrian government monitored internet content, extracting IP addresses and then tracking down and arresting critics of the regime. Assad supporters also stole opposition activists' online identities and impersonated them in online forums, distorting information for their own purposes.[77]

Nevertheless, enough information about the war reached the outside world to stir outrage about the conflict, and particularly about the Syrian government's tactics, which included the use of chemical weapons on civilians. We will see in the next chapter that Syrian "citizen journalists" courageously kept open some channels of information from combat zones. No government could claim "We didn't know" what was happening within Syria.

But what did knowledge – even of undeniable atrocities – produce? Of the world's major powers that could have made a difference in the war, only Russia and Iran intervened in a significant way, and that was in support of Assad. As the euphoria of the Arab uprisings dissipated, it became clear that "new media" – satellite television and online venues – would not necessarily be able to counteract more traditional elements of geopolitical strength.

It is important to keep in mind that information's policy-related value is primarily as a stimulus to political and/or military action; it helps to shape the intellectual environment within which policymakers and the public make decisions about priorities and courses of action. Beyond that it can do little. In cases such as Syria and in other humanitarian emergencies, information per se is a factor only to the extent that it can educate about the situation and perhaps stir the collective public conscience. That latter task can be extraordinarily challenging, especially when the public is receiving mixed messages, as when information from news media, non-governmental organizations (NGOs), and other sources seems to mandate action, but governments – for whatever reasons (sometimes good ones) – are determined not to be pushed into "doing something" in response to the crisis of the moment.

Such are the instances when competition for information control matters most – when it transcends questions of access and dissemination, and instead potentially has great effect on many lives. Those who wield influence in the information world do not always realize that they are not playing an insiders' game – "us" versus "the government" – and may forget that many in the public are not mere spectators, but can be profoundly affected by the information that they and others receive. Some of those who see innate value in sustaining the freest possible flow of information believe they have a moral duty to ensure that information channels remain open. In this way, they may shape the future role of information at war.

3

War Information Expands

The nature of warfare is rarely static. Change is driven primarily by technology and politics. We have "progressed" from swords and spears to the tools of present-day warfare, which include long-range sniper rifles for killing one person at a time and nuclear weapons that can obliterate millions in moments. Unchanged, however, is the horrific violence of conflict, including the victimization of innocents, and the willingness at times of state and non-state actors to rely on armed conflict to achieve their political goals.

How does information affect this evolution? Communication flow, like warfare, is in many ways dependent on technologies that help to determine the comprehensiveness of gathering and the speed of delivering information. It may also be influenced by political decisions that aid or obstruct this process.

What are the connections between communication and conscience? Casualties among noncombatants and the persistent abuse of women during war are sometimes dismissed as merely "collateral damage." News coverage of even genocidal terrors has often been superficial and belated. The scale of carnage can be numbing and, for distant onlookers, difficult to grasp.

This brings to mind a comment attributed to Joseph Stalin: "The death of one person is a tragedy; the death of a million is a statistic."[1] That observation, like most of Stalin's thinking, disregards elements of basic humanity, elements that information might help to reassert.

"Never Again"

Individual reporters and journalism as a profession have gradually accepted greater responsibility for calling the public's attention to the civilian suffering that accompanies war. When this suffering happens in remote locations such as Rwanda or Myanmar, the governments in those places may find it politically inconvenient to acknowledge even massive losses of life or to allow information about the situation to reach the outside world. Journalists therefore find themselves facing difficult but essential responsibilities as sentinels of conscience. Their work might alert global publics to what is happening and generate pressure on policymakers who could come to the aid of the victims.

Since the World War II Holocaust, which went largely unremarked by news media and governments as it took place, political leaders have been quick to pledge that such an atrocity will "never again" happen. But genocide keeps happening ... again and again.

Genocide can be defined simply as targeted actions aimed at destroying particular groups of people. The 1948 United Nations Convention on the Prevention and Punishment of the Crime of Genocide defines it more formally this way:

> In the present Convention, genocide means any of the following acts committed with intent to destroy, in whole or in part, a national, ethnical, racial or religious group, as such:
> a. Killing members of the group;
> b. Causing serious bodily or mental harm to members of the group;
> c. Deliberately inflicting on the group conditions of life calculated to bring about its physical destruction in whole or in part;
> d. Imposing measures intended to prevent births within the group;
> e. Forcibly transferring children of the group to another group.[2]

Some of these acts have occurred in places outside the areas from which information regularly flows to the larger public, and governments that might have intervened have claimed that they had not received sufficient information to enable them to respond. Visiting Rwanda in 1998, four years after 800,000 persons were murdered there, President Bill Clinton told an audience, "It may seem strange to you here, especially the many of you who lost members of your family, but all over the world there were people like me sitting in offices, day after day, who did not fully appreciate the depth and the speed with which you were being engulfed by this unimaginable terror."[3]

Clinton's implied excuse for inaction was that he hadn't been fully informed about the events in Rwanda, but United Nations Secretary-General Kofi Annan said: "The fundamental failure was lack of political will, not the lack of information. If it is lack of information that prevents action, that prevents the solution of crises, then I think we would have very few crises in the world today."[4] Information is abundant; political resolve less so.

Annan's point about the availability of information and the weakness of "political will" is important. To stimulate political action, information must be delivered with enough quantity, frequency, and urgency to capture and hold the public's attention. Beyond that, the information must be of a kind that touches the emotions of people who are far removed – physically, politically, and culturally – from the genocide. That can be a steep hill to climb.

Countering the notion that there is too little information available about a particular event is the reality that, in the ever-growing flood of information in which the public tries to swim, it is difficult to motivate information consumers and policymakers to care enough about a particular situation to manifest the political will that might affect policy.

Timeliness on the part of journalists and other information providers is also important. General Romeo Dallaire, who commanded the United Nations Assistance Mission for Rwanda in 1994, later wrote: "Looking back, it seems that the dearth of in-depth media reporting of a conflict before it actually went catastrophic was an absence that permitted and even encouraged those who were going to pursue a more extreme position to actually do so – and enabled them to believe that they might even escape the condemnation of the international community."[5] Everything moves quickly today; the murder of 800,000 Rwandans took place in just 100 days. When information is delayed, it has minimal value beyond offering sad lessons, and even timely reporting must contend with the information overload that is so prevalent today.

The Rwandan genocide also illustrated how information purveyors can sometimes act as *de facto* combatants, contributing to rather than helping to alleviate slaughter. Dallaire observed that:

> the local media in the country, in particular the extremist radio station Radio Télévision Libre des Mille Collines (RTLM), were literally part of the genocide. The genocidaires used the media like a weapon. The haunting image of killers with a machete in one hand and a radio in the other never leaves you … . To my mind it is indisputable that the use of hate media by proponents of the genocide had an impact on events.[6]

Related to this, another lesson from Rwanda cited by Dallaire is the need for a military force such as his UN troops to be able to monitor local media, which requires equipment and translators. This might have enabled him and his superiors at UN headquarters in New York to recognize the level of viciousness that was being communicated through RTLM and other information venues, and so anticipate the violence that followed.

The best way to characterize the international news media response to Rwanda is as too little, too late. Superimposing today's technologies on the 1994 events, one can speculate about possible responses by news organizations and publics that might have occurred if Rwandans had had access to 21st-century social media and had used YouTube and other media forums to provide real-time graphic evidence of the mass murder that was taking place.

Another factor to consider when looking back at information about the Rwanda genocide (among other conflicts) is racism. Is there a tendency in white-majority cultures to be dismissive of violence among people of color? "Tribalism" is the kind of condescending characterization that helps to push some wars toward the outer boundaries of public attention.[7]

Political diffidence amidst crisis will always be with us, but perhaps it will be less prevalent with information being shared more quickly and broadly. That might be wishful thinking, but clearly the *lack* of information is likely to diminish the chances of a constructive public response in times of crisis.[8] Journalist Charlayne Hunter-Gault wrote, "What is important is that there be a record that helps provide the outline of lessons learned, so that, for example, the world will not be allowed to forget the consequences of doing nothing in Rwanda."[9]

Aside from speculation about what might have been, the history of recent decades offers numerous lessons about wartime tragedies and the information that accompanies them. One instance: for several years preceding the Rwanda slaughter, journalists and others had witnessed horrific crimes in the former Yugoslavia, especially in Bosnia. Correspondents' experiences there led to considerable introspection among some journalists and new consideration of the significance of information at war.

Information Challenges in Bosnia

The shattering of what had been Yugoslavia is a complex story best told elsewhere. But the importance of gathering and delivering information about the war there is in itself significant in the evolution of wartime journalism and the nature of how and when information becomes available to global publics. In such conflicts, even with abundant information flowing, sad ironies abound. One Bosnian Muslim told an American journalist: "We can watch CNN. We can watch reports about our own genocide!"[10]

How do information gatekeepers respond in such situations as they try to remain objective amidst misery? Peter Maass of the *Washington Post* wrote: "Journalists observe other people's tragedies; we rarely experience them. The difference is immense."[11] And *Newsday*'s Roy Gutman said: "Your number one concern on earth is getting the full story, getting out of there, and getting the story out. You don't have time for emotions. You really just simply concentrate on what you're doing."[12]

A commitment to emotional distancing might seem appropriate for journalists, but among those covering the Bosnia War were some who questioned this. David Rieff wrote that in his view the "lack of objectivity is a badge of honor," adding:

> I do not think that we had the obligation to be objective about the Bosnian War any more than a journalist in 1940 would have had the obligation to be objective about the Second World War ... One would hope that had a reporter managed to get [into the Warsaw Ghetto], he or she would not have written a piece that tries to present the German and the Jewish points of view as if they were morally of equal weight.[13]

Rieff's example underscores the fact that, as long as information is being gathered by human beings, not robots, moral judgments will influence content. In terms of journalistic practice, criticizing stark objectivity is easiest when you are on the ground in the midst of bloody chaos and you believe that "good" and "bad" sides are clearly identifiable. But information consumers far removed from a conflict may have a less sharply focused view of events, and they may prefer information to be presented without being passed through someone else's moral filter (even if that filter is designated as "fairness" or "neutrality"). Governments are expected to provide information that serves their own interests rather than being resolutely objective, but if the news media also stray from objectivity, the already imperfect balance between government and journalistic information providers may become severely skewed, as can be seen in cases in which governments overtly control the information flows to the public.[14]

Most journalists would admit – even if just to themselves – that they want their news products to have *effect*; they want news consumers to pay attention and respond to the information they receive, especially when lives are at stake. The BBC's Martin Bell wrote about Bosnia: "We were drawn into this war as something other than the witnesses and chroniclers of it. We were also participants." And when he was asked by Bosnians about how the world was reacting to events there, "I could hardly answer that it was none of my business. It was everybody's business ... perhaps *especially* that of the journalists, because if the world didn't know, its ignorance was our failure."[15]

But perhaps journalists covering the Bosnia War overestimated their influence. David Rieff took a hard look at the supposed connection between information and political action:

> It was the conceit of journalism that if people back home could only be told and shown what was actually happening in Sarajevo, if they had to see on their television screens images of what a child who has just been hit by a soft-nosed bullet or a jagged splinter of shrapnel really looks like, or the bodies of citizens massacred as they queued for bread or water, then they would want their governments to do something. The hope of the Western press was that an informed citizenry back home would demand that their governments not allow the Bosnian Muslims to go on being massacred, raped, or forced from their homes.[16]

Despite reporting that was often graphic and heart-wrenching, outcry from much of the "informed citizenry" during the fighting in Bosnia was muted – too quiet to outweigh the risk analyses that governments' policymakers relied on to maintain their distance from meaningful involvement. This war provided examples of the tensions that may exist between an increasingly aggressive press corps and governments that were trying to avoid being pushed into intervention. Because these governments were not on-the-ground parties to the conflict, they had limited ability to control the information flow or shape the information content their publics were receiving from the news media. And so, their policymakers had to live with news-generated pressure of varying intensity.

These policymakers also knew, however, the sentiments of their own constituencies. How were news accounts affecting the voters who might determine the policymakers' futures? How attentive were they to news reports, and how susceptible were they to the moral arguments – implicit and explicit – in the information they received?

For their part, journalists, often at considerable personal risk, were shaping the information they provided within a context of moral outcomes that they hoped would induce governments and publics to respond. Some journalists did not shy away from forcefully framing inaction as political failure. Peter Jennings, anchor of ABC's principal television newscast, introduced one report from Bosnia this way: "Once again, Bosnian civilians forced to flee their homes in terror while the Western European nations and the United States do nothing about it."[17]

In 1992, journalists themselves were still learning about the scope of atrocities being perpetrated in Bosnia. *Newsday* reporter Roy Gutman told of receiving a telephone call one night from a Bosnian Muslim political leader in Bosnia's second-largest city, Banja Luka. The source told Gutman:

> They are shipping Muslim people through Banja Luka in cattle cars. Last night there were twenty-five train wagons for cattle crowded with women, old people, and children. They were so frightened. You could see their hands through the openings. We were not allowed to come close. Can you imagine that? It's like Jews being sent to Auschwitz. In the name of humanity, please come.[18]

Gutman went. He was able to confirm his source's information and he found leads to two additional stories: mass murder in Serb-run concentration camps, and systematic rape by Serb troops. He did what he was supposed to do – he wrote about it, and the additional publicity his reporting stimulated led to the Serb government closing one of its biggest concentration camps and allowing Red Cross access to some prisoners.

A constructive step, albeit a relatively small one. The breadth and severity of a war's horrors are likely to be first recognized by on-the-scene information gatherers – men and women who may find it difficult to comprehend why it is that what they are seeing and reporting is eliciting only tepid response from potentially powerful publics and policymakers. Part of the difficulty is that these audiences are distant physically and emotionally. Information can sometimes make the remote seem proximate, but bridging emotional distance is particularly challenging. It is important to remember that, between the gathering of information and delivering it to the public, lies a multifaceted process over which the initial gatherers have only limited influence. The information will pass through numerous hands and be subject to various objective and subjective pressures before reaching the public. If news correspondents are the ones doing the gathering, there may be a series of editors or producers through which the material must pass. News organizations, especially major ones, are often formidably bureaucratic.

Further complicating the information-gathering in Bosnia was the political reality that the war's protagonists understood how information could be manipulated. Martin Bell wrote that, when reporters were nearby, Bosnian Muslim officials might provoke the Serbs:

> And where the shells landed and did their indiscriminate damage, the cameras would never be far away. Nor would the [Bosnian] government spokesmen demanding action. This was the way that wars were waged in the age of satellite television and UN peace enforcement: a military victory could be a political defeat. The Muslims could win the war by losing it. And vice versa the Serbs.[19]

In this environment, journalists faced the challenge of delivering the narrowly defined "news" while also presenting broader truths.[20] Information at war is a mix of these, with each bit of news and parcel of truth being like pieces of a jigsaw puzzle. The puzzle is of indeterminate size, and what it will finally look like when (and if) completed is uncertain. Human strengths and frailties are part of this process, affecting the speed and agility with which the puzzle is assembled.[21]

Myanmar

It is tempting to look at cases such as the wars in Bosnia and Rwanda and dismiss them as twentieth-century problems that arose when information did not move as promptly and pervasively as it does today. Information is plentiful in our current century, and it is comforting to believe that concentration camps and mass murder cannot take place without being immediately discovered and stopped. But indulging in such intellectual contentment is a costly and misleading luxury. If a war zone is remote enough, if a government suppresses information forcefully enough, and especially if the victims are not known well enough by the rest of the world, then genocide can still occur.

In Myanmar (also known as Burma), the predominantly Muslim Rohingya people have been killed or driven from their homes in massive numbers.[22] Beginning in August 2017, more than 800,000 Rohingya fled Myanmar, most of whom made their way to Cox's Bazar, Bangladesh, which became the site of the world's largest refugee settlement.[23]

Various relief organizations have provided assistance to the refugees in Bangladesh, but in much of the world voices of outrage have been muted or sporadic. Part of the reason is that information has been only occasionally available; the military-dominated Myanmar government imprisoned their own journalists who tried to report about atrocities, and barred most foreign reporters from the Rohingyas' home territory in Myanmar's Rakhine state.[24]

New York Times columnist Nicholas Kristof was allowed into Myanmar in 2018 with a tourist visa that came, he later reported, "with a stern warning that I must not do any reporting." He added, "In general, I believe that journalists should obey the laws of countries they visit, but I make an exception when a regime uses its laws to commit and hide crimes against humanity."

Kristof visited Rohingya villages and told his readers what he found: "Sometimes Myanmar uses guns and machetes for ethnic cleansing ... but it also kills more subtly and secretly by regularly denying medical care and blocking humanitarian aid to Rohingya." Kristof also found that new information tools were being used by the government to further its objectives. He wrote that "hatred toward the Rohingya has escalated because of the arrival of smartphones and Facebook, resulting in virulent anti-Rohingya propaganda depicting them as murderous terrorists who commit atrocities against Buddhists."[25] (Buddhists constitute 88 percent of the Myanmar population, Muslims 4 percent.[26])

Kristof presumably had influence, being one of America's best-known newspaper journalists and having regular access to the powerful pulpit of the *New York Times* op-ed page. He took personal risks to report about the Rohingya (he visited Rakhine several times) and in his columns he skillfully combined human-interest and political aspects of the story. But, other than within the international aid community, information about the Rohingyas' situation produced little in the way of substantial policy change or meaningful pressure on the Myanmar government.

The reason for this may be that information about conflict and other humanitarian emergencies has limited impact when members of the information audience perceive that they have little direct connection to the events in question and little stake in their outcome. Even exceptionally informative and evocative reporting might not affect policy if the public is reluctant – for whatever reason – to support even non-military humanitarian assistance (which can be expensive). Exceptions to this may occur if there is an information deluge on multiple media platforms – print, broadcast, online – about a particular situation. There are cases when assistance is provided, at least temporarily, due to a spurt of information that stirs the public's and policymakers' consciences. A single television news report about the 1984 famine in Ethiopia triggered a surge in governmental and private aid; images of starving people in Somalia in 1992 were cited by President George H. W. Bush when he sent US troops to support

United Nations relief efforts; photographs of dead civilians in Bosnia were factors in President Bill Clinton eventually ordering air strikes against Serb forces.

But episodic responses do little to alleviate deep-rooted, long-term problems. The plight of Myanmar's Rohingya is a case in point, and their situation is exacerbated when access to information is obstructed. In Myanmar, such obstruction was partly engineered by the government, which tried – with considerable success – to keep its own and foreign journalists away from the conflict zone. Accurate information also was in short supply because outside journalists who tried to cover the story lacked background knowledge and reliable sources.[27] A report by the East Asia Forum noted that information gatherers in this instance tended "to walk a well-trodden path – one that takes journalists to the same interviewees and the same sites, all of which serve to reinforce dominant accounts of the situation."[28]

A case can be made that the efforts of the Myanmar government to kill Rohingya or drive them into exile constitute genocide. Samantha Power, who served as US Ambassador to the United Nations during the Obama administration, told an interviewer in 2019 that "in the last two years, we have seen the Myanmar military's systematic campaign of destruction against the Rohingya, using murder, rape, and forced expulsion to rid the country of a Muslim minority that had long been persecuted."[29] Power and others have argued about whether diplomatic measures, such as economic sanctions, to force the Myanmar government to stop its violence, are effective, but such debates receive little attention from broader publics. If their constituents seem uninterested, political actors will feel little pressure to address the problem.

It is not fair to place all blame for the public's inattention on those who should be providing information. On the other hand, without adequate information the public will likely remain disengaged and the fate of the Rohingya may remain far down the list of policy-makers' priorities.

This is despite the 2005 United Nations adoption of principles related to the "responsibility to protect." These principles call for "the international community" to build ways "to protect populations from genocide, war crimes, ethnic cleansing, and crimes against humanity."[30] This is relevant to information at war in two ways. First, it makes it incumbent on states to respond to "the worst forms of violence and persecution" through the United Nations Security Council. Maybe (and only maybe) if enough information reaches global publics, recalcitrant Security Council members might be more inclined to act.[31] But, even then, politics may intervene, as when China, criticized for its treatment of its own Muslim minority, blocked Security Council action regarding Myanmar's Rohingya.

Second, information per se may help break up political logjams if it is presented powerfully and persistently. Consider the composition of the "international community" on which the UN principles place responsibility. During the twentieth century and earlier, that "community" took the shape of a pyramid with an elite, relatively small number of policymakers, financial powers, and others at the highest reaches of the structure. The diverse constituencies occupying the lower parts of the pyramid were often uninformed and uninterested in distant matters, and they had few means of acting effectively even if they wanted to. The increased availability of information has changed that, at least somewhat. The international community remains a pyramid, but the upper regions are more accessible because so many more people are able to know what is going on in the world and, if they so choose, can be empowered by that knowledge. Over time, as more and more information becomes available to more and more people, the responsibility to protect may become an effective factor in international affairs and the plight of Myanmar's Rohingya might be replicated less often.[32]

Even this cautiously hopeful outlook depends on there being a connection between information availability and moral reasoning. How do people digest information about distant tragedies? Do they skim a newspaper's front page, shake their heads in sorrow when seeing a shocking headline or photograph, and then just move on to the Sports section? For them, that is certainly the path of least resistance. If information of this kind is to have meaningful moral impact, it needs to be reinforced by varied sources. Perhaps clergy will address that front-page story during religious services. Perhaps a family member or neighbor will have read the story carefully, pondered it, and discussed it with others. Perhaps popular culture will weigh in (as with movies such as *Hotel Rwanda*). Perhaps when people's exposure to information occurs in multiple facets of their lives, the impact of that information may become stronger. Perhaps, perhaps, perhaps.

Journalism of Attachment

Writing in the *Los Angeles Times* in 1995 about news coverage of the war in Bosnia, Howard Rosenberg asked, "Have we, the U.S. public, watching all of this securely from across the sea, gotten so used to these now-nightly pictures of violence and sorrowful victims that they've become abstractions?"[33]

That is a reasonable question, and it might be asked not just about Americans, but also about people around the world, more and more of whom can "watch all of this securely" on their televisions, their laptops, and their phones. What does it take to move them? Are there ways in which information can better resonate and stir individual and collective conscience?

The BBC's Martin Bell, after covering the war in Bosnia, wrote a book, *In Harm's Way* (1995), about his experiences there and his recognition that those who provide the public with information have special moral obligations. He wrote: "In the news business it isn't involvement but indifference that makes for bad practice. Good journalism is the *journalism of attachment* [emphasis in original]. It is not only knowing, but also caring."[34] He added:

> But if ... it is possible to create and maintain a climate of opinion in which the saving of lives is thought to matter, and governments are committed to it because their people support it, and survivors in the war zones are given some hope when they would otherwise have none, then something more than mere hand-wringing is being achieved. And if journalists do it, they are committing useful journalism. There is a point to it.[35]

Once again, clean-shaven objectivity is challenged. Questioning it is not new, but articulating challenges about its validity and about a need for exceptions to it are becoming more common. (Among American journalists, in a different context, Donald Trump's presidency also led to an expansion of boundaries, to the extent that some major news organizations began regularly labeling some of his statements as "lies" and "racist," not just in editorials but also in regular news stories.)

What Bell and a few of his colleagues were doing was not attempting to skew information to pluck at heartstrings, but rather to broaden war-related information in ways that better defined a continuum: news to public opinion to policy. This involved making clearer to information consumers that publics and governments should view information not as existing in a freestanding silo, but rather being an integral part of their own lives and work, and of their community, broadly defined. Ideally, according to this approach, information can act as a moral stimulus to action.

Two decades later, Bell revisited his earlier journalism in another book, *War and the Death of News* (2017). In it, he reflected on a broadcast he did for the BBC news program *Panorama* in 1993, during which he voiced his frustration with a peace process that was achieving nothing while more Bosnians died. In the broadcast he said:

> The policy of the outside world till now has been one of drift and inadequate measures taken too late ... . The case for intervention is not to help one side or the other, but the weak against the strong, the unarmed against the armed; to take the side of the everyday victims who, till now, have had no protection. It is, fundamentally, a question of whether we care.[36]

After the *Panorama* program, complaints poured in, from fellow journalists as well as from those with political interests in the war. Bell was accused of displaying "fashionable bias," but the BBC stood by him. He later cited this episode as an instance of letting the journalism of attachment come to the surface, wholly visible, and "not stand neutrally between the victim and the aggressor." This kind of war reporting, Bell added, "is the reverse of bystander journalism, indifferent and unfeeling."[37]

In the eyes of some, Bell had committed a mortal sin for a journalist: he had taken sides, abandoning objectivity. But a case might be made that Bell was, in a humanistic if not a journalistic sense, being fully objective in his evaluation of the suffering in Bosnia. Objectivity does not require, and arguably does not benefit from, blindness to reality.

Bell was not alone in challenging tenets of objectivity. Christiane Amanpour, who covered the war in Bosnia for CNN, asked what "objectivity" really meant. "I have come to believe," she wrote:

> that objectivity means giving all sides a fair hearing, but not treating all sides equally. Once you treat all sides the same in a case such as Bosnia, you are drawing a moral equivalence between victim and aggressor. And from there it is a short step toward being neutral. And from there it's an even shorter step to becoming an accessory to all manner of evil; in Bosnia's case, genocide. So, objectivity must go hand in hand with morality.[38]

While such views affect gathering and presenting information, their ripple effects also impact policymaking. For their part, policymakers may dig in their heels as they resist media-influenced public demands to "do something." When this situation arose during the war in Bosnia, British Foreign Secretary Douglas Hurd said, "We have not been and are not willing to begin some form of military intervention which we judge useless or worse simply because of day by day pressures from the media."[39]

Hurd was by no means alone among policymakers who have resisted media-generated pressure for policy change, particularly when that change would involve armed intervention overseas. Many senior policymakers operate on the principle that they must not risk the lives of their nation's military personnel unless that nation's security is at stake. This is a judgment more complex than those that information gatherers face. Deploying troops should usually be a last resort – an exception might be to contribute to a peacekeeping force – despite the transient allure of martial glory. As American diplomat William J. Burns observed: "The militarization of diplomacy is a trap, which leads to overuse – or premature use – of force, and under-emphasis on nonmilitary tools. 'If your main tool is a hammer,' as Barack Obama liked to say, 'Then every problem will start to look like a nail.'"[40]

Information has its own kind of power. It is very different from a military weapon, but ideally it can still have profound effect. Motivation for taking personal and professional risks and for defining the significance of information varies among those who place themselves in the midst of war. Photojournalist James Nachtwey, after covering combat for several decades, spoke to an interviewer about the "collective conscience" information can nurture:

> I believe in the power of information in the mind of the public. [Information stops people's opinion simply being] monopolized by the powers that be. The process of change is dependent upon that. There's empirical evidence that the work of the press – not my work, or the work of any one journalist, but the work of all of us together – creates a critical mass of information that helps create change. There are wars that people think are hopeless and will never end, but they do, and one of the reasons for this is because of information and the collective conscience it creates. When the war in Iraq began, the American public was overwhelmingly in favor. Fast forward a few years and the majority of Americans are overwhelmingly against it. What made that difference but information?[41]

In another interview, Nachtwey discussed why getting information to a large public is so crucial for those who are caught up in a war:

> When there's a war there's so much at stake for the people involved in the war and for the rest of the world. Photographs can get behind the political rhetoric that is always surrounding a war ... And photographers are on the ground; they are seeing what is happening to individual human beings. They are showing the effect of the war and holding accountable the decision makers and policy makers that are

conducting the war. And this is a way in which public opinion can be brought to bear, to pressure for change ... I think that, in a way, a picture that shows the true face of war is an anti-war photograph. In my experience in seeing what war does to people and societies it would be very difficult to promote that. So, I think that photographs that show the true face of war, in a way, are mediating against using war as a means of conducting policy.[42]

In *War Photographer*, a documentary film about Nachtwey and his work, Nachtwey talked about his relationship with the people in war zones whom he photographed:

Those pictures could not have been made unless I was accepted by the people I'm photographing ... They understand that a stranger has come there with a camera to show the rest of the world what is happening to them. It gives them a voice in the outside world that they otherwise wouldn't have. They realize that they are the victims of some kind of injustice, some kind of unnecessary violence. By allowing me there to photograph it, they are making their own appeal to the outside world and to everyone's sense of right and wrong.[43]

In these instances, Bell, Amanpour, and Nachtwey were describing a relationship between information and the public that transcends the neutrality with which much journalistic information is not only gathered and presented, but also received. The foundation of this approach remains accuracy, and if that foundation is solid it may be able to support the kind of information that constitutes journalism of attachment.

Journalistic empathy is not always viewed favorably by those who are doing the fighting. Journalists can become targets, sometimes with bounties placed on them. More broadly, those who plan and carry out military operations must increasingly consider information that is totally outside their control. A soldier shoots an unarmed civilian, and another soldier takes a photo that is instantly moving across the internet. An artillery barrage misses its target and hits a school, and soon a YouTube video from a teacher at the school is delivering the anguish to much of the world. Or a freelance journalist tells the story of soldiers left unprotected by faulty equipment. This is the kind of documentation that not many years ago would never have reached the public. Today, this is just another aspect of information at war.

Information from War-Zone Occupants

First-person reporting is an essential element of information at war. Over the years, many war correspondents have bravely done their best to secure the stories of combatants and civilians on the front lines of conflict. But sometimes this is not possible – the fighting is too intense or forces in control of an area refuse to allow journalists into their territory. This has meant that information about many crucial aspects of conflict reached the public belatedly, or never.

In enemy-occupied territory, underground information dissemination has ranged from reliance on word-of-mouth, such as Paul Revere's ride to warn of English troops on the move near Boston in 1775, to conventional news operations, such as during the 1944 Warsaw Uprising, when patriotic Poles printed newspapers describing their desperate efforts to drive Nazi forces out of their city.

As with many aspects of information at war, technology is driving change. It still is impossible in some situations for regular journalists to reach the heart of a conflict, but sometimes information may be available from "citizen journalists."

That term itself generates controversy. Citizen journalism is provided by persons who usually do not have much, if any, academic or professional training in journalism. They might not know how a conventional news story is structured, and they might not consider certain ethical and other issues that professional journalists deal with. But they possess a valuable, offsetting qualification: they are on the scene and are determined to deliver information.

Sometimes, the citizen journalist's task is of brief duration and consists of providing information to established news media. After a terrorist attack, for instance, news organizations might ask – through their online or other venues – for anyone who was present to contact them to describe the event or provide photographs or video. Once this information is received and vetted, it can be delivered to the public. If no professional journalists were at the scene of the attack, this can be a useful method of describing or showing what happened.

An example of this was the BBC's appeal for information immediately after the July 2005 terrorist bombings of the Underground and a bus in London. The broadcaster's request garnered 50 photos from the public within an hour of the first bomb going off; 1,000 images and dozens of video clips within the next few days; and around 22,000 texts and emails with personal accounts of the attacks that arrived on the first day.[44] Most of the photos and videos came from mobile phone cameras, and with nearly 3 billion smartphones in use around the world as of 2020, such outpouring of citizen reporting is likely to become more widespread.

Citizen journalism related to a single incident is one thing; continuing coverage in wartime conditions is something very different. The Syria War that began in 2011 defied the efforts of many news organizations to provide comprehensive reporting about what was going on. Many places in the war zone – especially those occupied by Islamic State (IS) – were virtually inaccessible. Any journalists who were discovered in IS territory were likely to be executed. Nevertheless, some civilians who lived in these areas wanted to tell the world about the horrors they were enduring, and some of them found ways to deliver that information.

In Raqqa, Syria, proclaimed by IS in 2014 as the capital of their caliphate, citizen journalists organized, calling their group "Raqqa Is Being Slaughtered Silently" (RBSS). Their story was told in the 2017 documentary film *City of Ghosts*. The film's director, Matthew Heineman, told an interviewer: "The name of the group says it all ... there's no information going into the city, there's no information coming out. So, if it wasn't for them we truly wouldn't know what was happening."[45]

RBSS split into two teams: one team, comprising 17 correspondents, remained in Raqqa, with the assignment "to film, record, and deliver urgent news," and the other, based initially in Turkey and then in Germany, assembled the reports and distributed them online to news agencies around the world. Story topics included the violence with which IS controlled the city, the persistent food shortages, and the lack of medical supplies in the local hospitals.

For its part, IS produced its own videos that often met high professional technical standards, patterning some after violent video games such as "Grand Theft Auto." IS also used videos to recruit; one video showed an IS spokesman saying, "The Islamic State is in great need of men with media skills so they can bring the real news to people." IS also pursued RBSS personnel with a vengeance, offering rewards for information about or the assassination of RBSS leaders. They arrested the father of two members of the RBSS external team and posted online a video of his interrogation, which concluded with his execution. They used checkpoints in Raqqa to examine contents of individuals' mobile phones, arresting and executing anyone they deemed to be a "media activist." They also pursued RBSS members outside Syria, murdering one on a street in Gaziantep, Turkey.

Eventually, IS was driven out of what was left of Raqqa. RBSS remained at work, documenting the vicious tactics of various other parties in a war with no end. Abdelaziz Alhamza, the main RBSS spokesman, said: "Our words are stronger than their weapons. Either we will win, or they will kill all of us."[46]

The film makes clear that citizen journalism can be invaluable, particularly when offsetting the voice of a malignant but media-savvy organization such as Islamic State, which has proved that it possesses considerable skill in creating its own version of "news." The Syrian War has been fought by an array of forces in addition to IS, including the Assad regime's military, Russian air power, Hezbollah fighters, and others, all of whom contribute to an environment so extremely dangerous that news organizations must rely heavily on information gathered by citizen journalists and disseminated through social media. British journalist Lindsey Hilsum wrote that "a meticulous sifting of testimony, videos, and photographs conveyed by social media, to be cross-checked with government propaganda, satellite imagery, and whatever other sources are available, is a crucial part of twenty-first-century conflict reporting." She noted that she was part of a WhatsApp group linking journalists to doctors in a Damascus suburb, who reported what results they saw of Russian and Syrian-government bombardment of civilian areas.[47]

Does citizen journalism affect the course of a conflict? In the case of the Syria War, apparently not in a significant way. The Assad government continued to rely on exceptionally brutal tactics, including using airstrikes and chemical weapons against Syrian civilians. The Russian military also seemed unbothered and unleashed their air power against population centers. Islamic State did not back away from viciousness, and it mounted information counterattacks, trying to sustain its obviously false self-portrayal as champions of the world's Muslims. Political leaders elsewhere condemned the combatants' behavior, but with little result. Global publics may have been appalled by the fighting that produced hundreds of thousands dead and millions of refugees, but not to the point at which they mounted noticeable pressure on governments to undertake meaningful political or military measures that might deter the combatants.

Elsewhere, long-term projects have been designed to make citizen journalism a more reliable and consistent source of information. The Sudan Media Capacity-Building Project, supported by the British government and the Thomson Foundation, had by early 2019 trained more than 700 people in skills such as publishing on various platforms and using mobile phones as reporting tools. Local reporters used their new skills to capture footage and report stories about uprisings in Sudan and disseminate their content via Twitter and other social media. Some of these reports reached broad audiences after being picked up by international media organizations. One important result of such efforts is that news about Sudan is being reported by Sudanese, rather than depending on outsiders whose perspectives on Sudan might be narrower than those of locals.[48] Another example is found in Nigeria, where real-time video and accounts from citizen journalists have documented attacks by the Boko Haram terrorist organization. These reports have also been used by news organizations around the world.[49]

The trade-off for such expertise is possible localized bias affecting the reporting, something of which news organizations must be aware when deciding whether to use citizen-journalists' coverage. As with other aspects of news gathering, cost–benefit decisions must be made, but overall, when a news organization is searching for credible on-scene reporting, citizen journalists' work can provide useful depth and expertise.

Crowd-Sourced Information

Another technology-enhanced method for scrutinizing armed conflict is crowd-sourced research. Information is like an iceberg: only the tip may be visible at first glance, but there is much more to be explored beneath the surface.

The internet has made investigating the information iceberg – notably the policies and actions of governments and others – far more accessible. The speed and depth of such investigations can enrich the overall supply of war-related information. Searching official records, analyzing satellite and other imagery, and generally digging deeply into stories behind events can be done by anyone with time, internet access, and a certain amount of skill. When individual efforts are organized into a collaborative venture, important information may be pulled together with valuable results.

An example of this is Bellingcat, which describes itself as being "an independent international collective of researchers, investigators, and citizen journalists using open source and social media investigation to probe a variety of subjects," among which have been the 2014 shooting down of Malaysia Airlines flight MH17 over Ukraine; the 2018 chemical attack in Douma, Syria,; and the poisoning in Britain of the Russian double-agent Sergei Skirpal and his daughter.[50]

In one typical case, Bellingcat studied an attack by the Somali terrorist group Al Shabaab on a Kenyan military base in Kulbiyow, Somalia, which is just across the border with Kenya. Kenyan officials claimed that their troops were able to repel the attack with few casualties among their soldiers, while Al Shabaab reported that they had overrun the base and inflicted a large number of casualties on the Kenyans. The detailed Bellingcat research, relying on analysis of drone footage, television news video, and statements from persons involved, found that the Al Shabaab account was the more accurate.[51]

For another case – this one involving an air attack, possibly targeting civilians, in Yemen – Bellingcat explained its methods and findings:

> On the morning of the 6th of July 2015, an airstrike killing around 40 people took place on a market in the Southern governorate of Lahj, according to Amnesty International. Through satellite imagery, Bellingcat was able to establish that the location of the attack was a bustling livestock market near to a petrol station and multiple other services, such as a Qat market and restaurant. The tarpaulin market stalls were visible in the middle of the road on images by satellite image service provider Google Earth Pro in both 2015 and 2016. Bellingcat also examined photographic and video content uploaded by local journalists who documented the site shortly after the attack, positively identifying two large impact craters. This may indicate a "double-tap" strike, a practice where one strike is followed by a second hitting those that respond or gather in the aftermath. Such strikes often kill civilian responders or rescue workers.[52]

The Bellingcat report made clear that the damage was done to, and casualties were inflicted on, non-military targets.

Bellingcat's methods are similar to those used by intelligence agencies and other government entities, but they are not constrained by the political exigencies under which government investigators often must work. The researchers' reports are available online and serve as valuable supplemental information to official and news media accounts, which are sometimes contradictory.

Private sources of information about war extend today to formerly government-only content including precise imagery from satellites and, more recently and pervasively, drones. Universities, research organizations, collectives such as Bellingcat, and other bodies focused on information are helping make war a more transparent enterprise. This will presumably affect the conduct of armed conflict because fewer elements of warfare, such as war crimes, will escape public notice. This is another instance of how changes in the availability of information may alter the nature of war.

News organizations themselves have also made significant advances in digital forensic journalism. The *New York Times*, beginning in 2017, tracked repeated bombing of hospitals in Syria. Russia had long been viewed as the culprit in these attacks, but that was unproven, and Russia denied its involvement. In October 2019, the *Times* published a lengthy account of the attacks supported by convincing evidence. *Times* reporters wrote:

> We collected hundreds of photos and videos from Facebook groups and Telegram channels … . During our investigation, we obtained tens of thousands of previously unpublished audio recordings between Russian Air Force pilots and ground control officers in Syria. We also obtained years of flight data logged by a network of Syrian observers who have been tracking warplanes to warn civilians of impending airstrikes. The flight observations came with the time, location, and general type of each aircraft spotted.

In examining the attacks on Syria's Kafr Nabl Surgical Hospital, the *Times* team relied on geolocation to verify video evidence: "Using Google Earth, we labeled minarets and water towers, and kept track of the nearby hills and mountain ranges." These were corroborated with satellite imagery. Further, "the Russian Air Force communications gave us the clearest evidence of Russia's responsibility because we had the exact time of the explosions from the video metadata."[53]

This kind of information gathering and analysis may impose a new level of accountability on those who wage war, perhaps making outrages such as bombing hospitals more politically costly for the perpetrators. (It is worth noting, however, that Russia, for one, seems unmoved by such revelations, embracing a "deny and proceed" approach.)

Women's Stories and Women's Storytelling

For many centuries, women have been considered spoils of war, to be enslaved, raped, and murdered. Precedents can be found even in the *Iliad*, in which women such as Briseis, Chryseis, Priam's daughters, and other women are treated with offhand cruelty.[54] Today – more than 3,000 years later – such treatment remains an all-too-common facet of war, with its brutality fortified by the systemic misogyny that pervades so many societies.

Information about women in wartime is gradually gaining more attention, for a number of reasons. Women's issues related to many matters have become more visible, and responsive actions have gained political and social momentum in many parts of the world. The presence of women journalists in war zones is becoming more common, and the coverage they provide has, in many instances, benefited from their respect for and access to the women who find themselves in the midst of conflict.

This expansion of information at war has produced mixed results so far, with conflicts in Iraq, Myanmar, and elsewhere replete with horrific attacks on women. But at least these situations have been presented to the world, to shame the perpetrators and those who fail to respond.

As for wartime information gathering, women journalists have long been present, but their numbers were small. During World War I, Mary Boyle O'Reilly and Peggy Hull were among the few female American reporters to cover the fighting in Europe. Martha Gellhorn covered the Spanish Civil War, Clare Hollingworth captured the "scoop of the century" with her reports for the *Daily Telegraph* about Germany's invasion of Poland in September 1939, and there were others. A turning point was during the Vietnam War, when there were about 70 women journalists who took it upon themselves to join the "mythic male pursuit" of war coverage, and, according to Joyce Hoffman, "the female war correspondent was transformed from a novelty into the norm."[55]

The path was not easy. Martha Gellhorn, who covered the fighting in Vietnam in the mid-1960s (until the South Vietnamese government refused to renew her visa) focused in some of her stories on civilian casualties and the anguish of children. She was derided by Associated Press photographer Horst Faas, who said of her work: "Here we go again. We've seen this before; we know all this. Why do women always have to look for orphanages?"[56] Women journalists often felt special pressures. When covering her first firefight, NBC correspondent Liz Trotta thought, "If I fail, they'll say it's because I'm a woman."[57]

As policies of news organizations and war departments evolved, women combat reporters' numbers grew. By the time of the 21st-century wars in Afghanistan and Iraq, it was not unusual for women to be covering the fighting. Pentagon guidelines for embedding journalists with the invading force in Iraq in 2003 stated that "gender will not be an excluding factor under any circumstance."[58] By this time, correspondents such as Kate Adie, Lyse Doucet, Janine Di Giovanni, and others had established themselves as among the best frontline journalists.

More important than progressive regulations was the excellence of women journalists' work and the price some of them paid. This was exemplified by the reporting of Marie Colvin (who was killed covering combat in Syria in 2012), the photography of Leila Alaoui (who was killed in a terrorist attack in Burkina Faso in 2016), and many others. Further, women's reporting brought new breadth to the information delivered from areas of conflict. Hannah Allam, who reported from Iraq for McClatchy Newspapers, wrote that "reporting on Iraq through the eyes of its women ... was more representative of the population as a whole. Years of bloodshed had left Iraq with a population that was more than half women, many of them heads of households because their men were dead or missing or exiled." She cited the car bombings of 2006 that would sometimes produce daily death tolls of 80 or more, and she wrote: "Consider those numbers for a moment: eighty dead men meant eighty new widows and dozens of newly fatherless children. Every day. That meant that each week, more than five hundred Iraqi women suddenly became the sole providers for their families, setting their own devastation aside to keep their children fed and housed."[59]

That perspective had long been a rarity in information at war, but now Allam was not alone in providing this kind of reporting. Also covering the war in Iraq, Jane Arraf wrote about accompanying American troops on a raid in search of jihadist fighters and how women gravitated to her: "With their children screaming in terror, weeping women would ask me where the men were being taken, or beg me to tell the soldiers that their sons, husbands, and brothers had done nothing wrong, and there were no insurgents hiding among them."[60] Reflecting on her work in Syria in 2015, Zaina Erhaim wrote that she found advantages as a woman journalist. "If I wasn't a woman," she noted, "I wouldn't have been invited to the closed segregated women's community of Idlib. And I certainly wouldn't have been able to film the women there moving about freely in their houses and as they worked."[61]

This kind of information is essential for comprehending the essence of warfare and how armed conflict wreaks havoc on so many lives – those of the combatants and many others. It isn't that all men are devoid of empathy, but rather that women bring, in addition to their basic skills in combat coverage, a perspective and sensitivity to certain aspects of war that information consumers need if they are to fully understand the scope of war's impact on society.

Romy Froehlich wrote that "the most prominent role of women during wartime seems to be that of victims – politically or militarily instrumentalized," and that "the regular annihilation, trivialization, and marginalization of women in the media is further enhanced in war coverage by the myth of the peaceful and weak female who is in need of protection."[62] One way in which such condescending portrayals of women are being offset is through depictions of women on the battlefield as fighters.

Women as combatants are not new factors in warfare. To again cite the *Iliad* as precedent, Homer refers to Amazons as "a match for men in war." Herodotus also describes their fierceness. Today, numerous armed forces (such as those of the United States and Israel) include women in all branches, and Kurdish all-female units have recently fought in areas of Syria and Iraq. These YPJ (an acronym for the Kurdish term "Women's Protection Units") were reportedly much feared by their Islamic State enemies who believed it was a disgrace to be killed by a woman and a barrier to entering paradise.[63] Information about women engaging in combat has gradually been moving from the "feature" category into standard news content.

Fleeing War: Refugees and Information

In addition to those civilians who are killed or wounded during war, victims of conflict include those who are driven from their homes. The United Nations defines refugees as those who flee their countries because of war, violence, or persecution. Their numbers are staggering, particularly when combined with those of persons who are internally displaced (forced from their homes and living elsewhere in the same country). According to the UN, as of late 2019 nearly 71 million persons worldwide had been driven out of their homes. Roughly 41 million were internally displaced, 26 million were refugees (having left their own countries), and more than 3 million were seeking asylum. The three principal home countries of these refugees were Syria, Afghanistan, and South Sudan.[64]

For as long as there has been armed conflict, there have been refugees. As they seek safety, many refugees today rely increasingly on online tools, and in so doing they provide an example of the expanding effects of new media. They use smartphone maps, global positioning apps, messaging applications such as WhatsApp, and other connections to plot their journeys; to stay in touch with distant family members; to keep informed about locations of border guards, crossing points, and predatory gangs; and generally to diminish the isolation of life on the run. These tools have also reduced the need to rely on illegal traffickers, because Facebook sites and other online content may give them enough information to travel independently. To assist in this process, the United Nations High Commissioner for Refugees, in the early years of the war in Syria and the fight against Islamic State within Iraq, distributed 33,000 SIM cards to refugees in Jordan and gave away more than 85,000 solar lanterns that can be used to charge cellphones.[65]

Based on her study of refugee communication, Professor Marie Gillespie told an interviewer in 2018 that "water, phone, food," in that order, are the three most important items refugees take with them when they are forced from their homes. Illegal escape techniques are often faster than legal ones, and so, Gillespie said, refugees often find themselves turning to the "dark digital underworld," using encrypted channels to connect with smugglers and others who might aid their escape.[66]

Smartphones are multifaceted assets, providing internet connection, a Global Positioning System (GPS), and a digital camera (which can help document the legitimacy of someone's status as a refugee or asylum-seeker). Using these tools, however, is not always easy, as access to WiFi, SIM cards, and battery-charging can be expensive or unavailable. Also, using smartphones can facilitate surveillance of the refugees by state and non-state actors.

Through their smartphones, refugees can also find news about which countries are most likely to accept them. But they also must deal with misinformation that flows online, such as false reports about Syrian refugees being deported to Iraq.[67]

Charitable organizations and other NGOs have used new media technologies to assist refugees. The Clooney Foundation for Justice, with a grant from Google, created pop-up schools in Lebanese refugee camps and provided laptops pre-loaded with teaching materials.[68] InfoMigrants is a collaborative effort by three major European media organizations – France Medias Monde, Deutsche Welle, and ANSA (with co-financing by the European Union) – to provide refugees with accurate reporting that can offset misinformation.[69] Refugee.info, which is staffed primarily by refugees and asylum-seekers, assists refugees with information about asylum procedures, work permissions, registering children for school, finding a doctor, and other such matters.[70] This organization – which works with refugees in Europe – along with CuentaNos in El Salvador and Khabrona in Jordan, are parts of Signpost, which was created in 2015 by two major NGOs: International Rescue Committee and Mercy Corps. Signpost has reached more than a million refugees, and its credo is, "Information is power. Our vision is that all people fleeing crisis and conflict have the information they need to be safe, access vital services, and rebuild their lives."[71]

Many more NGOs, as well as governments and international organizations, have worked to reduce the burdens on refugees by helping them to take advantage of the connectivity that information technology allows. The Emergency Telecommunications Cluster (ETC), created under United Nations auspices, coordinates information availability in conflict zones and in other humanitarian emergency situations. It considers communication as a form of emergency aid, and it works with technology companies and local telecoms providers to offer timely, resilient, decentralized communication capabilities. ETC has been active in South Sudan, the Central African Republic, Libya, and other conflict zones.[72]

The ultimate goal, of course, is that no one should need to become a refugee. That is a noble, but for now unrealizable, aspiration. In the meantime, expanded availability of information can help to alleviate some of the conditions refugees endure while on the move.

What Has Changed?

Information at war is an always-evolving field. Change is driven by technology and by professional maturation that is, for the most part, constructive. But as the events described in this chapter illustrate, progress takes place slowly. At best, advancing justice and peace through war-related information gathering and dissemination happens only incrementally. Of course, information in itself cannot bring about change; that task belongs to those who consume and act upon information. Further, as the next chapter explains, new media tools themselves can be used not just in constructive ways, but also for disruptive and even deadly purposes.

4

Social Media Go to War

Information at war has traditionally flowed through channels controlled in one way or another by governmental, political, and business elites. War-related information considered controversial by these elites has sometimes been withheld, altered, or purposely left incomplete. Even the most diligent journalists and other investigators have found themselves occasionally (or even persistently) frustrated by obfuscation and bureaucratic manipulation of information. The degree of obstruction varies from country to country, but it happens everywhere to some extent.

When truth is a casualty, the public is also wounded. Journalists or dissidents of various stripes can occasionally deliver information that the powers-that-be would prefer to keep out of view, but information-hungry members of the public may have found themselves, like Oliver Twist, begging for additional gruel: "Please, may I have some more?" In a democracy, a public desiring information should not be reduced to this.

Then, during the first years of the twenty-first century, digital social media platforms arrived, and with these new information venues came a level of empowerment that helped to elevate the public from beggars to players able to collect and disseminate information themselves with unprecedented ease. Initially, this change was almost wholly technology-driven, with steadily expanding internet accessibility at its heart. Gradually, these new media reshaped the nature of information at war and much else.

As of early 2020, out of a global population of roughly 7.8 billion persons, 4.6 billion (59 percent) were internet users. Twenty years earlier – late 1999 – only 248 million people were accessing the internet. During the first years of the new century, internet usage was highest in developed countries, especially in tech-savvy nations in East Asia, North America, and Europe. Recently, the usage figures have become more balanced; the fastest internet access growth rates between 2000 and 2020 were in Africa (11,567 percent), the Middle East (5,477 percent), and Latin America (2,411 percent).[1] Those three regions still trail other parts of the world, but as the gap continues to close, global information access becomes more equitable and information-based empowerment expands.

Being able to use the internet is just a first step, opening the door to perusing a vast array of information sources, including diverse news media. The meaning of "local" news has changed dramatically; most news products are no longer confined to their geographic homes but rather are available – sometimes for free, sometimes for a fee – to anyone on the planet with full internet access and curiosity. This availability has led leading news organizations in countries where English is not the principal language to offer versions of their content in English, which is the world's most widely spoken language. So, if you live in the American Midwest and are interested in the war in Ukraine that began in 2014, you can tap into English-language products of the Kyiv-based Unian news service for a Ukrainian viewpoint, and the Russian RT (formerly Russia Today) for a Russian interpretation of events in the war. If tensions in the South China Sea interest you, a few clicks will bring you news reports in English from China, Japan, Vietnam, the Philippines, and elsewhere in the region. Depending on the commercial and political interests of the news providers' home countries, content may also be available in additional languages.

Despite the breadth of information now at hand, this system still basically adheres to the conventional provider–consumer relationship, with news recipients constituting a mostly passive audience for the content. It remains primarily a one-way process. Changing this is one reason why social media have become so important.

It is worth keeping in mind how new the internet-based social media are. The oldest of the dominant social media venues is Facebook, which was created in 2004, followed by YouTube (2005), Twitter (2006), Sina Weibo (2009), Instagram (2010), and countless others – many short-lived and many still scrambling to attract and retain users. New players are always entering the information marketplace and joining the competition for audience.

The rise of social media brought with it the enabling of publics to participate in the information process as providers themselves, as well as consumers. Much content being delivered is second-hand – such as a tweet of a news story – but much also originates with the individual user. Some of this is trivial ("Look at this cute picture of my cat!"), but much is substantive, such as the "citizen journalism" discussed in chapter 3, or stimuli for online discussions and activism about important issues. Organizing rallies locally or around the world to address climate change or other issues is far more feasible (and far less expensive) today because of social media's speed, accessibility, and pervasiveness.

In the context of armed conflict, this expansion of the information universe means that it has become far more difficult for any given government or non-state actor to monopolize the flow of information to and from a war zone. Instead of a limited stream through which information can move (and be controlled), many channels may exist, and the sheer number of voices makes it almost certain that at least some of them will be heard.

An example of the value of online access is the *Washington Post*'s 2019 "Afghanistan Papers" project, which included analysis of 2,000 pages of "lessons learned" interviews conducted by the US government, and several hundred confidential memos written by Secretary of Defense Donald Rumsfeld. The *Post* acquired these through a three-year legal battle and presented them in the newspaper, in podcasts, and on a website. The collective output offered, according to the *Post*, "new insights into how three presidential administrations have failed for nearly two decades to deliver on their promises to end the war."[2]

This project was a descendant of the "Pentagon Papers," published in 1971, which exposed US policymakers' persistent lying about the reasons behind the Vietnam War and the ongoing conduct of that war. The *New York Times* and other news organizations published this information, and much of the content became available to the public in book form, but at the time there was nothing comparable to the technology used as part of the *Post*'s Afghanistan project. Anyone with internet access could take advantage of numerous search tools on the *Post*'s website that facilitated deep dives into the Afghanistan database. For the researcher, this was a treasure trove, and it was all free.

Many countries do not have legal systems that would allow a news organization – even one prepared to engage in a lengthy and expensive court contest – to acquire and publish government documents of the kind the *Post* uncovered. Nevertheless, those involved in war-related policymaking must recognize that venues such as WikiLeaks are increasingly likely to be joined by established news organizations, public interest groups, and even individuals who can put information that once would have been closely held into the public's hands. How much of a constraint on policy decisions that proves to be remains to be seen, but for those seeking information, "secret" is taking on a less forbidding meaning.

This new information marketplace may, at times, lend itself to manipulation. In 2010, when WikiLeaks released a quarter of a million classified US State Department cables, news organizations thought they had found a gold mine of previously hidden documentation about government actions and cover-ups. But, a few years later, it became clear that WikiLeaks itself was being used. As is detailed in chapter 5, Russian disinformation campaigns fed material – much of it invented – to WikiLeaks, which disseminated it to news organizations that then delivered it to the public. With WikiLeaks as a "cut-out," the Kremlin's interference with the 2016 US presidential election became more effective.

Aside from WikiLeaks, part of the reason that accessing such information is becoming more commonplace can be found in the nature of the technology so many people use constantly. The smartphone is the Swiss Army knife of personal communication and information gathering. It has many of the tools found in desktop and laptop computers, but it fits easily in a pocket, allowing users to drench themselves in information ranging from the latest weather report to news bulletins and much more, including "research" into whatever topic piques their curiosity. For many people, applications ("apps") make smartphones computers first, telephones (for conversations) often a distant second.

Ease of use means increased frequency of use, so an individual's inclination to seek information is likely to be strengthened by having a smartphone. And as smartphone availability grows, the device will take precedence over regular cellphones – among more affluent users first, until competition drives prices down. Of the estimated 6.8 billion mobile phone users in early 2020, 3.5 billion were using smartphones. By 2021, the number of smartphone users is expected to more significantly exceed 50 percent of all mobile phone users.[3]

With tools such as these, constituencies for war information are almost certain to grow in number and assertiveness. Governments will continue to keep secrets related to war, but doing so will become increasingly difficult. The once-rare "leak" will become more common, with more groups and individuals – including some on the frontlines – gathering and disseminating information about conflict.

Much of this process will be constructive, bringing more scrutiny to war-related policymaking and enhancing democratic oversight of the many elements of warfare. Other kinds of information will also become more easily obtainable by large publics who will, if they so choose, be able to see more realistically complete depictions of war. Photography is among the media that will foster this.

Merging Old and New: Photography at War

For the onlookers of war, understanding the true nature and status of combat can be difficult. Who is winning and losing? How much damage is being inflicted on our enemies and on our own troops and homeland? Is the struggle worth it? What is the war really like? Is there such a thing as honorable warfare?

Words, official and journalistic, even if truthful, cannot tell the entire story because the true savagery of conflict is so far outside the life experience, and even the imagination, of most among the watching public. How can someone who wasn't there really understand the firebombing of Tokyo and Dresden near the end of the Second World War as more than just cold statistics about the dead? How can someone who has never been to war appreciate what a soldier endures slogging through a jungle or across a desert?

Photography can take the public somewhat closer to the uncomfortable reality of war. Barbie Zelizer wrote that images of war "are haunted by the stubborn inevitability and proximity of death. Combining the cool mechanics of the camera with the hot passions of wartime, they offer visual statements about circumstances much of the world prefers not to see."[4]

Seeing war may allow the observer to more fully grasp the heroism, brutality, and other aspects of the fighting. From the mid twentieth century onward, television and online video platforms have provided vivid depictions of elements of war ranging from the gallant to the excruciating. But a century before such moving images became an integral part of daily life, artists and photographers offered the public frozen moments from wars. And even today, with so many venues available for video, the still photograph retains its power. Andrew Hoskins and Ben O'Loughlin wrote, "Television is relentless in its immediacy, in its delivery of the present and its selective redelivery of the past, but this real-time temporality and apparent flow may function to obscure its impact, unlike the indelible marking associated with the medium of the photograph."[5] Susan Sontag observed: "A photograph passes for incontrovertible proof that a given thing happened. The picture may distort, but there is always a presumption that something exists, or did exist, which is like what's in the picture."[6]

Modern photography was born in the early nineteenth century, but decades passed before printing technology advanced to the point at which photographs could be presented to general audiences. By the time of the Crimean War (1854–6) and the American Civil War (1861–5), photographers were venturing into war zones, but because of the state of printing, newspapers and magazines had to rely on artists to illustrate reports from battlefields and to provide sketches based on photographs.[7] To view the work of war photographers such as Mathew Brady, people stood in line outside their studios in New York City and elsewhere to see photos (some of them staged), including soldiers' bodies strewn across fields and trenches.

By the time of the Second World War, photographs had become an integral part of wartime information. Newspapers and magazines (such as photo-heavy *Life*), brought images of combat to the public. Governments of nations fighting in the war recognized the power of this visual journalism and, to varying degrees, controlled what the public could see. Morale-boosting images, such as the raising of the American flag on Mount Suribachi after a bloody victory on the Pacific island of Iwo Jima, were favored, while photos of dead home-country soldiers were often censored.

The Vietnam War produced photographs that still possess searing intensity, and some remain as icons of that conflict. Eddie Adams's 1968 photo of a South Vietnamese police general executing a Viet Cong fighter on a Saigon street, and Nick Ut's 1972 image of a young Vietnamese girl running down a road with her clothes burned off and her body seared by American napalm are among the foundation-stones of collective perception of that war. Of this latter photograph, Susan Sontag wrote that it "probably did more to increase the public revulsion against the war than a hundred hours of televised barbarities."[8] Even many young people born long after the Vietnam War ended recognize those photographs, although they may not fully understand the war from which they emerged.

Photojournalists' work reached the public when news organizations – sometimes hesitating when influenced by the government or fearing "patriotic" political backlash – decided to publish them. Ron Haeberle's photographs of the March 1968 My Lai massacre, during which American troops murdered up to 500 Vietnamese civilians (including women and children), were not available for public view until November 1969. When the photos were finally published (shortly after print reporter Seymour Hersh's story about My Lai had appeared), the impact was profound. Evelyn Theiss wrote: "The images graphically undercut much of what the U.S. had been claiming for years about the conduct and aims of the conflict. Anti-war protesters needed no persuading, but 'average' Americans were suddenly asking, '*What* are *we doing in Vietnam?*'" (emphasis in original).⁹

Contrary to a long tradition of morale-bolstering images of the Iwo Jima type, the My Lai photographs were precedent for what might be called "anti-heroic" photography. In chronicling sordid aspects of American war-making, the new images' harsh realism undermined the myth of flawless military honor and the righteousness of the American cause.

But American and global publics did not always see such photographs, at least not in timely fashion. During the 1991 Gulf War, as the retreating Iraqi army was being pounded by American and allied forces, photographer Kenneth Jarecke, on assignment for *Time* magazine, came across an Iraqi military truck that had been destroyed by an American bomb. The truck's driver and his fellow soldiers were now nothing but charred remnants of human beings. Torie Rose DeGhett, in a magazine article published several years later, described what Jarecke's photo showed:

> The Iraqi soldier died attempting to pull himself up over the dashboard of his truck. The flames engulfed his vehicle and incinerated his body, turning him to dusty ash and blackened bone ... the soldier's hand reaches out of the shattered windshield, which frames his face and chest. The colors and textures of his hand and shoulders look like those of the scorched and rusted metal around him. Fire has destroyed most of his features, leaving behind a skeletal face, fixed in a final rictus. He stares without eyes.¹⁰

This was visual information about the reality of war. *Time* and the Associated Press decided not to publish it. This decision, wrote DeGhett, "denied the public the opportunity to confront this unknown enemy and consider his excruciating final moments." It was published at the time only by the British newspaper the *Observer* and the French daily *Libération*.¹¹

British journalist Harold Evans defended publication of the photo, suggesting a test for use in such cases: "Is the event portrayed of such social and historic significance that the shock is justified? Is the objectionable detail necessary for a proper understanding of the event?" Evans contended that these questions had been answered affirmatively in this instance, stating: "It is right that we should contemplate the results of our beliefs [about going to war]. No action can be moral if we close our eyes to its consequences. Here, in charred flesh and grinning skull, was the price of patriotism. That was the service that publication of this photograph performed." Of the protests directed to the *Observer*, Evans wrote: "They suggest that even now, at the end of the bloodiest century the world has known, even now after the trenches, and Hiroshima, and My Lai, popular culture is still largely imbued with a romantic conception of war and resents a grimmer reality."[12]

Along similar lines, David Carr, writing in the *New York Times* in 2003, observed that war photography has "an ability not just to offend the viewer, but to implicate him or her as well."[13] Perhaps that is the essence of decisions to avert the collective public gaze from such images.

The next step in painful, anti-heroic photographs was the growing dissemination of images collected not by journalists but by frontline troops themselves. Donald Matheson and Stuart Allan noted that "the image of war is suddenly out of the hands of the political marketer or the cautious editor and in the hands of others – among them soldiers, citizens, activists."[14]

Soldiers have long had cameras to take snapshots to send home to family and friends, and their photos rarely traveled beyond that limited audience. But digital cameras and internet access changed that, and suddenly the most unpleasant truths of war were in wider circulation, such as so-called "trophy photos," showing soldiers grinning beside dead enemy combatants, sometimes in horribly gruesome poses. A particularly loathsome case was the array of photos showing American soldiers torturing Iraqi prisoners in Abu Ghraib prison near Baghdad in 2004, during the Iraq War.

The photographs, taken by another American soldier, showed Iraqi prisoners stripped naked and tormented by their jailers; threatened by snarling dogs; sexually humiliated; and in probably the most widely seen of these images, a hooded prisoner appears held up by wires in a mock crucifixion. Senior American military and civilian officials tried to dismiss all this as the actions of a few "bad apples," but the photographs did great damage by undermining the US claims of nobility of purpose in launching the war to "liberate" Iraq. Writing in the *Washington Post*, Philip Kennicott noted, that despite official efforts to downplay the significance of the photos, they would be perceived elsewhere in the world as evidence of American malfeasance. "World editorial reaction is vehement," stated Kennicott. "We are under the suspicion of the International Red Cross and Amnesty International."[15]

With the Abu Ghraib photos easily available in cyberspace, fighting the Iraq War became even more burdensome for American military commanders, who were quickly finding that any notion of "mission accomplished" was an illusion. When a country's civilian policymakers and its military lose, even incrementally, their ability to control information during wartime, eventually prevailing in the conflict becomes considerably more difficult. As information becomes ever more likely to escape from boundaries channeling it in particular directions, its impact in wartime becomes more difficult to predict.

Social media are especially important in ensuring the diversity and broad reach of war-related photography. One of the largest social media platforms for photographs is Instagram, with (as of early 2020) more than 1 billion monthly active users, more than 100 million photos and videos posted daily, and more than 50 billion photos shared since its founding in 2010.[16] Most Instagram users post personal photos – family, pets, and such – but many professional news photographers also post on this site, displaying an array of photos that tell a more complete story of the events they cover than their limited number of published photos can convey. Social media and other online venues also can help these images reach larger audiences. Combat photographer Lynsey Addario wrote, "In a time when the space allotted to photographs in magazines was shrinking, a slide show was a consolation prize; images that didn't fit into the print edition were at least viewed by the public online."[17]

In many ways, new photo-related technologies have helped the public gain a greater understanding of what war actually looks like. But some of the new tools can infringe on the accuracy of the image. The photographer Edward Weston once wrote, "Only with effort can the camera be forced to lie; basically it is an honest medium."[18] Weston worked during the first half of the twentieth century, a time when technology had not yet made many inroads into the honesty of the medium. Today, however, with just minimal effort, the camera's work can be made into a lie.

A wartime example of this occurred when freelance photographer Adnan Hajj doctored photographs distributed by Reuters during the 2006 war between Israel and Hezbollah. In one of the photos, Hajj thickened the smoke rising from downtown Beirut after an Israeli airstrike, and in another showed three flares (misidentified in the caption as "missiles") dropped by an Israeli military jet when just one flare was actually dropped. After independent websites showed how the first picture had been altered, Reuters apologized and removed the picture from its archives. Reuters then examined other photos by Hajj and discovered the doctored image of the flares.[19]

There is no telling how many such phony images have traveled through social media or been otherwise published. News organizations try to police themselves, and independent "photo detectives" help to identify fakes. In addition to the damage inflicted on news media credibility, bad information – photographs and other material – victimizes the public. Information consumers are, to a considerable extent, at the mercy of information providers, especially when the topic is one which the consumers are not personally familiar with and cannot verify on their own. Technology-enabled fakery is certain to become more sophisticated and more difficult to detect. It can poison the well of information at war.

Terrorists' Information Warfare

Terrorism is war. Rather than large armies and sophisticated weaponry, terrorist groups may rely on a few individuals with homemade tools, targeting civilians to amplify their savagery. Sometimes terrorist organizations can take on the trappings of more traditional militaries, as was the case of Islamic State (IS) beginning in 2014. IS at its strongest controlled cities such as Mosul in Iraq and Raqqa in Syria, and it claimed territory estimated at 81,000 square miles, not much smaller than the area of Great Britain.

But the planners of the IS "caliphate" as a physical entity miscalculated their relative strength. Once major powers – such as the United States – brought their military strength (particularly air power) to the fight, IS-held territory rapidly shrank. Nevertheless, terrorist organizations are very much alive, and present challenges to conventional military planners. What are the targets to be attacked? How can a war against terrorists be "won" and what role can information play?

Terrorists depend on weaponized information just as they rely on assault rifles and explosives. When Al Qaeda attacked the United States on September 11, 2001, they killed approximately 3,000 persons. (The number remains approximate because more than 5,000 persons have been diagnosed with cancer linked to toxins at the attack scenes.[20]) These are, of course, significant numbers, but consider how many millions of people were *terrorized* by information about the attacks and found their lives shadowed by terrorism-related fears. Television news video of the airplanes crashing into the World Trade Center, individuals falling to their deaths, the towers collapsing, frightened onlookers on the run ... the images from that day were seen across the globe, constituting an information victory for Al Qaeda over the world's most powerful nation.

This is a primary goal of terrorists. Joseph Nye defined terror as "a psychological drama in which violence is used by nonstate actors to capture attention, shape the agenda, and shock the stronger players into counterproductive actions. On all three dimensions, Al Qaeda succeeded."[21]

Satellite television and the internet give terrorist organizations global clout by delivering information about their actions to huge audiences. Some in these audiences react with horror, others with applause. The information is delivered to global publics by different providers: conventional news media and, increasingly, by terrorists themselves. The ranks of Al Qaeda, Islamic State, and others include persons skilled in packaging and disseminating information. When terrorists attacked the airport and a metro station in Brussels in March 2016, it was uncertain at first who was behind the bombings. But, within hours, the Amaq News Agency, Islamic State's in-house news service, posted (first in English) IS's claim of responsibility. The news quickly spread, first through Telegram, the favorite social media platform of IS, and then news organizations around the world picked up and reported the claim.[22] (Telegram is a messaging service offering public and encrypted private channels. Amaq used it regularly to make "news" announcements, and Islamic State terrorists sometimes used it to communicate with each other and with prospective recruits.)[23]

Islamic State has stressed the importance of jihadi media activism and has recruited "media operatives" with publications such as "Media Operative, You Are Also a Mujahid." The recruiters state that the operative's job is to "buoy the morale of soldiers, spread news of their victories and good deeds, encourage the people to support them by clarifying their creed, methodology and intentions, and bridge the intellectual gap between the mujahidin and ordinary Muslims." All this, wrote Charlie Winter, "is ideal for popularizing the Islamic State brand."[24]

Al Qaeda had earlier built an online library of training materials that would teach its readers how to make ricin poison, how to build a bomb from commercial chemicals, and other advice. The online magazine *Muaskar al-Battar* (Camp of the Sword) told potential recruits, "Oh, Mujahid brother, in order to join the great training camps you don't have to travel to other lands. Alone in your home or with a group of your brothers you too can begin to execute the training program."[25] The Al Qaeda-affiliated Global Islamic Media Front, primarily serving sympathizers living in Europe, featured online videos showing how to plan a roadside assassination, fire a rocket-propelled grenade and a surface-to-air missile, blow up a car, take hostages, and master other tactics.[26]

Terrorists' use of information became more intense through the work of Abu Musab al-Zarqawi, leader of Al Qaeda in Iraq (AQI), which – after Zarqawi was killed in 2006 in a US airstrike – evolved into Islamic State. In 2004, AQI kidnapped American businessman Nicholas Berg, and Zarqawi himself beheaded the captive on camera. The video of this murder was posted on the web, and within 24 hours it had been copied onto other sites and downloaded more than 500,000 times.[27] Soon the number of viewers was in the millions.

This incident was an early indicator of the value of the internet to terrorists. Mainstream news organizations would not show such graphic footage to the public, but the internet provided a way for Zarqawi to avoid traditional media filters and deliver whatever images he wanted. Based on the number of downloads, Zarqawi correctly gauged the tastes of those he wanted to reach. This is in large part a hard-core audience, not a general one, and Zarqawi had apparently decided that he would play to his strength, connecting with those who approved of his methods, rather than soften his appeal to make it more acceptable to a wider audience.[28] (Islamic State later broadened this approach, especially for its recruiting.)

Jihadists soon came to appreciate the value of online publication. *Jihad Recollections* was an online, English-language magazine created in 2009 by American extremists. It first achieved notoriety by threatening the producers of the *South Park* television show because of an episode that included a satiric portrayal of the Prophet Mohammed. It was succeeded by another online magazine, *Inspire*, which included articles such as "How to Make a Bomb in the Kitchen of Your Mom." These instructions were reportedly followed by the Tsarnaev brothers, who made bombs in pressure cookers that killed 3 and injured 264 others at the 2013 Boston Marathon.[29]

Some terrorists have presented, on their own, their attacks in real time through social media venues. Video of the March 2019 attacks on mosques in Christchurch, New Zealand, in which 51 persons were killed, was streamed in real time on Facebook Live by the murderer, and then was posted by others on YouTube, Reddit, and additional sites. There is an audience for terrorist violence: within 24 hours of the attacks, Facebook had blocked viewing of the video 1.2 million times by stopping uploads, and another 300,000 times by removing the video after it had been posted.[30] YouTube officials relied on software to identify and delete videos of the murders, but the content was being posted at the rate of one upload per second immediately after the attacks, and some people posting the videos were making small changes in the content to defeat the artificial intelligence system that YouTube has relied on to screen out extreme violence, child pornography, and other such content.[31]

Later in 2019, a terrorist attacked a synagogue in Halle, Germany, and using a head-mounted camera livestreamed his attack on Twitch, a platform owned by Amazon. (The terrorist was partially foiled by a locked synagogue door, but nevertheless killed 2 persons and injured 2 others.) Twitch reported that only 5 persons had watched the livestream, but 2,200 viewed a recording of the attack during the 30 minutes before the video was removed. At the time of the attack, Twitch was the most popular livestream service, with more livestream viewers than YouTube or Facebook. From Twitch, the video of the incident moved onto other platforms, including Twitter and Streamable, and it reached more than 15,000 Telegram accounts, and from there even more viewers.[32]

In some countries, legislative bodies have considered criminal penalties for social media purveyors who fail to block such postings, but despite the massive amounts of money and technology available to social media companies, many tech-savvy individuals – including terrorists and terrorism voyeurs – have proved that they can outsmart Silicon Valley. Even platforms committed to rigorous monitoring of their content face challenges, given the speed and diversity of languages in online postings.

Because terrorists can use online venues to "self-publish" reports about their actions, news organizations are also faced with self-policing responsibilities. Emily Bell of Columbia University's School of Journalism wrote, "While the ambition is always to have the best possible reporting in difficult situations, there is inevitably debate about where the line should be drawn in terms of coverage and focus – now, that balance must also take into account the fact that the press no longer controls what information is available." This applies not only to reporting about terrorist attacks, but also to contributing – even if inadvertently – to the information environment that facilitates terrorism. Bell noted that "where there is a saturation of inflammatory rhetoric about ideology or particular groups ... it becomes statistically likely that some lone wolf will take the bait."[33]

Journalists may face difficult decisions about how to cover terrorism. In the aftermath of the New Zealand murders, that country's prime minister, Jacinda Ardern, refused to mention the perpetrator's name. Her goal was to impose anonymity to avoid any glorification of the killer. Some news organizations responded differently. In Britain, the editor-in-chief of the *Guardian*, Katharine Viner, said:

The role of a news organization is different from the role of a politician or a political party; our responsibility is to report the facts, contextualize events, and work with our readers to understand what's going on. Not reporting the terrorist's name would undermine those efforts. However, we do think it's important to ensure that the terrorist's identity is not overly represented in our coverage, and that our coverage also focuses on the victims.

Viner's view was endorsed by the *Guardian*'s readers' editor, Paul Chadwick, who wrote: "Rumor and conspiracy thrive in closed information loops. Professional journalism, by circulating verified information and giving context, breaks them open. If journalists choose to be silent, conspiracists fill the void and turn the silence to their purposes."[34]

Chadwick's point about conspiracists' ability to widely disseminate their views again underscores the significance of an evolving media environment in which access to information platforms is wide open and lacks the filtering process that news organizations once imposed on a large part of the information flow. Terrorists, conspiracists, and others can reach much bigger audiences than in the past, and they can do so quickly and easily.

Secondary effects of information also can work to terrorists' advantage. Terror attacks on tourists, for example, are likely to receive extensive news coverage and social media reporting, and they can seriously damage a country's tourism industry, which is a vital part of many nations' economies. Similarly, international corporations considering investing in a country may be deterred by reports about terrorist activity there, thus depriving it of a valuable infusion of funds. Further, consider how air travel has been affected not only by actual attacks on aircraft but also by speculation about the vulnerability of this kind of transportation. Even security measures at airports may frighten at least as much as reassure.

Responding to terrorists' information tactics requires a multipart strategy that involves limiting terrorists' access to media channels (such as Twitter) and creating content to counter the recruiting efforts of terrorist organizations. Such a strategy is essential if at least some of terrorist organizations' recruiting efforts are to be defeated. Recruiting relies on information that is delivered face-to-face as well as through assorted media, and this is related to the larger task of constituency-building. Islamic State was able to sustain its physical caliphate for several years because it could recruit enough supporters to offset battlefield losses, and its resurgence (as of 2020) in places such as Afghanistan and the Sinai Peninsula is dependent on its ability to expand its supply of fighters. Beyond nurturing fighters and other activists, Islamic State (like Al Qaeda and others) has always been conscious of the need to use carefully crafted information to maintain a popular base that could affect political opinion in contested territory and elsewhere.

Combating terrorism requires a combination of information and kinetic methods. As in all warfare, the balance must be carefully designed, particularly because some terrorist organizations manipulate religious and cultural, as well as political, beliefs to serve their ends. Creating counternarratives along these lines has sometimes confounded secular governments and limited the effectiveness of their information operations. The cultural lenses through which information is viewed help to determine its clarity and effectiveness.

As non-state actors such as Al Qaeda, Islamic State, Boko Haram, Al Shabaab, and others expand their capacity to wage war, their opponents' mastery of information as a tool of warfare must evolve at least at the same pace. In chapter 5, an analysis of Russia's use of information warfare will present strategic and tactical examples that offer lessons that can be applied in dealing with terrorist groups as well as with major powers. Before that, it is worth examining recent developments in the uses of information in conventional warfare environments.

On the Battlefield: Hamas versus Israel

The persistent conflict between Israel and Hamas only occasionally attracts much attention beyond its own region, but for the women, men, and children on the ground this is not a "small" war. When fighting flares up, civilian casualties are abundant, mainly on the Palestinian side.

Gaza, or the Gaza Strip, has been governed by Hamas since the Palestinian Legislative Council elections of 2006. Israel and Egypt control Gaza's land borders, and Israel has imposed a maritime blockade. About 2 million people live in Gaza's 139 square miles (about twice the size of Washington, DC), 65 percent of whom are age 24 or younger.[35]

The Gaza War of 2008–9 (the Israeli military named their effort "Operation Cast Lead") began in late December 2008, when Israel claimed there had been an increase in rocket attacks from within Gaza. The fighting lasted just three weeks. Casualty figures vary, depending on their source, but approximately 1,400 Palestinians were killed, while 13 Israelis died (10 of whom were soldiers, 4 of these killed by friendly fire). These numbers were evidence of Israel's military superiority, but they also raised legal and ethical questions about proportionality. This imbalance was a factor in Israel's determination to influence the content of news reports and other information about the war, and in Hamas's resolve to narrow the information gap between itself and the Israelis.

For Israel, which controlled access to the combat zone, a first step was to prevent foreign journalists from entering the area. Then the Israeli military began disseminating videos on YouTube, including footage of Israeli bomb strikes against Hamas. These appeared to show that only combatants were targeted. For its part, in terms of what was then considered "new media," Hamas relied on blogs and websites to present its version of events.

This was early "social media warfare." As with its military might, Israel far outdistanced the information capabilities of Hamas, controlling the war narrative through media content and global public relations efforts that were more sophisticated than anything Hamas (or its supporters in the Arab world) could muster.

The next Israel–Hamas war in Gaza came in summer 2014. Israel named its air and ground assault "Operation Protective Edge." The conflict began after the kidnapping and murder by Hamas of three Israeli teenagers, followed by the arrest of the alleged criminals, and then barrages of Hamas rockets fired into Israel. Once again, the Palestinians suffered far greater losses than the Israelis. During Israeli airstrikes and its ground invasion, approximately 2,200 Palestinians were killed while 72 Israelis died (of whom 67 were soldiers).

By 2014, social media tools, which had been in their infancy during the 2008–9 war, had entered a robust adolescence. Also by 2014, Hamas had recognized that having a social media-oriented information strategy was a wartime necessity. During the week leading up to the fighting, the Twitter hashtag #gazaunderattack was used 375,000 times, and during the month that the war lasted it was used 4 million times, outpacing the IDF account about the conflict more than twenty-fold.[36]

Sometimes the Hamas tweets included photos purportedly showing damage to civilian areas. The BBC, however, found that some of these photos were actually from fighting in Syria and Iraq years earlier. Some verified photos that were published online caused their own furor. One posted on Twitter by a Danish journalist showed Israelis on a hilltop – with camp chairs and popcorn – celebrating as they watched Israeli airstrikes in progress.[37] That photo was retweeted more than 8,500 times.

Graphic and politically controversial images that mainstream news organizations might decide not to publish can still reach large audiences through social media venues. By 2014, Hamas and its supporters had learned this. They established a Twitter account, @alqassambrigade, posted photos of Palestinian casualties, and issued threats directed at the IDF. (Twitter later removed that Hamas account.) IDF has been on Twitter since 2009, and as of mid-2020 @idf had 1.2 million followers.

Lt. Col. Peter Lerner, head of the IDF's Foreign and Social Media office within the IDF Spokesperson's unit summed up his task this way:

> If you are absent on the social media space, you cede that space to the enemy. You have to be there to lead the conversation, especially in wartime. If you're silent on social media, you're not putting anything in your enemy's way that prevents their message from gaining steam; if you're silent on social media, you're not getting your own message across; and if you're silent on social media, you're not giving your supporters ammunition to use.[38]

Social media also provide a way to put civilians to work in assisting a war effort. In 2014, at a university in Israel, as many as 400 students worked at banks of computers to send pro-Israel messages to the world. Writing in 30 languages, they targeted online forums while trying to be seen as ordinary forum participants. They also lobbied Facebook to remove content inciting violence against Israel and posted drawings of Hamas rockets made by Israeli children who had been under attack.[39] The student effort also created a website in 13 languages with updated war information, videos, testimonials, and other pro-Israel content.[40]

As of 2020, a tense standoff between Israel and Hamas continued, with spurts of violence occurring from both sides. In purely military terms, Israel remains far superior; its weaponry and the capabilities of members of its armed forces cannot be matched by the Hamas fighters (or, for that matter, by any of Israel's other neighbors). Because of this superiority, Israel acts with a certain amount of restraint, knowing its political footing is always precarious. If Israel were to try to "conquer" Gaza, it could almost certainly do so, but this would involve vicious urban combat with massive physical destruction and many Palestinian civilian casualties. Much international public opinion would gravitate toward the underdog Palestinians.

As David Patrikarakos observed: "Asymmetric warfare is not so asymmetric anymore. The IDF would have to meet Hamas not just on the battlefield but in cyberspace. War would have to be fought at the narrative as well as the physical level."[41] Competition among war-related narratives is not new. Virtually every war has narratives driving it: slavery or states' rights in the American Civil War; the presence or absence of weapons of mass destruction in the Iraq War; and countless others. What has changed is the involvement of global publics in shaping these narratives. No longer the exclusive domain of bards and presidents and generals, the wartime narrative may now incorporate contributions from millions of individuals using social media to help to shape the cases for and against a conflict's protagonists. Lt. Col. Lerner's points cited above illustrate how seriously one of the world's top military organizations takes the business of narrative and the need to wisely use new media tools in this venture.

Information at war can serve as something of an equalizer, but only to a certain extent. Between the Gaza wars of 2008–9 and 2014, Hamas became considerably more sophisticated in its approach to using information, particularly via social media, and this helped Hamas to generate international political pressure on Israel. Analyzing social media use in Israel's 2012 Operation Pillar of Defense, an eight-day exchange of airstrikes and rocket attacks that was a prelude to the 2014 war, Thomas Zeitzoff found that "shifts in public support reduce conflict intensity, particularly for Israel. This effect is greater than the effect of the key international actors." As online support for Hamas increased, Zeitzoff wrote, Israel significantly reduced the number of its airstrikes.[42]

Nevertheless, as Hamas moved toward greater social media expertise, it was important to remember that war comprises varied constituent elements. The *political* facets of conflict are, in most cases, important, but, although the information–politics nexus can (as in the Pillar of Defense case) affect combatants' tactics, this transient influence does not necessarily mirror the actual combat capabilities of the warring parties. The virtual battlefield is global, and in 2014 most IDF and Hamas twitter followers lived abroad.[43] Hamas tried to take advantage of information-enhanced political efforts, but a tweet is far from being the equivalent of an Israeli Air Force F-15.

The influence of information at war extends only so far. This case was an instance of information affecting the course of conflict, but only within relatively narrow limits.

Public Diplomacy Goes to War

Information at war plays varied roles, ranging from being an integral part of kinetic combat operations to strengthening the political position of a warring party. This latter task may take information strategy into the realm of public diplomacy, for which a boiled-down definition is a government's effort to influence foreign publics. Rather than government-to-government diplomacy, this is government-to-public. Much public diplomacy has traditionally been information-based, such as through international broadcasting, and it has often relied on soft power, meaning the ability to get others to do what you want through attraction rather than coercion.

Public diplomacy can be important during wartime because it may influence the political environment on which both adversaries and allies depend for support for their war efforts. In conflict zones, reaching out to civilian populations can affect the levels of resistance or support the military may encounter. Given that politics and public opinion are integral facets of war, public diplomacy should not be underrated.

As the examples from the Hamas–Israel conflicts illustrated, influencing global public opinion can be an important element of overall wartime strategy for major powers and for non-state actors. Related to the latter, Michele Bos and Jan Melissen have described "rebel diplomacy" undertaken by rebel groups in Africa's Sahel as being "at the core of their survival strategy." Ansar Dine, based in northern Mali, was formed in 2011 and merged with Al Qaeda of the Islamic Maghreb in 2017. Ansar Dine initially relied on mainstream digital platforms such as YouTube, but after being labeled a terrorist group it was banned from such venues and relied instead on "deeper" online services such as Telegram to disseminate its message. Ansar Dine sought to portray itself as nobly fighting against foreign oppression, sending photos via Telegram that showed its "heroes," such as the young men who carried out a suicide attack in Timbuktu.[44]

Similarly, the National Movement for the Liberation of Azawad (MNLA), also operating in northern Mali, used online venues to distribute videos showing purported battlefield successes against the Malian army. The MNLA used this approach, wrote Bos and Melissen, as a means of "framing the conflict in its own image and increasing its legitimacy in the eyes of foreign observers," and "raising the MNLA's profile among interested foreign publics and leading to its being taken seriously by relevant external actors." Emphasizing news management, MNLA was successful "in securing its exposure on French television, giving it the opportunity to appeal directly to French and other Western audiences."[45]

Neither Ansar Dine nor the MNLA was capable of sustaining a military campaign, much less carving out a lasting secessionist state from northern Mali. They were, however, sufficiently skilled in using information tools to be able to raise their organizations' profiles in ways that enhanced their credibility as politico-military actors. In the judgment of Bos and Melissen, "Weak or ineffective violent non-state rebels or terrorist groups can use media to give the appearance of strength and capability ... . Public diplomacy became for Ansar Dine and the MNLA a way of keeping up the appearance of power," although "only for a very short period did these groups' digital self-representation reflect their actual power and influence on the ground."[46]

Larger military organizations, such as the US armed forces, rely on public diplomacy in a number of information-related ways. For years, the American military has used psychological operations (PSYOPS), now renamed military information support operations (MISO), as part of their array of tools. MISO has been defined by the US Department of Defense as "planned operations to convey selected information and indicators to foreign audiences to influence their emotions, motives, objective reasoning, and ultimately the behavior of foreign governments, organizations, groups, and individuals in a manner favorable to the originator's objectives."[47]

For some countries, military public diplomacy has a significant advantage over conventional diplomatic efforts because of the greater funding available to military programs. According to a 2009 US government report, in Somalia the State Department's public diplomacy programs had a $30,000 budget at that time, while the US military's information support team – part of the US embassy-based public diplomacy effort based in Mogadishu – had a budget of $600,000.[48]

Matthew Wallin observed that, "in fighting counterinsurgency campaigns in Iraq and Afghanistan ... on a daily basis soldiers were committed to a deliberate effort to influence the opinions and actions of the general public."[49] Part of this venture, as with any public diplomacy project, should heavily rely on *listening* to determine what factors are shaping public attitudes. Questions can be raised, however, about the effectiveness of such work in war zones when undertaken by uniformed, heavily armed soldiers. Intimidation – even if unintended – constrains the flow of information. Gender can also prove to be an issue in cultures in which female populations will not interact with males who are not members of their families. The

US military's response to this latter concern was to create Female Engagement Teams specifically to allow exchanging of information with the 50 percent of a population that might otherwise be off limits.[50]

There are boundaries that affect the military's effectiveness in such matters. Gathering information is sometimes more a matter of diplomacy than of soldiering. Marc Grossman, former US Under Secretary of State and special envoy to Afghanistan and Pakistan, suggested that the State Department create "a new personnel specialty: the 'expeditionary diplomat,'" who would serve "in the hardest places at a moment's notice," working primarily on reconstruction and stabilization projects. The skills needed for this kind of task would be partly acquired through training provided by the Department of Defense and the Central Intelligence Agency.[51] Some might criticize this approach as militarizing diplomacy and endangering the diplomats doing this work. But many valuable information sources often go untapped because no one is tasked with seeking them out. Diversification of information-gathering responsibilities might, in some instances, be worth the effort and risk.

The cases discussed in this chapter illustrate the developing maturity of social media as instruments of information at war. In something less than two decades, social media progressed from being a novelty to becoming an essential tool for states and non-state actors involved in conflict. Among the most adept users of these venues was Islamic State, which made a point of recruiting tech-savvy jihadists to its ranks. The alliance of anti-IS nations took considerable time to devise their own online strategies that could adequately counter the terrorists' efforts, and – although the physical IS caliphate was destroyed through conventional combat – IS and other groups will certainly rely on online media as they rebuild.

Meanwhile, a powerful new player was emerging in the use of information in conventional conflict as well as in aspects of modern war that do not rely exclusively on bullets. Russia has used information tools in its war against Ukraine and in its efforts to disrupt its adversaries' politics, most notably in the 2016 US presidential election. Russia's success with different levels of information-based tactics marks the arrival of new dimensions of information at war. As we will see, these new factors raise questions about how "war" should be defined. Can the definition go beyond "blowing things up" and include political destructiveness? Can a "war" of this kind be "won" by doing significant damage to an adversary's political system?

5

Russia and New Dimensions of Information at War

Nations are always searching for ways to take advantage of other nations, devising political, economic, and military strategies to do so. Some of these strategies have a specific, visible goal, such as carving out a piece of another country's territory, seeking an upper hand in trade relations, or just seeking to change a particular policy in a way that will benefit the government that is initiating the action. Other efforts might be malign and covert, such as aiming to disrupt a country's civic stability, perhaps setting the stage for a more conventional form of hostilities.

Probing for other countries' fault lines is ongoing. Sometimes a characteristic generally perceived as a strength, such as a democratic political process, can be transformed into a weakness by a determined adversary that is able to find and exacerbate flaws in that process. The targets in such competition need not be subjected to the physical harm that might befall them in traditional warfare, but inflicting systemic damage on a rival may amount to a non-military kind of victory ... winning a war without a shot being fired.

The information-laden environment of the twenty-first century is especially hospitable to those who wish to pursue non-kinetic tactics to advance their own interests by damaging those of others. A case can be made that "war" is not solely a matter of physical destruction or capturing territory. Today, information can be weaponized and targeted with unprecedented precision – a new kind of stealthy "smart bomb." It can be used to achieve a nation's policy goals, sometimes without the adversary state knowing exactly what has been done to it. With relatively little bloodshed or physical devastation (or none at all), this nevertheless can be considered war, and should be taken seriously as such.

As of this writing in 2020, the most accomplished information warrior is Russia, with its strategy built to advance the foreign policy of its president, Vladimir Putin. With negligible regard for truth or other nations' sovereignty, the Kremlin appears intent on using information to help it to claw back parts of the lost Soviet empire and in other ways rebuild its global influence. This Russian enterprise is at the heart of information at war today.

Manipulating information and influencing other nations' public opinion are far from new. History is replete with examples, as the following two cases illustrate. One is from the period shortly before America's entry into the Second World War, and the other involved superpower antagonisms during the Cold War.

"Draw America into the War!"

As we saw in chapter 1, pro-British reporting from American radio journalist Edward R. Murrow and some of his colleagues helped to strengthen interventionist sentiment among Americans in 1940 and 1941. Although he clearly sympathized with Great Britain and hated Nazi Germany, Murrow received little more than implicit encouragement from Franklin Roosevelt's White House.

In desperate straits, the British government needed to rely on more than a few friends' good will, and so it created a sophisticated information operation on American soil targeting the American public. In July 1941, Winston Churchill had appointed a close aide, Brendan Bracken, as head of Britain's Ministry of Information. Bracken's approach was mainly to cater to the needs of friendly American correspondents in the UK and to cajole visiting American publishers and other news executives. This was helpful to the British cause, but it had only indirect impact on American voters, whose opinions mattered most to Roosevelt.

To reach them without seeming to be relying on easily dismissed propaganda broadsides, the British initiated a covert information campaign headquartered in New York City and led by Canadian William Stephenson, an officer in Britain's Secret Intelligence Service, MI6. For public consumption, the midtown Manhattan office was labeled "British & Overseas Features," and its task was purportedly to provide British news articles to foreign newspapers. In reality, the office was, according to Henry Hemming, "dedicated to spreading fake, distorted or inaccurate stories, a rumor factory so big" that on average it was disseminating 20 stories every day.[1] Some of these rumors, wrote Hemming, "went straight to friendly contacts at interventionist pressure groups, others might go to sympathetic newspaper columnists, influential academics, or to political figures within powerful émigré groups."[2]

To find homes for their stories in American publications that might be suspicious of British ties, Stephenson and company made a deal with an established American news agency, ONA (Overseas News Agency). For a monthly fee, ONA would send the Stephenson team's "creative journalism" to ONA subscribers in neutral European countries, such as Sweden and Switzerland, where ONA staffers would rewrite them (while retaining the Stephenson writers' intent) and send them, now with foreign datelines, to ONA's US subscribers, such as the *New York Post, Herald Tribune,* and *Baltimore Sun.* These newspapers considered ONA reliable and ran many of the stories.[3]

As Roosevelt continued to lead the United States ever closer to intervention, Stephenson's rumor factory increased its production. Because some isolationists had argued that Germany was certain to win the war, Stephenson's writers described purported German weaknesses. Among its stories in late 1941 were those describing a typhoid epidemic behind Nazi lines; wounded German soldiers on the Russian front being left to die; Nazi generals plotting to assassinate Hitler; and so on.[4] If these reports turned out to be true, it was only a coincidence.

All this was taking place with the quiet approval of the White House. Roosevelt confidant Colonel Bill Donovan recognized that he and Stephenson had a common goal, and together the two men were principal architects of intelligence cooperation between their two nations. (Donovan later became head of the Office of Strategic Services, the precursor of the Central Intelligence Agency.) Meanwhile, real British news agencies were stepping up their outreach to American audiences, and actors and other representatives of the British movie industry were hard at work in Hollywood, making films sympathetic to the British cause and spreading the British message among West Coast "influencers" of the day.[5]

The British effort – sometimes American-assisted – to subdue isolationist sentiment and inspire support for the UK's war effort finally saw its goal achieved in December 1941, when the Japanese attack at Pearl Harbor led to America declaring war on Japan, Germany, and Italy.

The British exercise in propaganda is nevertheless instructive because it illustrates that information at war is a tool that can be used not just against enemy targets. Connecting with friendly (and prospectively friendly) information audiences can be crucial to a war effort. Over a long term, this would generally be a good situation for public diplomacy (presumably without duplicity), but in this case the British needed to produce results quickly.

In retrospect, the British tactics may appear to have been heavy-handed interference in domestic US political affairs. This could have provoked damaging blowback, but the stakes were such that the risk – which was somewhat lessened by FDR's covert approval – had to be taken. The US–UK partnership, supported by the relationship between Roosevelt and Churchill, proved to be a determinative factor during the remaining years of the war.

Compared with most instances of information at war, the British–US case is an anomaly. Friendly relations between protagonists do not always exist and are even less likely after the information-based meddling has occurred. Far more common are tensions that are edging ever closer to the precipice of armed conflict. During the Cold War, with the omnipresent specter of nuclear arsenals heightening those tensions, information gamesmanship could always be perilous, even if irresistible.

The Kremlin's Cold War Information Tools and US Response

Especially for those whose lives are several generations removed from the end of the Second World War, the demarcation between the conclusion of that conflict and the beginning of the Cold War may seem fuzzy (and, in reality, a case can be made that the latter was a continuation of the former). The Soviet Union, having lost 25 million of its citizens during the war, immediately sought to forcefully extend its influence into as much of Europe as possible, in part to ensure it would have a buffer against future adversaries and partly to advance the spread of communism.

Of the major Western allies, only the United States was physically unscathed and in an economic and military position to counter Soviet efforts. America, however, was gripped with uncertainty about how to deal with communism abroad and at home. The US responses ranged from the generosity of the Marshall Plan to the fearfulness that accompanied McCarthyism.

Aside from tactical maneuvering, the Cold War was a contest of ideas. John Lewis Gaddis wrote, "The issue at stake was almost as big as that of human survival: how best to organize human society."[6]

The philosophical competition between the West, led by the United States, and the communist bloc, led by the Soviet Union, sometimes extended beyond ideas and veered frighteningly close to direct armed conflict between the two powers. For the better part of a half-century, covert operations, proxy wars, and ill-advised gambits by both sides could have spiraled into the scarcely imaginable consequences of a global nuclear war.

Policymakers who embraced sanity recognized that, although military preparedness was essential, a less dangerous but still effective means of winning acceptance of their respective systems' superiority was through information. Narratives would be designed to elicit support from global audiences – those with preexisting loyalties who might be swayed, and those who were uncommitted but might be enticed into one or the other superpower camp.

Allen Dulles, who was director of the Central Intelligence Agency (CIA) from 1953 until late 1961, warned in his memoir (published in 1963) that the Kremlin

> vigorously uses all the instrumentalities of its propaganda machine. In one year, according to the Soviet Ministry of Culture's report, the Soviets published and circulated approximately thirty million copies of books in various foreign languages ... . In many countries throughout the world, they control newspapers and have penetrated and subsidized a large number of press outlets of various kinds which do not present themselves openly as Communist. With some of the most powerful transmitting stations in the world, they beam their messages to practically every major area of the world. They step up their propaganda to the particular target areas which they consider to be the most vulnerable.

This apparatus, wrote Dulles, constituted "Moscow's orchestra of subversion."[7]

On the American side, broadcast and print media were targeting audiences in communist and non-aligned nations. Also, wrote Frances Stonor Saunders, the CIA directed a program of cultural propaganda directed at US allies in Europe that was designed to "nudge the intelligentsia of Western Europe away from its lingering fascination with Marxism and Communism towards a view more accommodating of the 'American way.'"[8] The CIA maintained a "Propaganda Assets Inventory" that included organizations, publications, and other vehicles for countering Soviet – and even just left-leaning – information. Senior officials at the CIA decided when and how to deploy these assets.[9]

More overt US government efforts were led by Edward R. Murrow,

who had retired from CBS and joined the Kennedy administration as
director of the United States Information Agency (USIA), a position
that Kennedy elevated to include ex officio membership in the
cabinet and National Security Council.[10] Remaining a journalist at
heart, Murrow faced the task of preserving "the balance between his
agency's presentation of news and its championing of America, since
the USIA could opt out of neither." He said, "I do not mind being
called a propagandist so long as the propaganda is based on truth."[11]

An example of the USIA's work can be seen in its response to the
erection of the Berlin Wall in summer 1961. As described by Gregory
M. Tomlin:

> Murrow insisted that the USIA refer to the "Khrushchev crisis" and
> explain how Soviet intransigence in Germany endangered free people
> across the globe. Voice of America aired a three-part program titled
> "The Manufactured Crisis," and it rebroadcast Kennedy's July 25
> Berlin speech in thirty-five languages, which an estimated twenty
> million people heard. The agency's Motion Picture Service distributed
> nine hundred reels of the president's two addresses to ninety-five
> countries. USIA library managers reported "very heavy local usage" of
> an illustrated pamphlet containing fifteen articles related to the crisis.[12]

For their part, the Soviets were creating messaging that attacked
the United States, emphasizing topics such as racial conflict within
America, an issue the USSR spotlighted consistently, especially in
content directed to Africa.

Worth noting is the importance of using the word "propaganda"
with care. Its literal meaning – derived from the definition of the
Latin *propagare*, "to spread" – does not imply untruthfulness. In
modern usage, however, a pejorative connotation usually attaches to
the word, equating it with political falsehood. Propaganda, however,
is not always wholly false; the message may be fundamentally true
but adulterated by exaggeration and spin.

The Kremlin also gave high priority to managing information in
countries it considered to be within its sphere of influence. Finland,
with its 830-mile (1,340-kilometer) border with the Soviet Union,
has long been a target for Soviet (and then Russian) influence operations. Finland has consistently stood up to its giant neighbor. The
Finns fought the Soviets in the "Winter War" of 1939–40 and,
although greatly outnumbered in troops, tanks, and aircraft, killed or
wounded more than 300,000 Soviet soldiers while sustaining 70,000
total casualties of their own. Despite those figures, the war ended
with Finland ceding territory to the Soviets.

After the Second World War concluded, Finland – given its location – had no choice but to sign a "friendship treaty" with the USSR, which opened the way for a growing Soviet presence in Finland. During the Cold War, Finland was a testing ground for Soviet information tactics, and the fraught relationship gave rise to the term "Finlandization," referring to a country being allowed to retain nominal independence while under the influence of a more powerful nation. Esko Salminem described how the Soviet embassy in Helsinki strong-armed Finnish news media, and how the Western powers watched warily, out of concern that the Soviets might have Finlandization in mind for Western European countries.[13] (Later in this chapter, we will see how information-related tensions continue between Finland and Russia.)

During the final years of the Cold War – especially during the presidency of Ronald Reagan – the United States became more forceful in exerting information-related pressure on the Kremlin's Warsaw Pact satellites. Of particular interest to the Americans was Poland, where the Solidarity labor movement was pitted against the communist government. Part of the US effort involved funding Polish-language publishers outside Poland and smuggling their products into the country, as well as delivering cash to underground publishers within Poland. Seth G. Jones reported that, in 1985 alone, the CIA sent roughly 500,000 publications and US$900,000 into Poland.[14] The CIA also developed a clandestine broadcasting tool that allowed Solidarity backers to override Polish government-run television news and broadcast their own calls for workers to participate in public protests.[15] In addition to benefiting from the CIA's assistance, anti-regime efforts in Poland received help from US labor organizations such as the AFL-CIO, and Catholic charities, and overt broadcasting support from Radio Free Europe and the Voice of America.[16]

Uses of information by the Soviet Union during the Cold War – in general terms and in specific cases such as that of Finland and other targets – are historical antecedents of Russia's 21st-century fine-tuning of ways to wield information as a valuable tool of hybrid warfare: valuable, but not to be relied upon exclusively. Frederick C. Barghoorn, in his book about Soviet use of propaganda in foreign affairs, observed that "Moscow's appreciation of the political significance of propaganda does not imply any underestimation of the role of other instruments of domestic and international politics." Barghoorn added that Moscow "has never explicitly repudiated Lenin's dictum that great political problems are decided, in the last analysis, by force."[17]

In the twenty-first century, as the Kremlin has increased its reliance on information weaponry, Lenin's appreciation of force as the ultimate underpinning of policy has been supplemented and given a deceptively smoother edge, while still being a core value of Russia's strategic thinking.

Restructuring Russia's Information Arsenal

During the Cold War, many in the West became familiar with the Soviet Union's information organs, such as newspapers *Pravda* and *Izvestia*, which were the leading news services within the USSR, and the international news service TASS, which after its founding in 1925 enjoyed the "exclusive right to gather and distribute information outside the Soviet Union, as well as the right to distribute foreign and domestic information within the Soviet Union, and manage the news agencies of the Soviet republics." TASS news and photos were received throughout the USSR's constituent republics by "4,000 Soviet newspapers, TV and radio stations and over a thousand foreign media outlets. The news agency ran one of the biggest networks of correspondents in the world – 682 offices in the country and 94 bureaus abroad – and employed close to 2,000 journalists and photo correspondents."[18]

Another umbrella news agency – this one dating back to 1941 – was RIA Novosti (originally named the Soviet Information Bureau), which like TASS had bureaus around the world and a large staff that provided content for newspapers, magazines, books, and radio stations. The organization was especially responsible for delivering Russia's official messaging to global publics. In 2005, RIA Novosti launched Russia Today (as of 2009, simply RT), a multilingual television news network. In late 2013, President Vladimir Putin shut down RIA Novosti, leaving RT as Russia's dominant international media voice. (Ria Novosti has been successfully reconstituted for Russian audiences and is Russian-language only.[19])

Russia Today had proved its value to the Kremlin in 2008 with its coverage of the war between Russia and Georgia about the breakaway Georgian regions of South Ossetia and Abkhazia, over which Georgia sought to assert its authority. Initial Western news coverage portrayed Georgia as a democracy victimized by an aggressive Russia (a portrayal that a later European Union report discredited, stating that Georgia had started "an unjustified war"[20]). As Julia Ioffe wrote, that early coverage "was precisely the kind of anti-Russian reporting by the world's press that Russia Today was created to counteract." Ioffe noted that this conflict was "Russia

Today's crucible" as it was "the only press outlet available to a Western audience that had access to the Russian side of the fighting." The channel claimed its broadcast viewership rose to 15 million at this time and its YouTube views were more than a million.[21]

More recently, RT has become the Kremlin's principal propaganda outlet, but its success in building an audience is open to question. In terms of influencing Americans, for instance, RT claims that it can reach 85 million people in the United States.[22] But figures related to *reach* are mostly meaningless because they may have little relation to the number of people actually *watching* a broadcaster. By way of comparison, a major US television network such as NBC could claim a reach of more than 300 million Americans – basically everyone with access to a television – and yet only a relatively small portion of these would constitute the actual audience at any given time.

As Jim Rutenberg observed, however, "ratings are almost beside the point" because "in the new, 'democratized' media landscape," RT has "come to form the hub of a new kind of state media operation, one that travels through the same diffuse online channels, chasing the same viral hits and memes, as the rest of the Twitter-and-Facebook-age media."[23] Television as television is no longer the dominant information force it once was. Influence is now sourced by a composite media structure from which many people select bits and pieces to assemble their own reservoirs of information that feed their thinking about politics, consumer behavior, cultural choices, and much more. RT's managers have demonstrated sophisticated understanding of this multi-faceted approach.

RT's partner Sputnik began its work in 2014 as an international news agency, radio broadcaster, and news website operator. Like RT, Sputnik was created, in the words of Vladimir Putin, "to break the monopoly of the Anglo-Saxon global information streams."[24] Sputnik's radio broadcasts are available in 90 cities worldwide, but reach only a limited American audience through two Washington, DC stations and three small stations in Kansas City. Writing about Sputnik's radio content, Neil MacFarquhar observed that it is "a modern spin on propaganda," focusing on "sowing doubt about Western governments and institutions rather than the old Soviet model of selling Russia as paradise lost."[25]

What is the point of such efforts? Is it merely to use political mischief to annoy adversaries, without provoking too harsh a response? Or are tools such as RT and Sputnik more useful than they first appear, serving as chisels to chip away at nations' institutional foundations by spreading falsehoods? And, again, a question arises that is central to important strategic issues: is this war, or is it merely an aggressive form of public diplomacy? Whatever the answer, how much provocation should the targeted nation allow before responding? And should that response be on a similar, information-oriented level, or is an escalated response necessary?

Information as 21st-Century War

In 2013, Valery Gerasimov, a senior Russian general who has served as chief of the General Staff of the Armed Forces, wrote an article extolling the value of propaganda and subversion in warfare. Sometimes referred to as "the Gerasimov doctrine," it may be less a doctrine in itself than it is a contribution to existing military canon. (The writer who coined the term "Gerasimov doctrine," British scholar Mark Galeotti, has since recanted, saying that he used it only to have a snappy headline for a blog post and not to raise the general's pronouncements to the level of "a foundational set of beliefs as to what kinds of war the country will be fighting in the future."[26])

In his article, Gerasimov said: "The very 'rules of war' have changed. The role of nonmilitary means of achieving political and strategic goals has grown, and, in many cases, they have exceeded the power of force of weapons in their effectiveness." These nonmilitary means, added Gerasimov, should be "applied in coordination with the protest potential of the population," which could presumably be heightened through use of informational measures. Later in the article, Gerasimov noted that "the information space opens wide asymmetrical possibilities for reducing the fighting potential of the enemy. In North Africa [i.e., the 2011 "Arab spring"], we witnessed the use of technologies for influencing state structures and the population with the help of information networks. It is necessary to perfect activities in the information space, including the defense of our own objects."[27]

A key phrase in this article, used again by Gerasimov in a 2019 speech,[28] is "protest potential," a factor that is particularly susceptible to information pressure. A population's propensity to engage in destabilizing protests might be made more volatile by information designed to exacerbate political tensions. As we will see later in this chapter, Russia has developed its information technology capabilities to accelerate discord in specific places in order to take full advantage of protest potential.

To bring these tactics to the forefront of its military strategy, Russia announced in 2017 that it was creating a new branch of its military – information warfare troops. Defense Minister Sergei

Shoigu told the Russian parliament that "propaganda needs to be clever, smart, and efficient," but he was not specific about the new troops' responsibilities.[29] The previous year, a NATO study provided a sense of the direction in which the Russians were moving: "The Russian approach is much broader than simply sowing lies and denial, for instance maintaining that Russian troops and equipment are not where they plainly are. Instead, Russian state and non-state actors have exploited history, culture, language, nationalism, and more to carry out cyber-enhanced disinformation campaigns with much wider objectives."[30]

Those objectives presumably included significant destabilization of an adversary. Implementing this holistic strategy required tacticians, technology experts, and other skilled personnel to evaluate a targeted population, design the appropriate step-by-step plan, and conduct continuing evaluation. RAND technology expert Rand Waltzman told a US Senate committee in 2017 that such a process might comprise the following steps:

1. Take the population and break it down into communities, based on any number of criteria (e.g. hobbies, interests, politics, needs, concerns, etc.).
2. Determine who in each community is most susceptible to given types of messages.
3. Determine the social dynamics of communication and flow of ideas within each community.
4. Determine what narratives of different types dominate the conversation in each community.
5. Use all of the above to design and push a narrative likely to succeed in displacing a narrative unfavorable to you with one that is more favorable.
6. Use continual monitoring and interaction to determine the success of your effort and adjust in real time.[31]

Waltzman noted that this process might soon be automated (presumably relying on artificial intelligence), which would enable those using this approach to do so more broadly and faster. (Analysis based on these criteria would be useful not just in aiming at another country's population, but also in structuring campaigns for consumer products, political candidates, and other such efforts that would benefit from precise targeting.)

Among military practitioners, this process takes on a more severe edge. The Russian military has clearly come to view information as a dimension of war. The Russian Ministry of Defense's *Military Encyclopedic Dictionary* offers this definition of "information war":

An open and violent collision between states in which the enemy's resistance is suppressed by the use of means of harmful influence on his information sphere, disruptions or destruction of the normal functioning of his information and telecommunication systems, [undermining] the security of his information resources, [and] obtaining unauthorized access to them as well as using massive informational and psychological influence on the Armed Forces' personnel and the population of the enemy in order to destabilize society and the state.[32]

This approach to war requires a certain level of care in order to avoid plunging into the abyss of the "traditional" conflict that is so dangerous in the nuclear era. This involves giving information/propaganda a distinct priority in military operations. Russian Lt. Gen. Andrei Kartapolov wrote in 2015 that "a classical war of the twentieth century consisted usually of 80 percent violence and 20 percent propaganda. New-type wars consist of 80 to 90 percent propaganda and 10 to 20 percent violence."[33] Along these lines, Russia has developed information that, depending what is needed in a given situation, "entertains, confuses, and overwhelms the audience."[34]

Debate exists about the significance of the "Gerasimov doctrine" – whether information is truly a dominant factor in overall Russian military strategy. The Kremlin's intentions are always difficult to ascertain, but in this chapter and elsewhere in this book are enough examples of Russian deployment of military and quasi-military information mechanisms with hostile intent to make the writings and actions of Gerasimov and his colleagues worth pondering.

Not only the Russians are reevaluating the role of information at war. Other militaries are adapting to the increased use of information-based tactics. In a speech in early 2020, British army Major General Jonathan Cole described the British plan:

Information Manoeuvre involves the use of information in all its forms to understand the operating environment better than anyone else and subsequently to make the most of that advantage. The aim is simultaneously to shape perceptions to ensure the Army's activities and intentions are appropriately recognised by allies, populations and adversaries. This approach, combined with the fighting skills of ground manoeuvre and air manoeuvre forces, will pre-empt, dislocate and disrupt our opponent; thus delivering effects both physically and virtually.[35]

The British Army's 77th Brigade was mandated to implement this plan, which includes these tasks:

- Conducting timely and appropriate audience, actor and adversary analysis.
- Planning and integrating information activity and outreach (IA&O).
- Supporting and delivering IA&O within pre-designated boundaries.
- Supporting counter-adversarial information activity.
- Support to partners across Government upstream and post-conflict institutional development/reform.
- Collecting, creating and disseminating digital and wider media content in support of designated tasks.
- Monitoring and evaluating the information environment within boundaries or operational area.[36]

In one form or another, information capabilities such as these cited by the British army are becoming part of the tactical arsenal of militaries around the world, although their levels of commitment in terms of budget, personnel, and other such factors vary.

To a certain extent, this process is driven by "keeping up with the Russians" – understanding the Kremlin's strategies and tactics, and recognizing that in some ways Russia has had a head start in this field. Christopher Paul and Miriam Matthews, in their RAND publication *The Russian "Firehose of Falsehood" Propaganda Model*, provide insight into why the Russian information products are effective. Several of their findings are particularly useful in understanding the Russian information strategy:

- What matter most in audience acceptance of information are getting the message from numerous and a variety of sources; getting versions of the message from others whose views are similar to those of the recipient. ("Did you see this?")
- High volume will consume the attention of the audience, overwhelm competing messages, and will increase credibility if multiple sources are supplying the message.
- Information overload leads to lowered defenses regarding challenging truthfulness.
- Repeated exposure to a statement increases the likelihood that it will be accepted as true.
- Over time, information from a questionable source may be remembered as true, with the source forgotten. ("Where did I hear that?")
- Angry messages are more persuasive to angry audiences.[37]

Social media are among the most useful weapons in this kind of information assault. One facet of this (which will be examined later in this chapter as part of the analysis of the 2016 US presidential election) is the "echo chamber" phenomenon that provides reinforcement for one's views by presenting only content grounded in a similar outlook. There is nothing mysterious about this; if you are ultra-conservative, it is likely that many of your Facebook "friends" will also be ultra-conservative. Much the same will be the case with those you follow and those who follow you on Twitter. That familiar viewpoint will echo through the corridors of your online world. Repetition of that opinion and insulation from contrasting views can contribute to intellectual isolation and reinforcement of your established attitudes.

Social media venues are well suited to the creation of such insular communities. The echo chamber's existence is part of the fallout from the information explosion of recent decades. The breadth of choice that is now offered to information consumers replaces the limited (and largely centrist) options that were dominant in the mid-to-late twentieth century. In the United States then, news was provided by a local newspaper, perhaps some radio reports, and most significantly by the three big national television networks – ABC, CBS, and NBC. Especially the latter were designed to reach and hold broad, mainstream audiences. These providers could, of course, be ignored, but information alternatives that matched the narrow tastes of an individual were harder to come by.

Creating an "echo chamber" of sorts in that environment was possible, although anyone doing so was still unlikely to be wholly sealed off from the dominant civic conversation about public affairs. As noted earlier, during periods of national crisis – such as President Kennedy's assassination or the Vietnam War – the dominant information sources exercised a gravitational pull on the mass American audience, shaping attitudes and discourse. Conspiracy theories and other rumors still circulated, but they lacked the nurturing isolation provided by today's echo chambers. Similar situations existed in numerous other countries during the adolescence of television news, when choices of information providers were limited.

Susceptibility to the echo-chamber effect is debatable.[38] Becoming comfortable in an echo chamber may reflect a desire to reinforce biases without being bothered by alternatives.[39] A bit of intellectual exercise may be needed to escape (if one desires to escape), but with so much information available, being "locked into" an echo chamber unwillingly is rare, although the more autocratic the environment in which one lives, the more difficult it may be to find information alternatives.

Russian information warfare strategists understand these phenomena well, and they know how to take advantage of them. They have moved beyond reliance on TASS, or even RT and Sputnik.

They see the internet's many venues as the principal providers of the world's information, and as battlegrounds on which they are determined to use these tools to achieve strategic goals.

The Internet Research Agency

The true scope of Russia's commitment to information at war is unknown, with much activity shrouded in secrecy. When Russian military officials announced in 2017 that a corps of "information warfare troops" was being created, it presumably did not mean soldiers in uniform marching on a parade ground while clasping laptops. Military personnel working on computers constitute part of the effort, and they are supplemented by civilian efforts directly or indirectly backed by the government.

Only occasionally do elements of Russia's information warfare structure emerge into view. Such is the case with the Internet Research Agency (IRA), also known as Glavset. From its base of operations in St Petersburg, IRA personnel targeted domestic and foreign audiences. P. W. Singer and Emerson T. Brooking wrote that these "trolls" were tasked with creating "civil unrest" among Russia's foes. In doing so, they assumed fake online identities, known as "sockpuppets," and wrote "hundreds of social media posts per day, with the goal of hijacking conversations and spreading lies, all to the benefit of the Russian government."[40] Singer and Brooking reported that documents leaked in 2014 stated that each IRA employee, in the course of a 12-hour workday, was expected "to post on news articles 50 times" and to "maintain six Facebook accounts publishing at least three posts a day and discussing the news in groups at least twice a day .... On Twitter, they might be expected to manage accounts with up to 2,000 followers and tweet 50 times a day."[41]

Evidence of the IRA's sophisticated talents could be seen in the information about a series of incidents in the United States in 2014. One was an effort to spread news about a chemical plant explosion in Louisiana, another reported an Ebola outbreak in Atlanta, and one more claimed that an unarmed black woman had been shot by police, also in Atlanta. The online content was polished, using logos from CNN and other news outlets. The report about the chemical plant on #ColumbianChemicals included eyewitness accounts. The Ebola story featured video of medical workers in hazmat suits. The Atlanta shooting story, #shockingmurderinatlanta, offered fuzzy video of the incident. All this was enough to cause brief panic and force first-responder agencies to investigate and comment.[42]

None of these events had actually happened. The "news reports" and their dissemination were apparently the work of the Internet Research Agency. The value of the art form designed by the IRA employees depended on correctly judging the limits of believability. Members of the audience for the IRA product had to trust the content enough to push it into their own online information space. Singer and Brooking wrote: "By cleverly leveraging readers' trust, these engineers of disinformation induced thousands – sometimes millions – of people each day to take their messages seriously and spread them across their own networks via 'shares' and retweets. This sharing made the messages seem even more trustworthy since they now bore the imprimatur of whoever shared them."[43] By the time the IRA embarked on its most notable project – attacking the US presidential election process in 2016 – the exponential growth of its online messaging through retweets and such had reached surprising levels.

David Sanger observed that the creation of the IRA:

> marked a moment of profound transition in how the Internet could be put to use. For a decade it was regarded as a great force for democracy: as people of different cultures communicated, the best ideas would rise to the top and autocrats would be undercut. The IRA was based on the opposite thought: social media could just as easily incite disagreements, fray social bonds, and drive people apart.[44]

Did this Russian effort shape the results of the election and pave the way to the White House for Donald Trump? No definitive answer can be given; Trump's victory was attributable to numerous factors. But there is no denying that Russia was much involved in trying to push the American electorate in the Kremlin's preferred direction.

"Active Measures" and the 2016 US Presidential Election

The US Department of Justice *Report on the Investigation into Russian Interference in the 2016 Presidential Election*, submitted in March 2019 by Special Counsel Robert S. Mueller III (the Mueller Report), cites "active measures" undertaken by Russia with the goal of "sowing discord in the U.S. political system." The report noted that "active measures" is "a term that typically refers to operations conducted by Russian security services aimed at influencing the course of international affairs."[45]

Some of the most controversial material in the report concerned the actions of Russian agents that benefited the Trump campaign. The report stated that "the IRA and its employees began targeting the United States as early as 2014 ... By early to mid-2016, IRA operations included supporting the Trump Campaign and disparaging candidate Hillary Clinton."[46]

President Trump consistently and forcefully denied any collusion. The Internet Research Agency effort was not included in the charges brought against Trump in the impeachment proceedings conducted by the US House of Representatives in 2019. He was charged with abuse of power in his dealings with the government of Ukraine, and with obstruction of Congress by telling officials in his administration to ignore congressional subpoenas. He was impeached by the House, acquitted by the Senate, and continued to serve as president.

A principal part of the IRA strategy was voluminous use of social media. By late 2017, Facebook had identified 470 accounts that were controlled by the IRA and accounted for 80,000 posts between January 2015 and August 2017, perhaps reaching as many as 126 million persons. In early 2018, Twitter reported that it had found 3,814 IRA-controlled Twitter accounts that may have been in contact with 1.4 million people.[47] Further, the Mueller Report stated that "on multiple occasions, members and surrogates of the Trump Campaign promoted – typically by linking, retweeting, or similar methods of reposting – pro-Trump or anti-Clinton content published by the IRA through IRA-controlled social media accounts."[48]

The Mueller team developed detailed indictments related to its investigation, including *US v. Internet Research Agency et al.* The indictment named as defendants the IRA, oligarch and close Putin associate Yevgeniy Prigozhin (who allegedly bankrolled the IRA), 2 of Prigozhin's business entities, and 12 other Russian individuals. Among the charges leveled by the Grand Jury was that the defendants conspired "to defraud the United States by impairing, obstructing, and defeating the lawful functions of the government through fraud and deceit for the purpose of interfering with the U.S. political and electoral processes, including the presidential election of 2016."[49]

The indictment alleged, among other specifics, that the Russian conspirators had created a Twitter account, "Tennessee GOP," with the handle @TEN_GOP, that attracted more than 100,000 online followers, and that they had stolen Americans' identities, appropriating "the social security numbers and dates of birth of real U.S. persons without those persons' knowledge or consent."[50] Russian operatives also allegedly produced, purchased, and posted ads on US social media and other online sites. Among the ads' themes were these: "Donald wants to defeat terrorism ... Hillary wants to sponsor it"; "Hillary Clinton Doesn't Deserve the Black Vote"; "Ohio Wants Hillary 4 Prison"; "We cannot trust Hillary to take care of our veterans"; and so on.[51]

In November 2016, Trump won 306 electoral votes to Clinton's 232, while Clinton won the popular vote with 48 percent to Trump's 46 percent (a margin of nearly 3 million votes).[52] Did the Russian-orchestrated machinations affect the outcome of this extraordinarily close presidential contest, and if so to what extent? That will continue to be debated. Regardless of the effects of the Russians' involvement, and assuming they were de facto Russian state actions, should the United States have retaliated in some way? No terrorist bombs exploded, and no bullets were fired, but an integral part of the political structure of the United States was attacked. House of Representatives Speaker Paul Ryan accused those indicted of "a sinister and systematic attack on our political system."[53]

At what point does such activity cross the line separating "mere politics" from an act of war? And if it is determined that this line *has* been crossed, what is to be done about it? Ways that information consumers can help in responding are reviewed in chapter 6. A preview of one kind of government response may have been seen in November 2018.

The US Cyber Command Attack

In the aftermath of Russia's election tampering, the United States military's Cyber Command, which collaborates with the National Security Agency, began targeting Internet Research Agency operatives with electronic communications (emails, pop-ups, texts, and direct messages), putting them on notice that the US government knew their real names and online handles.[54] With their covers blown, these Russian agents could expect that their ability to work and travel freely outside Russia might be affected.[55]

Cyber Command's commander, General Paul M. Nakasone, in a 2019 interview, outlined some of the strategic issues that shaped his role. He noted that threats in cyberspace persist "because the barriers to entry are low and the capabilities are rapidly available and can be easily repurposed," adding that "unlike the nuclear realm, where our strategic advantage or power comes from possessing a capability or weapons system, in cyberspace it's the *use* of cyber capabilities that is strategically consequential. The *threat* of using something in cyberspace is not as powerful as *actually* using it [emphasis in original]."[56]

Nakasone labeled the weaponizing of information in influence campaigns a "corrosive threat," and said:

> We've learned that if we're going to have an impact on an adversary, we have to *persistently engage* [emphasis in original] with that adversary, we have to understand that adversary, and we have to be able to impose cumulative costs on that adversary, and we have to be able to understand where that adversary not only is but also where he is going.

This involves, said Nakasone, "defending forward: How do we warn, how do we influence our adversaries, how do we position ourselves in case we have to achieve outcomes in the future?" According to Nakasone, this means "operating outside our borders, being outside our networks, to ensure that we understand what our adversaries are doing. If we find ourselves defending inside our own networks, we have lost the initiative and the advantage."[57]

In his analysis of Nakasone's approach, David Ignatius observed that this new doctrine "moves the United States closer to Russia's approach of treating cyberspace as part of a continuum of warfare. Rather than a binary on/off switch, conflict is now seen as something closer to a rheostat, which can be dialed up or down as conditions require."[58]

Cyber Command's tactics were in evidence in November 2018, when it blocked the Internet Research Agency's internet access on the day of the US congressional elections and for several days thereafter to prevent the Russians from using disinformation to cast doubt on the validity of the results. Ellen Nakashima reported that a presidential order in August 2018 had given Cyber Command the "latitude to undertake offensive operations below the level of armed conflict – actions that would not result in death, significant damage, or destruction."[59]

It is worth noting that the Cyber Command attack on the IRA was a balanced retaliation rather than an escalation. Erica Borghard observed that "the United States does not appear to have targeted the much bigger fish here: the Main Intelligence Directorate of the General Staff (GRU), Russia's military intelligence agency ... . Planners may choose less ambitious targets because they're easier to attack, to avoid revealing what they know, or because they want to prevent an escalatory spiral."[60]

Presumably neither the United States nor Russia wants their information battles with each other to lead to armed conflict. A premise of information at war is that information warfare can accomplish tasks that once were within the domain of traditional military activity, and do so without incurring the losses or inflicting the physical damage inherent in "real" war. But information tactics are designed to be more than mere irritants – they aim to significantly weaken an adversary to the point at which it is politically debilitated and/or may be susceptible to conventional attack.

As we will see later in this chapter, Russia is the nation most inclined today to embark on information adventurism, but it is not alone. Similarly, the United States is not alone in developing strategies and tools to respond to information aggression. Several NATO members number among current or prospective Russian targets, which was a reason that NATO in 2013 created a Strategic Communications Centre of Excellence based in Riga, Latvia (based on a Latvian initiative[61]) that develops and improves strategic communication capabilities. NATO defines the Centre's role this way:

> Strategic communication is an integral part of the efforts to achieve the Alliance's political and military objectives, thus it is increasingly important that the Alliance communicates in an appropriate, timely, accurate and responsive manner on its evolving roles, objectives and missions. The mission of the Centre is to provide a tangible contribution to the strategic communications capabilities of NATO, NATO allies and NATO partners. Its strength is built by multinational and cross-sector participants from the civilian and military, private and academic sectors and usage of modern technologies, virtual tools for analyses, research and decision making. The heart of the NATO StratCom COE is a diverse group of international experts with military, government and academic backgrounds – trainers, educators, analysts and researchers. The Centre is staffed and financed by its sponsoring nations and contributing participants. The Centre was initially founded by Latvia, Estonia, Germany, Italy, Lithuania, Poland, and the United Kingdom in 2014. The Netherlands and Finland joined in 2016, Sweden in 2017, Canada in 2018 and Slovakia in early 2019. France and Denmark are set to join in 2020.[62]

According to an analysis by *The Economist*, the Centre "tracks the 'weaponization' of social media, including the use of bots and a growing trend towards 'hybrid' activity involving both humans and machines." This unit also "helps with training, introduces information warfare into NATO exercises, and gets involved in operational support beyond the military sphere, such as election resilience. Tracking Russian propaganda efforts to undermine NATO's new multinational battlegroups in the Baltics" allowed NATO to promptly push back. Among the NATO center's tasks has been to evaluate the influence of "cognitive warfare," which involves video and voice recordings that seem genuine but are actually phony.[63]

As technology advances, so too will politico-military strategists expand their abilities to deploy and defend against these elements of conflict. Already, much is happening.

Targets

Ukraine

David Sanger wrote that "every technique Americans soon worried about began in Ukraine: manipulated election results, fictional online personas who widen social divisions and stoke ethnic fears, and what was called 'fake news' before the phrase was twisted into new meaning by an American president."[64]

In Ukraine, after protesters who were part of the Euromaidan movement chased pro-Russian President Viktor Yanukovych into exile, Ukraine's new government flirted with the EU and NATO, angering Putin. Underlying this was Putin's personal goal of reconstituting as much of the old Soviet empire as possible. (Putin in 2005 had described the collapse of the Soviet Union as "the greatest geopolitical catastrophe of the [20th] century.") In February 2014 – soon after the conclusion of the Winter Olympic Games in Sochi, Russia – Russian military forces, described by the Kremlin as Ukrainian "self-defense groups," seized the Crimea peninsula of Ukraine and then moved westward into Ukraine's Donbas region. The troops appeared to be "irregulars," in that they did not wear Russian insignia. These were referred to by some as "little green men" because of their unmarked green uniforms, but some Ukrainian news organizations labeled them "Russian invaders" and "occupiers from Russia."[65]

When the Ukraine military fought back, Russia in 2015 sent regular troops to engage in the fighting. As of this writing in mid-2020, 14,000 Ukrainians had been killed in this war. Russia also directed a sustained information campaign against Ukraine, supplemented with cyberattacks on the country's economic and administrative infrastructure.

Parts of eastern Ukraine, including Crimea and Donbas, are largely Russian-speaking and some residents are well-disposed to being part of Russia or separating from Ukraine into a new, pro-Russian state. These residents tend to be receptive to Russian political messaging, which the Russians provide in quantity, especially through Russian television channels and social media. (Ethnic Russians constitute about 17 percent of the Ukrainian population. Ukrainian is spoken by roughly 68 percent of the country, Russian by 30 percent.[66]) Overall within Ukraine, favoring absorption by Russia is definitely a minority sentiment.

In Ukraine, about 74 percent of the people rely on television as their primary source of news.[67] Given their location and the fact that for many Ukrainians Russian is their first or second language, they often ingest information provided by Russian channels. Facebook is also solidly popular, with 18.5 million users (as of December 2019) out of a population of 42 million. In the run-up to Ukraine's 2019 presidential election, pages set up supposedly by Russian individuals criticized Ukrainian schools, spread disinformation about NATO and local protests, and targeted President Poroshenko. In the next election, Poroshenko lost to television comedian Volodymyr Zelensky. Alerted by American law enforcement officials to these pages, Facebook shut down many of them.[68]

Five years before that election, as Russia began its war against Ukraine, General Philip Breedlove, the supreme allied commander of NATO, called the Russian media effort "the most amazing information warfare blitzkrieg we have seen in the history of information warfare."[69]

The breadth of the Russian effort was enabled by adding social media to the traditional mix of broadcast and print information. When journalist David Patrikarakos arrived in Ukraine to cover the war in spring 2014, he quickly found that "Twitter contained more up-to-date information than the *New York Times* or NBC." Further, as Russian information providers flooded social media with their version of events – mostly disregarding truthfulness – Patrikarakos recognized that "it wasn't propaganda I was witnessing. It was the reinvention of reality."[70] If "reality" is defined more by perception than by reliance on substantive facts, those who rely on information as a tool for war have added incentive to be even more persistent and outlandish in their messaging. An example is a 2014 news story on Russia's dominant television channel about Ukrainian army personnel crucifying a 3-year-old boy as his mother watched. It never happened, but the story was "out there" and was passed around on social media and in conversation, so it did its damage.[71]

Russia's military intelligence organization, the GRU (the Russian acronym of Main Intelligence Directorate), was apparently busy on social media as the invasion began, posting on Facebook and the Russian equivalent, Vkontakte. The GRU posts pushed the Kremlin narrative that Ukraine's newly elected government was being manipulated by the United States. Thomas Rid reported that the GRU's goal "was to stir up negative feelings toward the new government in Kyiv and to alienate the Crimean population from pro-Western parties and organizations."[72] The Internet Research Agency was also active, disparaging the new Ukraine President Petro Poroshenko, whose term had begun in June 2014.[73]

In addition to such information tactics, Russian forces moving into Crimea jammed cellphone networks and cut internet connections between Crimea and the rest of Ukraine.[74] Julia Summers reported that the FSB (Russia's Federal Security Service, a successor of the KGB) had already secured access to information about roughly 16 million Ukrainians by taking over Vkontakte servers. Those whose information came into FSB hands included Ukrainian soldiers who were fighting in the east against Russians. These information penetrations were supplemented in late 2016 by 6,500 cyberattacks that extended into western Ukraine, which was outside the physical reach of the Russian combat troops but susceptible to the economic damage the cyberattacks caused.[75] The combination of information and cyber warfare strengthened the Kremlin's efforts to undermine public confidence in the new Ukrainian government. This heightened political instability, deterred foreign economic investment, and generally undermined the idea that the "Ukraine model" of representative government could pose a significant threat to the Kremlin's interests.

Once it occupied parts of Ukraine, Russia took control of many news outlets, concentrating on advancing a narrative that Russia was protecting Ukraine from the machinations of Western-backed "fascists" – a favorite, all-purpose label. Beyond catch-phrases, the Kremlin benefited from unsophisticated coverage by some Western news organizations. Alan Yuhas wrote in the *Guardian*: "The one thing the Kremlin loves more than misinformation is when the Western media pushes oversimplified stories. The idea that Ukraine is evenly split between a pro-European west and a pro-Russian east actually fits with Putin's preferred version of events."[76] Most Ukrainians would forcefully argue against Putin's view, stating that Ukraine is one nation and that they firmly oppose any Russian-backed secessionist movement.

The determination of both sides and the ineffectiveness of international efforts to secure a lasting peace have ensured that the battles of words and battles of bullets will continue to plague Ukraine. With more than 14,000 dead as of mid-2020,[77] the bullets (and related tools of conventional combat) have been plentiful. And so have the words that convey disinformation. EUvsDisinfo – a project of the European Union's Stratcom Task Force – established a database in

2015 to track Ukraine-related Russian disinformation. It reported in October 2019 that, since it began operating, it had recorded around 100 cases targeting Ukraine's statehood, around 700 aiming at the country's leadership, about 150 concerning language (Russian versus Ukrainian), more than 700 about Crimea, 200 accusing Ukraine of being fascist or Nazi, 300 instances along the lines of "NATO forces Ukraine to adopt anti-Russian foreign policy," and more than 30 claiming connections between Hitler and the current Ukrainian leadership.[78]

At the time of this writing, Russia continues to polish its information warfare skills in various parts of Ukraine while it pursues its ground war in Donbas. Ukraine remains in a precarious position. It is not a member of NATO or the EU, and all parties know that a Ukrainian effort to join these alliances (especially NATO) would likely elicit new military and economic retaliation from the Kremlin. Although the Western powers may offer soothing words, supporting Ukraine to the extent of further provoking Russia is, at least for now, unlikely.

Russia has benefited from the fact that, in the words of Lawrence Freedman:

> conflict was now conducted in a gray world of acts that were hard to attribute, and indeed often carried out by private individuals and groups acting as agents of the state ... Responsibility was always denied, without much attempt to make the denials plausible, and often with a knowing sneer. Refusal to be accountable for actions was combined with an impression of deliberate menace.[79]

It is in this "gray world" that the definition of 21st-century war is being shaped.

The Baltic States

Additional Russian information targets – the Baltic States of Estonia, Latvia, and Lithuania – are a very different matter. These countries, like Ukraine, are former Soviet republics, but now all are members of NATO. From Putin's standpoint, the level of risk in tampering with them is much higher than that of tormenting Ukraine. If Russia were to push too forcefully (such as by sending "little green men" across a Baltic State's border), one or several of the Baltics could invoke Article 5 of the NATO founding treaty, which calls for collective defense – if one member is attacked, all are attacked and all must respond. (The only time this article has been invoked was after the 2001 terrorist attacks on the United States.) But Russian aggression could also present NATO with an existential crisis. Would NATO members, especially the United States and other leaders such as Germany, be willing to go to war to protect a former Soviet republic? If not, Russia's influence would expand, NATO would be seen as toothless, and the balance of power in Europe could shift dramatically.

As we will now see, Russia is using information tactics to explore strengths and weaknesses in the Baltics, and those countries are strengthening their information defenses. SACEUR General Breedlove observed that Russia's "hybrid approach to war is to use all the tools they have ... to stir up problems they can then begin to exploit through their military tool."[80]

The Baltic States – Estonia, Latvia, and Lithuania – are former Soviet republics with ethnic-Russian minorities: Estonia and Latvia each have a 25 percent Russian minority; Lithuania has just 6 percent. The languages spoken are: in Estonia, Estonian 69 percent, Russian 30 percent; in Latvia, Latvian 56 percent, Russian 34 percent; in Lithuania, Lithuanian 82 percent, Russian 8 percent. Levels of internet access are: in Estonia, 87 percent; Latvia, 80 percent; Lithuania, 74 percent. Per capita GDP (2017) is: in Estonia, US$31,700; Latvia, US$27,700; Lithuania, US$32,400. The countries are small; their populations vary in size: Estonia 1.2 million; Latvia 1.9 million; Lithuania 2.7 million. Each country is a member of the European Union as well as of NATO.[81]

The economic statistics are important because they indicate that, individually and collectively, the Baltic States have been faring relatively well. They are stable and prosperous, and therefore presumably not particularly good targets for subversion, although two of the three have substantial ethnic-Russian minority populations. All three share borders with Russia. (Lithuania borders Russia's Kaliningrad province, which is sandwiched between Lithuania and Poland.) Although their EU and NATO memberships align them firmly with the West, the Kremlin covets them, or at least enjoys harassing them occasionally.

Lawrence Freedman observed that Russia's aggressive use of information was grounded in "the idea that public opinion could be moved using compelling but manufactured evidence, inserted into popular discourse by means of social media."[82] In the Ukraine case, social media were valuable to Russian efforts to destabilize the country, but in looking at the larger picture of information at war it is important not to underestimate the influence of what is now considered by many to be an old-fashioned medium: television. In each of the Baltic countries, the leading television networks are publicly owned, although digital broadcasting has opened the way for private TV and radio stations.

The Baltic governments and broadcasters recognize the need to guard against Russian-inspired tampering. They also understand the impact of the proximity of Russia and its own broadcasters, which could conceivably be a disruptive influence on the countries' ethnic Russians. Latvian journalist Aija Krutaine wrote:

> In the Baltics, it is a fact known for years that Russian speakers watch Russian TV channels, not local. It has also been common knowledge that information presented by those TV channels might not always be considered fair journalism. At the same time, until Russia's annexation of Crimea in March 2014, Estonians, Latvians and Lithuanians have cared little what Russian TV channels were broadcasting and what their neighbors were watching. Balts and Baltic Russians have been living in parallel information universes for over two decades. From time to time the issue was raised over how to reach and speak with Baltic Russians, yet no relevant actions followed.[83]

In 2015, Estonian Public Broadcasting began its own Russian-language channel, ETV+, to give Russian-speaking Estonians an alternative to Russian channels, but as of late 2017 the new channel was capturing less than 1 percent of the Estonian viewing audience.[84] Latvia also considered establishing its own Russian-language channel, but the government determined this might be counterproductive because it would be a disincentive for the country's Russian speakers to learn Latvian, and because there appeared to be little interest on the part of the prospective audience.[85]

Lithuania, which has the smallest percentage of Russian speakers in the Baltics (8 percent), took the strongest action to counter Russian broadcasts, banning several Russian channels from Lithuanian airwaves for three months. The commission regulating the country's media stated that "the goal our commission achieved by suspending those programs was that it stopped incitement to hatred, instigation of war, spreading of disinformation and violation of Lithuania's laws."[86] Lithuania's public broadcasting company (LTV) considered creating a program as counterpoint to Russian broadcasts, but decided against doing so because, in the words of LTV Director General Audrius Siaurusevicius, "anti-propaganda is very close to propaganda." Instead, LTV aired Russian-language programs produced by others, such as Germany's Deutsche Welle and the Voice of America.[87] (Whether these substitutes were themselves propaganda was apparently not addressed.)

Russian outreach is not wholly media-based, and some of it is decidedly low-tech. In Lithuania, displays of Putin's image, pro-Kremlin and anti-NATO graffiti, vandalism, and even certain tattoos are tracked by the country's defense ministry to see if trends related to such signs are emerging.[88] Is a tattoo "information"? In a way, yes; it conveys a message to those who see it. Granted, any one tattoo has a very limited audience, but those analysts at the Lithuanian defense ministry see such micro factors as pieces of a large puzzle.

Lithuania has also seen a relatively new tactic used by Russian disinformation specialists: hacking the content management systems of legitimate news websites to post their own stories, which they then spread using spoofed emails, social media, and even op-eds on sites that accept user-generated content. Among the Lithuania-related stories spread this way were reports about a US army vehicle colliding with and killing a child on a bicycle, about a NATO plan to invade Belarus, and one about German NATO soldiers desecrating a Jewish cemetery. Each one of these stories was false and had reached the public through hacking news sites.[89]

In Estonia in April 2007, the government decided to relocate a memorial to Soviet soldiers who had fought in World War II. Reaction came swiftly. Two nights of street rioting began, involving ethnic-Russian Estonians and Russian protesters who had come across the border to decry "Nazism" and "blasphemy" related to moving the statue.[90] The situation was exacerbated by false Russian news reports that the statue and Russian war graves were being destroyed. During the disorder, 1 person died, 156 were injured, and 1,000 were detained. The next day, Estonia was hit by a major cyberattack that took down online operations of government offices, media outlets, banks, and others. This, according to the BBC, was the first known cyberattack on an entire country.[91] This might be considered a "hybrid-hybrid" event: disinformation coupled with cyberattacks on infrastructure.

The events in Estonia in some ways foreshadowed the invasion of Ukraine in 2014: take a relatively minor event; use "fake news" to stir up local sympathizers so they will take to the streets; launch cyberattacks to damage the country's economy and government; and then, in the Ukraine case, follow up with a military invasion. This final step did not happen in Estonia in 2007, but Estonia and its Baltic neighbors began building information defenses. Meanwhile, Russia kept up the information pressure; by 2016, Kremlin-backed Sputnik News was operating in all three Baltic languages.[92]

Among the social media weapons in Russia's arsenal are internet trolls, such as those working for the Internet Research Agency. It doesn't take much for someone to become a troll; anyone with internet access who wants to persistently criticize, cause disagreement, or foment more serious trouble by using online tools can be a troll. "Hybrid trolls" are another matter. A NATO Stratcom Centre of Excellence study of trolls targeting Latvia found the hybrid trolls to be acting in concert, delivering pro-Russia content, and to be identifiable through "intensively reposted messages, repeated messages posted from different IP addresses and/or nicknames, and republished information and links ... For pro-Russian hybrid trolls, one important identifier is their frequently poor language skills when posting comments in languages other than Russian."[93]

The NATO study recognized the value of trolls as parts of a larger information scheme:

> The strengths of pro-Russian trolling do not lie in manipulating a limited group of people who read web comments or actively post in social media, but rather in its ability to reinforce Russia's narrative, which is already being communicated via other information channels – TV, blogs, propaganda websites run by pro-Kremlin activists, etc. Thus trolling, despite the direct evidence of its limited effects seen in isolation, is still a small but important part of a larger machinery aimed at influencing the public in NATO member and partner countries.[94]

The report added that trolling's effects should not, however, be underestimated: "A serious threat here is the creation of a false perception of hybrid trolls being real Russian people, leading to mutual distrust between different ethnic groups in Latvian society."[95]

What is to be done about trolls? Enter the elves.

Elves are volunteers who trace trolls and challenge their propaganda. Elves have flourished in the Baltic States, where they have partnered with government responders to debunk disinformation. In Lithuania, elves are armed with a valuable tool – Demaskuok ("debunk" in Lithuanian) software developed by a Lithuanian-headquartered media company, Delfi, in partnership with Google. First used in 2018, Demaskuok examines thousands of pieces of online content in Lithuanian, Russian, and English, comparing suspicious material to previous items found to be disinformation. In addition to keywords, Demaskuok analyzes the "virality" of an item – the number of times readers share it or write about it. Images are also examined, and sometimes they are found to have originally appeared before the events they supposedly document.[96]

Lithuania's elves – about 4,000 of them -- then bring a human dimension to the software's findings. Some read flagged material and pass along content they consider suspicious to colleagues with relevant expertise who fact-check it. After that, they send the flagged items with their comments to journalists who consider these evaluations as they construct news stories for the public. On occasion, elves have completed this entire process in just two hours.[97]

Pushing back against trolls makes sense, but an issue for journalists to consider is whether their own government might sometimes be using a "disinformation" label on content about topics that are merely politically sensitive. In Lithuania, this happened with material related to Lithuania's complicity in the Holocaust, a valid if controversial subject. Dismissing historical criticism as disinformation blocks news consumers from receiving important information. Also, questions have arisen about whether someone whose name turns up related to disinformation automatically deserves to be called "vatnikas," a slur denoting pro-Kremlin sympathies, in news stories.[98]

When a government becomes involved in determining what is "good" and "bad" information – what is real and "fake" news – it is possible (perhaps likely) that de facto censorship will find a foothold. And then ... the public might begin thinking that nothing is true.

When the Soviet Union was headed toward its 1991 implosion, the Baltic States gave it a shove by declaring their independence in 1990. The USSR and then Russia were reluctant to give up the former Soviet republics; the last Russian troops did not leave Lithuania until 1993, and Latvia and Estonia until 1994. The Baltics remain tempting targets for those in the Kremlin who want to reassert control over what was once the USSR. As noted earlier, deterring an attempt to forcibly do this is the NATO membership of the three countries, which – unlike with Ukraine – presumably protects them. That protection does not extend, however, to persistent efforts to create instability through information methods or cyberwarfare.

At the time of the major cyberattack that Estonia suffered in 2007, such an action would not trigger Article 5 of the NATO treaty unless there had been a loss of life comparable to the results of traditional military action. As a BBC report noted, retaliation after a cyberattack would be complicated by difficulty in identifying the source of the attack. In 2007, the strike on Estonia was launched from Russian IP addresses, online instructions were in Russian, and Estonia's appeals to Moscow for help were ignored. But there was no concrete evidence that the attack was actually carried out by the Russian government.[99]

Despite these ambiguities, NATO policy has changed since the 2007 Estonia attack. In 2016, NATO ministers designated cyber as an official operational domain of warfare, and NATO Secretary-General Jens Stoltenberg said: "A severe cyber attack may be classified as a case for the alliance. Then NATO can and must react. How will depend on the severity of the attack."[100] In meetings in 2018 and 2019, NATO officials added hybrid warfare as a possible cause for activating Article 5. A statement from NATO outlined its policy:

> Hybrid methods of warfare, such as propaganda, deception, sabotage and other non-military tactics have long been used to destabilise adversaries. What is new about attacks seen in recent years is their speed, scale and intensity, facilitated by rapid technological change and global interconnectivity. NATO has a strategy on its role in countering hybrid warfare and stands ready to defend the Alliance and all Allies against any threat, whether conventional or hybrid.[101]

For the NATO policy to effectively deter Russia, and perhaps other states, from cyber aggression will require more specificity and firm endorsement from the most powerful NATO members, such as the United States and Germany.

Poking and probing with information and cyber weaponry characterizes information at war today. The Baltic States' experience with Russia is instructive, but it does not stand alone. Others among Russia's neighbors, including those that were not part of the Soviet Union, have been targeted.

Sweden

Sweden may seem an unlikely target for Russian information attacks. It does not border Russia, it has not been a military power since the seventeenth century, it was neutral during both World Wars, and it is not a member of NATO.

It is the possibility of a change in that last characteristic that concerns the Kremlin. Authors of a study for the Swedish Institute of International Affairs found that "the overarching goal of Russian policy towards Sweden and the wider Baltic Sea is to preserve the geostrategic status quo, which is identified with a security order minimizing NATO presence in the region." The authors, Martin Kragh and Sebastian Asberg, writing in the *Journal of Strategic Studies*, expanded on this:

> Increasingly since 2014, Sweden has been the target of a wide array of active measures: disinformation, forged telegrams and fake news items have surfaced in the information landscape; Russian politicians and diplomats have intervened in Swedish domestic political affairs

on NATO and Baltic Sea security; pro-Kremlin NGOs and GONGOs [government-organized nongovernmental organizations] have become operative in Sweden and revelations of a Russian-owned company in Sweden connected to party financing in the European Union have emerged in media. In social media, troll armies are targeting journalists and academics, including the 'hijacking' of Twitter accounts. Russian state TV has castigated Swedish politicians as agents of Washington and falsified interviews with Swedish citizens, and Swedish journalists and diplomats working in Russia have been targets of harassment and espionage activities. Lastly, there exist examples of actors in Sweden, such as politicians, academics and newspapers, who wittingly or unwittingly perform a role as agents of influence or interlocutors of disinformation.[102]

An additional tool the Russians tried was a Swedish-language version of the Sputnik News website, but after being started in 2015 it was closed in 2016 because apparently few Swedes were visiting it.[103] Nevertheless, Russian-supplied disinformation continued to target Swedish news consumers through social media. It alleged that, if Sweden entered a military partnership with NATO, the alliance would secretly base nuclear weapons on Swedish soil; NATO could attack Russia from Sweden without the Swedish government's approval; NATO soldiers, immune from prosecution, could rape Swedish women without fearing criminal charges. Forged letters on convincing-looking stationery also appeared online; one on the letterhead of Defense Minister Peter Hultqvist encouraged a Swedish firm to sell artillery to Ukraine, which would violate Swedish law. The defense ministry promptly proved this was a forgery, which was effective within Sweden, but Hultqvist continued to be questioned about it when he attended international conferences.[104]

In September 2018, the Swedish foreign ministry, to counter Russian provocations, appointed its first ambassador and special envoy for countering hybrid threats, veteran diplomat Fredrik Lojdquist. He wrote: "Over the last decade or so, certain governments have clearly lowered their inhibitions to the use of malign and malicious actions. At the same time, the opportunity presented by our own vulnerabilities has increased, thanks to increased digitalization and dependencies but also underinvestment in internal and external security."[105]

Lojdquist's recognition of the importance of *internal* as well as external security measures is an important element in defending against information threats. They don't necessarily come flying across borders from elsewhere, as ballistic missiles do. Rather, they may be delivered by domestic media – traditional or social – that in hard-to-detect earlier stages were influenced by external actors. Lojdquist also noted that disinformation does "not have to be illegal or contrary to international law."[106] This fosters uncertainty that may contribute to a government pausing in its response while pondering issues such as a "chain of evidence" related to the threat, and whether principles of free speech might be at risk.

In most countries, defending against information attacks has not yet been accorded an appropriate level of coherent doctrine, such as Russia has devoted to its rationale for launching such attacks. Sweden's designation of a point person to organize response mechanisms is a useful step, but further consistent and sophisticated measures will be essential in developing effective defense.

Finland

During and after the Cold War, Finland has worked carefully to maintain a relationship with Russia that, if not cordial, is at least free of provocation. Finland has done this well, remaining prosperous and peaceful. An EU member, it has one of Europe's highest per capita GDPs, and it remains resolutely unenthusiastic about joining NATO. A 2017 survey by Finland's leading newspaper found 59 percent of respondents opposed to becoming part of NATO, while 22 percent supported joining the alliance.[107]

Nevertheless, Russia, its neighbor to the east, has been unable to resist meddling. (As noted earlier in this chapter, this has been going on for decades.) Russia pushes propaganda through Finnish information venues, sometimes coinciding with military exercises on the border, and its disinformation campaigns contend that Finland discriminates against its ethnic-Russian minority, which constitutes only 1.4 percent (about 78,000 persons) of the country's 5.6 million citizens.[108]

Russia's principal tool in trying to unsettle Finns has been trolling. Interviews conducted in 2014 and 2015 by Finland's public broadcaster Yle found that the trolls had succeeded in disrupting public conversation about Russia, and particularly about the Russian invasion of Ukraine. Those who criticized Russia in online forums were attacked repeatedly by trolls who accused them of being "Nazis," "fascists," and other such derogatory terms.

Jessikka Aro, the Yle reporter who led the investigation, received an exceptional amount of abuse once her stories appeared. This included trolls' allegations that she was a US intelligence agent and a drug dealer. She went to the Finnish police, and prosecutors brought criminal charges against the two ringleaders of the campaign against her. They were both found guilty, sentenced to jail time, and ordered to pay damages. The *New York Times* reported that this was the first time a European country had initiated legal action against persons spreading pro-Russian disinformation.[109]

Aro was also subjected to troll attacks that labeled her a prostitute and made her the subject of a music video depicting her as a "Bond girl." An article in *The Economist* about sexualized disinformation noted that sexual slander, such as that targeting Ms. Aro, "is a hallmark of disinformation campaigns," and "sex-themed lies pervade pro-Kremlin fake news."[110]

Aro reported that "many Finns describe they have been scared by trolling and stopped following topics concerning Russia and discussing Russia altogether because of it." One Finnish blogger told her: "In a war, buildings and the infrastructure of the society are destroyed. In information warfare, trust is destroyed." Another source remarked, "I rarely comment on anything anymore – because of trolls." Yet another said to Aro, "The whole comments section is starting to be full of untruthful news from trolls and personal attacks against those who correct them."[111]

Persistence and nastiness. These are the keys to trolls' ability to usurp civil society's online venues for conversation and debate.

There are more targets, and the number will grow as additional governments, non-state actors, individuals, and others decide to use information as a weapon. Speech is being used to deter speech, which is a perversion of the opportunities presented by an expanding media universe. Russia has distinguished itself by being the most thorough and remorseless player in weaponizing information, in some cases relying on information as an aggressive diplomatic tool when the Kremlin decides that overt conflict is not in its interest.

Turkey

As Russia has taken steps to extend its influence in former Soviet states, the Middle East, and elsewhere, it has consistently tried to reduce the corresponding influence of NATO, the EU, and the United States. In terms of geopolitical positioning, Turkey – a member of NATO and an ally of the United States – presents a tempting target for information-based assaults.

In November 2015, Turkey shot down a Russian Su-24 bomber that had entered Turkish airspace. In response, Russian media began emphasizing news reports that alleged not only that Turkey was turning a blind eye to Islamic State (IS) recruiting and transit through Turkey, but also that Turkey was helping to finance the terrorist organization by illegally facilitating IS sales of oil it was extracting from areas it controlled. The Russian coverage further accused Turkish President Recep Tayyip Erdogan and his family of being directly involved in the illegal oil trading.[112] Some Turkish news outlets picked up this story, and in early 2016 Turkey's government retaliated by blocking Turkish internet providers from accessing Russia's Sputnik news website.[113]

This case illustrates an important aspect of Russia's method of building audience for its media messaging. Sputnik created its Turkish website and radio channel in 2014. It also offers a Turkish-language Twitter account with close to a million followers.[114] Sputnik sometimes has had more leeway than Turkish journalism does in delivering critical news about the Erdogan regime, and presumably the Sputnik website "wants Turks, especially those who are critical of the Erdogan government, to come for decent coverage of Turkish politics and to stay for the pro-Kremlin spin."[115]

Once Russian media push a story to the surface of the sea of information, other news organizations may follow. The Turkey-IS oil story earned a *Time* magazine headline: "Is Turkey Really Benefiting from Oil Trade with ISIS?" The *Time* article concluded that the Turkish government was *not* involved in illegal oil dealings with IS, but the headline raising the question was a small victory for the Russian information purveyors.[116]

Relations between Turkey and the United States are frequently tense, and Turkish politicians sometimes find anti-Americanism to be politically useful. Sputnik has praised recent Russia–Turkey rapprochement and Turkey's purchase of Russia's S-400 missile system, a transaction that was strongly opposed by the United States. In a RAND report, Katherine Costello wrote that "Russian media are hard at work to inspire and reinforce such trends and promote the idea that Turkey's most valuable ally is actually Russia."[117]

Debate will continue about how much influence Russian media have had among Turks, but polling conducted by Turkey's Kadir Has University found that Turks who identified Russia as a threat to their country dropped from 34.9 percent in 2016 to 12.4 percent in 2018. Those who saw the United States as a threat rose from 44.1 percent to 60.2 percent in that same period.[118] Many factors contributed to this, including President Erdogan's penchant for irritating Turkey's NATO allies by flirting with the Kremlin, which has been reciprocated by Russia. The Turkish government also keeps tight rein on media within the country. Nevertheless, this is an example of how quickly the Russians will seize an opportunity to strengthen a foreign policy initiative by using information tools.

Libya

Much has been made in recent years about China's increased attention to African economics and politics, and to the vast amounts of infrastructure investment China has made in Africa related to its Belt and Road Initiative. In terms of using information as influence, China has primarily embraced the traditional soft-power method of counting on messages from state-run media, such as China Global Television Network (CGTN). But other global networks such as the BBC, CNN, and Sky News have maintained a significant lead in viewing audience within Africa.[119]

Russia, meanwhile, has relied on social media in Africa, especially Facebook. A Stanford University study (results published in late 2019) analyzed a network of 73 Facebook pages targeting six African countries: Sudan, Central African Republic, Madagascar, Mozambique, Democratic Republic of Congo, and Libya. These pages posted more than 48,800 times, received more than 9.7 million interactions on the posts, and were liked by more than 1.7 million accounts.[120] All the Facebook pages were connected to companies tied to Yevgeny Prigozhin, the Russian oligarch and ally of Vladimir Putin who provided funds to the Internet Research Agency (IRA), and who has mining interests in Africa.[121]

This Kremlin-engineered venture in Africa illustrates how Russia's approach to building influence is evolving and how it is using different tools to gain a foothold. For instance, the IRA efforts targeting the United States during the 2016 presidential campaign all emanated from the IRA offices in St. Petersburg, and often the English in which the content was written was filled with errors. In the Africa projects, noted Stanford's Shelby Grossman, the Russians appear to rely on a "franchising" method that uses local content producers. Grossman added that this technique creates localized context that resonates with information consumers, ensures a more familiar writing style, and makes it more difficult to identify the content as part of a disinformation campaign.[122] The Stanford report also pointed out: "Considered as a whole, these clusters of [Facebook] Pages were intended to foster unity around Russia-aligned actors and politicians. This distinguishes it from the IRA's operations in the US, which involved creating diametrically opposed groups and encouraging them to clash."[123]

Among the African countries where Russia is involved, Libya is a particularly interesting case because of the amount of effort the Kremlin has devoted to this oil-rich and strategically located nation. Russian information content has backed both Khalifa Haftar and Saif al-Islam Qaddafi (Muammar Qaddafi's son), who, as of mid-2020, are rivals in pursuit of control of the country. Both opposed the UN-endorsed Government of National Accord based in Tripoli, and Russian policymakers apparently believed they could broker a deal between the two. Either one would presumably be more friendly to Russia than the existing Tripoli government is. Even more important to Haftar than the information flowing through social media was the presence in Libyan combat zones of mercenaries employed by the Wagner Group, another of Prigozhin's enterprises. Equipped with new Russian weapons, they brought much-needed lethal professionalism to Haftar's militia.

Echoes of the war in Ukraine can be heard in Russia's Libyan campaign – barrages of words and barrages of bullets. The use of local content producers for the information part of the effort is part of the maturation of technique that Russia would need if it were to rely on hybrid war of this kind elsewhere. Backing up information efforts with military contractors moves information at war further into the realm of conventional armed conflict.

From Scandinavia to Africa, techniques of using information in warfare are evolving apace with advances in the technology of information production and dissemination. These techniques are being tested, sometimes with unprovocative caution and sometimes with ruthless ferocity, to measure their political and military effectiveness. Countries that might be targeted – and there are many – should be studying this evolution and planning their responses.

6

From Media Manipulation
to Media Literacy

As chapter 5 illustrated, information at war is becoming more sophisticated and more pervasive, keeping pace with (and sometimes outpacing) changes in geopolitics, communication technology, and warfighting. Policymakers around the world are finding new ways to use information to advance their interests, and global publics face the challenge of dealing with a still-rising tide of information and distinguishing between truth and falsehood, and between the important and the trivial.

Media literacy training is gaining traction in some places, but it mostly lags behind advances in disinformation tactics. Also, militaries are using information technology to enhance their capabilities in deterrence and combat.

How do these matters affect the nature of information at war? How can individual citizens make better-informed decisions about the value of information that they receive? Answers to such questions are not set in stone; they continue to develop.

Saudi Arabia and the United Arab Emirates versus Qatar

National leaders without scruples – there are a good number of them – are learning that using disinformation as a phony pretext for conventional warfare has become relatively easy. A close call in the Middle East in 2017 underscored the dangers involved.

On May 24, 2017, the website of the official Qatar News Agency (QNA) reported that Qatar's emir, Sheikh Tamim bin Hamad al-Thani, had given a speech praising Hamas, Hezbollah, the Muslim Brotherhood, and Iran. Quotes from the speech were then posted on QNA's social media accounts and on the news ticker at the bottom of the screen of the QNA YouTube channel.

Within minutes, the speech was denounced on Saudi-owned news channel Al Arabiya and on United Arab Emirates (UAE) channel Sky News Arabia. These reports accused Qatar of supporting extremist organizations and destabilizing the region. Qatar claimed that the QNA accounts had been hacked and blamed the UAE, which denied doing so. Both sides intensely used Twitter, as evidenced by a surge of retweets generated by "bots," automated accounts that generate material in such amounts and with such speed – sometimes hundreds of retweets in a matter of seconds – that their cumulative product may appear to reflect a groundswell of public opinion.[1]

This media duel quickly escalated, moving into a level of passion that made serious consequences increasingly likely. Although tensions among Middle East nations are common, and the relationship between Qatar and Saudi Arabia had long been particularly unpleasant, the Gulf States had been spared armed conflict. This crisis, however, was different.

Saudi Arabia, the UAE, Bahrain, and Egypt (dubbed "the quartet") initiated an economic and physical blockade (which can be considered an act of war), with the Saudis closing Qatar's only land border, through which approximately 40 percent of its imports entered the country, and stopping their air and sea shipments to Qatar.[2] The damage done by the blockade was somewhat alleviated by aid to Qatar from Turkey and Iran. Qatar's own vast wealth – the country is one of the world's leading producers of natural gas – ensured that the economic chokehold could be endured, at least for a while.

The quartet quickly followed up with a list of severe demands that included Qatar aligning its foreign policy with theirs, shutting down its renowned Al Jazeera broadcast network, cutting ties with Iran, and ending any support for the Muslim Brotherhood. As the quartet must have recognized, there was no chance that Qatar would agree to this, which would have amounted to a surrender of sovereignty.

During his visit to Saudi Arabia shortly before these events took place, US President Donald Trump apparently had given the de facto Saudi ruler, Prince Mohammed bin Salman, a green light to proceed against Qatar as an "anti-terrorism" measure. At this point, Saudi Arabia (perhaps joined by the UAE) appeared poised to invade Qatar, but reportedly backed down after intervention by the US secretaries of state and of defense, Rex Tillerson and Jim Mattis.[3] Among the numerous factors that would make any such invasion especially dangerous for the region and beyond was the presence in Qatar of the Al Udeid air base, the largest US military outpost in the Middle East and the forward headquarters of the US Central Command. Al Udeid is also the home of the Qatari Air Force, which could make it a target of any invading force. Consequences could quickly go from bad to worse.

In any event, last-minute diplomacy prevented armed conflict, but for our purposes it is worth noting how the spiral toward war began with phony information and how rapidly it accelerated. The fuse had existed for decades, but it was the 2017 disinformation episode that finally lit the match.

While the quartet and Qatar glared at each other, both sides were targeting American public opinion in an effort to move the US government in one direction or the other. In addition to pouring money into the wallets of Washington lobbyists and public relations firms, the countries spent millions on online and social media campaigns. These efforts included creating "The Qatar Insider," a website offering disinformation about Qatar, such as allegations that Qatar had been training Islamic State fighters. The site claimed to be "the comprehensive source for information on the truth about Qatar's funding, activities, and support for terrorist and extreme Islamist groups." The "Insider" also urged the United States to move out of the Al Udeid air base. This website was apparently backed by Saudi money funneled through an American consulting firm. Meanwhile, the UAE government hired a media firm to place anti-Qatar ads on Facebook, Twitter, and YouTube.[4]

Perhaps most concerning about this episode is the ease with which Saudi Arabia and the UAE were able to push their region to the brink of catastrophe. Hacking a news website – as was done to QNA – is not difficult. Even if the victim removes the disinformation promptly, which the Qataris did, the content can take on a life of its own, especially when aided by bots and other tools that expand dissemination and magnify impact.

This points to the need for governments to develop strategies for rapidly responding to information provocation (assuming it is too serious to be ignored) before a situation reaches the level of an uncontrollable crisis. Disinformation itself can be uncontrollable as various players – some whose identities are at least temporarily masked – jump into the fray, seeking to exacerbate a situation. Although Qatar possessed top-level communication and information-dissemination resources, it still was victimized.

Information and Prolonging Conflict: Afghanistan

Information can be used to push people toward war. There may be intervening factors that either hasten or slow that push, but as we have seen so far in this book information per se can often be a significant factor in leading up to, and during, warfighting.

But what about peacemaking? Can information facilitate reconciliation after a conflict's bloodshed, or is it more likely to serve as a bellows that keeps the fires of hatred alive?

In recent decades, Afghanistan has rarely known peace. The Soviet Union, the Taliban, the United States, the Afghan national government of the moment, various Afghan factions, and extraneous players such as Al Qaeda and Islamic State have fomented disruption within the country. In 2019, when hopes for peace between the Taliban and the government were surfacing, social media content proved a disruptive factor. For example, one video on social media at that time showed Taliban fighters executing a local judge, while another showed several Afghan army soldiers torturing Taliban fighters. Another video posted by Taliban supporters showed soldiers from the US-led coalition inappropriately searching Afghan women. And on and on.

As this was happening, the Afghan government and the Taliban were urging that neither side "fuel the conflict and revenge" with ill-chosen language and other messages.[5] This was a fine idea, but restricting public commentary is difficult to do. In Afghanistan as elsewhere, traditional media gatekeepers, such as broadcasters and publishers, are far less influential than they once were in terms of determining what information reaches the public. Afghan news organizations might decide that showing content such as these incendiary examples would not be in the public interest, but their control of the information flow is limited. Anyone can put those images on Facebook, YouTube, or other social media, and violent images and words can spread quickly, inciting still more violence. (A 2019 survey in Afghanistan found that 90 percent of households have at least one mobile phone, and 40 percent of households have internet access.[6]) Afghan historian Habibullah Rafi told the *New York Times*, "If the government keeps reminding of violence committed by the Taliban, and if the Taliban keeps sharing videos of violence by government forces, even if there is a peace deal the fighting could continue in the country because those fighting men will go after their revenge."[7]

Prospects for peace in Afghanistan have also been affected by Russian information efforts. The Russian information outlet Sputnik provides news in Dari, one of the country's official languages, and Sputnik Dari has more than 275,000 followers on Facebook. A narrative that Russia delivers through this and other venues is that the United States has neocolonial aspirations in the country and is the principal contributor to instability and extremism. This latter charge has been embellished with accusations of the United States forming an alliance with Islamic State to sustain turmoil in the country. The Russian message, meanwhile, stresses Moscow's willingness to contribute to Afghanistan's reconstruction.[8]

On a broader stage, how Afghanistan is portrayed by international news media also affects the country's prospects for peace and regeneration. Commitment of support from abroad is essential to Afghanistan's security and rebuilding, and the information about the country that reaches policymakers and their publics helps to shape the political feasibility of economic aid and other help.

Taken collectively, much of the information about Afghanistan that is delivered to global audiences tends to portray the country as a caricature – hopelessly bloody and corrupt. Writing about the linkage between news coverage and diplomacy related to Afghanistan, Katherine Brown reported that:

> Afghans said they largely do not recognize the country described in the Western press as theirs. They agreed US news stories give Americans, and the world, a distorted view of their country with an exaggerated sense of its violence and their people's cruelty. Some argued that by disproportionately reporting on the carnage instead of the character of the Afghan people, the U.S. journalists are making Afghans seem inhuman.[9]

This is something news organizations should consider when they evaluate the breadth and tone of their coverage. When such information becomes dominant in international discourse about Afghanistan, it can lower expectations about establishing and sustaining peace. This is one way that information at war remains important even in the aftermath of major conflict.

Caring about War

Should people care about what is happening in a war even if they watch the conflict from a safe distance and without any personal connection to the fighting? What kind of information stirs moral sensitivity? Why does all this matter? These questions have been raised earlier in this book in discussions about wars in Rwanda, Bosnia, and elsewhere, but definitive answers remain elusive.

Some journalists are deeply frustrated as they search for answers to such questions. During the Syrian War, NBC correspondent Richard Engel stated, "You would hope that by doing reports and putting them on TV and that talking about them that people would wake up, they would see, they would feel, and maybe call for action, and the calls are being made but the action isn't being taken."[10] The "action" Engel cited varies. It might be a symbolic but not particularly effective gesture, such as the American missile strike on a Syrian airfield during the Trump administration after a Syrian government chemical weapons attack that killed civilians. This was the kind of response that journalist Nik Gowing called "tactical and cosmetic."[11]

One might think that, in this era of constant news reports being available to the public, governments would be quicker to respond. President Barack Obama said in 2016: "If you were president fifty years ago, the tragedy in Syria might not even penetrate what the American people were thinking about on a day-to-day basis. Today, they're seeing vivid images of a child in the aftermath of a bombing."[12]

Obama implied that today the "tragedy in Syria" *was* affecting Americans, but if that was so, with what result? Information was available, but that does not ensure the sustained public interest that is necessary for a policy change. For journalists covering the story, and others who may truly care about such matters, how can links be forged between a broadened public consciousness of events and an awakening of conscience? Even though the Assad regime in Syria had crossed the "red line" Obama had defined concerning use of chemical weapons, and although there were plenty of pictures and other information about the toll of the Syrian attacks, Obama did not order a military response, in part because the American public and Congress seemed largely uninterested in such a forceful retaliation against Assad.

Such reluctance may be due to the public feeling overwhelmed by the amount of information they encounter and a resulting difficulty in deciding which pieces of information deserve priority attention. Richard Gowan of the International Crisis Group observed that there are "different images, different narratives, no facts beyond doubt … Because no one is ever certain whether that picture of a dead kid is real or whether it's going to be revealed to be a photo from two years ago that's been recycled, it creates cynicism."[13]

This issue has been present as at least a subtext in much of this book so far. A cynical reaction to information can lead to simply turning away from the crisis of the moment. Availability of information does not necessarily produce broader, more sophisticated public knowledge and caring about war, and it certainly does not necessarily produce activism related to substantive military intervention or even providing humanitarian relief.

One topic that would seem most likely to stir public interest is the welfare of a country's own warfighters – the individual members of the military – but even that topic only occasionally receives the attention it deserves from the news media and the public. One American journalist, Will Bardenwerper, who served as an infantry officer in the Iraq War, wrote: "The best reporting puts a human face on the implementation of our foreign policy, and with each passing year, there seems to be less of that kind of journalism. Only by communicating the humanity of the fallen – seeing them as their friends and family saw them – can the harsh reality of faraway war resonate back home."[14]

Part of the challenge for journalists, observed Bardenwerper, is "investing detached readers in the lives of strangers fighting in foreign lands." Citizens, he added, have a responsibility to pay attention to information about war because soldiers "are in harm's way because of us, our engagement (or lack thereof) as citizens, and ultimately our behavior at the ballot box." That leads, he wrote, to a further duty: "We owe it to them to try to learn what they are doing, why they supposedly are doing it, and to use this understanding to reclaim ownership of our foreign policy."[15]

Acquiring information about the reality of soldiers' lives and sacrifices can be difficult, because of problems of access, emotional as well as physical. Popular culture may fill part of this gap, with feature films such as *Platoon* and novels such as *The Things They Carried*, by Tim O'Brien. Documentary journalism, such as *Restrepo*, a film about the soldiers manning a remote outpost in Afghanistan, can also help to shape attitudes in ways that the daily flow of news might not.

From journalists' standpoint, the embedding policy during the early stages of the Iraq War seemed to stir empathy among many correspondents, who were often getting their first look at what soldiering involved: the daily risks, the prolonged separation from family, the uncertainty about the rationale for the war. Journalists on the ground with the troops may also have learned something about why soldiers are wary of – and sometimes hostile toward – the news media. Military culture is imbued with an "us-and-them" attitude about the press. This dates back to at least the Vietnam War era when many in the military embraced the notion that news coverage was undermining the efforts of those in combat.

Even when information about the troops can be acquired by journalists, conveying it can be challenging, particularly while avoiding jingoism and recognizing that, for much of the public, war is blessedly unfamiliar – something between an abstraction and a Hollywood spectacle. Nevertheless, the issues Bardenwerper addressed above remain important facets of information at war, and their frequent neglect is worth considering.

IoT and AI

The ever-increasing role of the internet in 21st-century society is reflected in the growing attention to the Internet of Things (IoT). By the end of 2018, an estimated 21 billion devices were connected to the internet. By 2030, that number is expected to reach 30 billion.[16]

In terms of the improved speed and convenience with which the tasks of everyday life may be accomplished, the Internet of Things may seem to be a transformation of science fiction into benign reality. Your refrigerator will tell your home computer when you are running low on milk, or it may just directly connect to an online grocery delivery service that will bring a fresh gallon to your door. You will not need to do anything other than drink the milk.

Undoubtedly, much good can come of this kind of machine intervention, such as using IoT to improve remote medical diagnosis and care. But many important advances in information technology also lend themselves to use by governments desiring to control their citizens' behavior, and still more will change the nature of the battle space and the impact of information-related methods in reshaping warfare. These changes will require profound adjustment of how the world's militaries go about their jobs.

The value of IoT (or IoMT – the Internet of Military Things) combined with AI (Artificial Intelligence) in combat depends on the quality of the advanced technology being used, but perhaps even more on the ability to construct networks that can put information, once gathered from various connected sources, to fast and comprehensive use.

Christian Brose wrote of this:

> What will matter far more than the things themselves is the connections between them – the ability of every sensor to share information with every shooter, every shooter to receive information from every sensor, and every machine to transmit information in real-time and at all times to every other machine … . The most important objective is

for the battle network to facilitate human understanding, decisions, and actions.[17]

Along similar lines, Lori Cameron wrote about how IoT might be used to identify enemy personnel:

> In asymmetric warfare, it isn't always easy to identify enemy combatants. They can appear as civilians or access restricted military bases with a stolen badge. Now, sensors can scan irises, fingerprints, and other biometric data to identify individuals who might pose a danger. Edge computing [processing data near the source rather than in a distant cloud] allows, for example, fingerprints from a weapon or bomb to be uploaded to the network and used to identify a combatant instantly. It can also confirm the identity of a target so a sniper can take him out.

Cameron also noted how IoT could monitor and help to respond to soldiers' physical state: "Sensors embedded in military uniforms and helmets can send information to a command center about a soldier's physical condition, helping him or her survive otherwise lethal enemy attacks. For example, pilots under g-force conditions or soldiers exposed to toxic chemicals can receive assistance."[18]

Another writer defined such innovations as being based on "software that can absorb more information from more sources than a human can, analyze it, and either advise the human how to respond or – in high-speed situations like cyber warfare and missile defense – act on its own with careful limits."[19]

"Acting on its own" is a concept that involves ethical as well as technological principles. It would be a significant step, relying on artificial, rather than human, intelligence to evaluate information and control weaponry. Even drones don't act on their own – they are controlled by human pilots, although they may be thousands of miles away. Humans are fallible, but they are human. They are susceptible to biases and other flaws, but they make judgments as best they can while adhering to rules of engagement in combat and presumably appreciating nuance under challenging circumstances.

"Autonomous weapon systems," however, move a step farther away from direct human control. The US Defense Department defines these systems as weapons "that, once activated, can select and engage targets without further intervention by a human operator." The Defense Department notes, "Autonomous and semi-autonomous weapon systems shall be designed to allow commanders and operators to exercise appropriate levels of human judgment over the use of force."[20] This is an important point. Although human judgment is always fallible, most people still prefer it rather than turning over important decision-making to autonomous machines.

A case for continuing research into the use of autonomous weaponry – especially in defensive measures – can be made based on the advent of hypersonic weapons. These could travel at speeds of at least 3,600 miles per hour, which is five times the speed of sound and could drastically reduce response time to an attack. Depending on the distance between launch site and target, the flight time could be just minutes. For the sake of speed, human decision-making about a response might need to be superseded by AI/IoMT tools.[21]

Someday, perhaps, armed robots will replace humans in advancing across battlefields, using massive chunks of information at amazing, non-human speed. P. W. Singer observed that AI might create "an environment where weapons are too fast, small, numerous, and complex for humans to digest – taking us to a place we may not want to go but are probably unable to avoid."[22]

A significant part of the future for war-related IoT and AI will depend on the quality of the information on which mandates and tasks for these new technologies will be based. AI, for instance, is not really "intelligent," in the way that human reasoning power is (to varying degrees), but once it acquires information it is exceptionally fast. Its value is based largely on its speed – its ability to rapidly sort through and organize the vast amounts of information it can access. Christian Brose observed that "faster information flows might not change the ways militaries operate. Intelligent machines will. They will interpret most of the information they collect independently, using artificial intelligence to identify critical pieces of intelligence within oceans of other data."[23] The usefulness of AI will depend largely on how well the machines are "taught" to identify appropriate data.

Similarly, the effectiveness of IoT depends on there being an information-driven network of connections that will produce worthwhile results. Without a foundation of accurate, useful information – a foundation designed by humans – these tools will do little more than showcase high-tech dazzle rather than truly assist those waging war.

Technology will continue to advance at a rapid pace, expanding the role of information at war. As that takes place, militaries will increase their reliance on information tools. American General Richard D. Clarke, commander of the US Special Operations Command (SOCOM), observed in early 2020 that US commanders in Afghanistan spend 60 percent of their time working on information-related issues. "Commanders think about how to use the information space to influence the Taliban's thought processes," Clarke said, "and how to influence the Afghan population."[24] This is in line with the ideas advanced by Russian General Gerasimov and others about using information more comprehensively, linking it more closely to current or prospective combat operations and political "active measures."

In light of this, strategies must be developed to defend against hostile information operations. These measures must extend beyond nations' militaries and become integral to the daily life of civil society. Dealing with disinformation is a big part of this.

Fighting Back against Disinformation

A longstanding adage from the news business remains pertinent today: "Your mother says she loves you. Check it out!"

In combating disinformation, "Check it out" is a basic rule on which an array of practices should be built. The concept is not difficult to understand, but it cannot always survive when it is so easy to simply accept information passed on from someone you know or when you see something online that elicits a "Wow!" If an information item is "too good to be true," it might not be true and should not be acted upon.

When we had just a limited number of information sources, and over time we had become familiar with these and trusted their content, challenging their validity may have seemed unnecessary. In the United States during the 1960s, if we saw a report from Walter Cronkite on the *CBS Evening News*, most of us tended to believe it. Sometimes the information was incorrect – purposely misleading from a government or the result of a journalist's mistake – and news has always been susceptible to errors of emphasis and nuance. But, most of the time, public trust in major news media institutions was not misplaced.

Today, is the same approach wise when news is delivered by Fox News or MSNBC or, going farther afield, by RT or CGTN, all of which pursue, to varying degrees, political as well as journalistic missions? Perhaps not. News consumers must now work harder to avoid being misled.

Many people today treat news consumption as a casual matter: glancing at a mobile phone when we are curious (or just bored), rather than having a fixed appointment – maybe a daily 6:00 p.m. newscast – that we have designated for receiving updates about events. A casual approach may be accompanied by inattentiveness that reduces healthy skepticism. That circumstance is perfect for false information to slip into our brains. Constantly being on guard against manipulation may be tiring, but it will increasingly be necessary.

Looking at countries subjected to information attacks (such as those examined in chapter 5), the record of defensive measures is decidedly mixed. Perpetrators, such as Russia's Internet Research Agency, can churn out massive amounts of disinformation at high speed and with persistence that can wear down even the most resolute defenders of truth. Responses are, by definition, reactive, not anticipatory. Considerable damage may have been done by poisoned information by the time responses come into play. In most instances, this imbalance works in favor of the attacker.

The most effective countermeasures are preventive – a protective vaccine, rather than an antidote used in desperation – and need not be draconian. Even well-meaning efforts must be devised carefully and with their own safeguards or they may slide into restraining free expression. In such a case, the price may exceed the value of the cure.

Understanding the audience and how it gets information

New media venues are perfect for disinformation because they are so accessible and so casually popular with users. It is possible to hack into CNN, the BBC, the *New York Times*, or other traditional information providers, but why bother? Social media are so enticing; they are attractive as "populist" alternatives to the gatekeepers of the past. Donald Trump's reliance on Twitter exemplifies the advantages of such venues to those who count on unfettered access to a mass audience. Rather than try to deal with media forums he considers hostile, Trump simply detours around them.

Online vehicles are also advantageous to those who want to spread rumors, conspiracy theories, and other false information quickly and broadly. A study conducted by Massachusetts Institute of Technology (MIT) researchers, with results published in *Science* magazine in 2018, examined 126,000 rumors spread on Twitter from 2006 to 2017 by more than 3 million people tweeting 4.5 million times. Dissemination of truthful news during the same time period was also analyzed. (Classification as "true" or "false" was based on information from six independent fact-checking organizations that had 95 to 98 percent agreement on the classifications.) The research found that

> false news reached more people than the truth; the top 1 percent of false news cascades diffused to between 1,000 and 100,000 people, whereas the truth rarely diffused to more than 1,000 people ... .

Falsehood diffused significantly farther, faster, deeper, and more broadly than the truth in all categories of information ... false news was more novel than true news, which suggests that people were more likely to share novel information.[25]

That is part of the story. Twitter is just one of the convenient and widely used tools for news distribution. It is used in reaching large publics by media organizations, governments, and individuals, among others. Reliance on it as an information source is pervasive among social media users, especially younger people.

Understanding the age gap in media usage is important in evaluating how and where to fight disinformation. A study commissioned by the Reuters Institute for the Study of Journalism at the University of Oxford found a disconnect between young people and traditional news content. According to this study, "Traditional news brands see news as what you should know, while young audiences see news as what you should know (to an extent), but also what is useful to know, what is interesting to know, and what is fun to know." The study also noted "an overarching finding that consuming news can often feel like a chore."[26]

This broadened definition of "news" in the context of audience expectations serves as both warning and guidance to news organizations working in various media. It also provides useful hints to those producing disinformation – how to design content to target particular information consumers. Shira Ovide observed that those providing accurate information have not learned to make their product "as appealing for internet audiences as have the worst online actors. And unfortunately, accurate information is often more complex than the appealing clarity of conspiracy theories."[27]

A 2018 Pew Research Center study about where Americans get their news found that "social media sites have surpassed print newspapers as a news source for Americans: one in five U.S. adults say they often get news via social media, slightly higher than the share who often do so from print newspapers (16 percent) for the first time since Pew Research Center began asking these questions." Television remained the most popular platform for news consumption, but its use had significantly declined, from 57 percent of adults using it often in 2016 to 49 percent in 2018. Particularly notable was the age gap illustrated by the study's findings. Among respondents aged 65 or older, 81 percent said they often get news from television, while in the 18–29 age group only 16 percent do so. For social media, in the 65+ group, 8 percent said they get news there often, while 36 percent of those 18–29 do so.[28]

A 2019 report in *The Economist* noted that young people's shift in choices of information providers was occurring throughout the world. In India, stated the report, "young Indians are half as likely to visit *timesofindia.com*, India's biggest English-language news site, as older ones; they are far more interested in videos and Bollywood news." In Britain, *The Economist* found, "younger teens are far less familiar with the BBC's brand than they are with those of YouTube or Netflix." In the Arab world, the report continued, "80 percent of Arabs aged 18–24 years old now get their news from social media, up from 25 percent in 2015."[29]

As with the evolving definition of "news," these data about age gaps are useful to those in the news business, but also helpful to those determining how best to push back against disinformation. Knowing who your consumers are, and what information platforms they rely on, is essential whether you are building an audience or designing a strategy to counter false information.

Media literacy

In many instances, those who dispense disinformation have the upper hand because the audiences they are reaching do not know how to deal with it. Even those who are quick to criticize "fake news" tend to base their complaint on their own biases, not on making an informed judgment about the truth or falsity of a given piece of information. Individuals or groups, such as Russia's IRA, that disseminate disinformation are predators that feast on the credulous.

Pushing back against this requires determination and a comprehensive structure to train the public in how to better evaluate information they receive. In chapter 5, we saw how Finland's government and news media have remained alert to Russian subterfuge, identifying Russian attempts to undermine Finnish political life. In 2015, as Russian disinformation campaigns directed at Finland became more pervasive, Finland's President Sauli Niinisto asked every Finn to join in the fight against false information.[30] Finns accepted that challenge, and today Finland is doing more than counterpunching; it is educating its citizens in how to spot, challenge, and prevent the spread of malign information that targets them.

Media literacy is the key to Finland's approach. The US-based Center for Media Literacy defines the term this way: it "provides a framework to access, analyze, evaluate, create and participate with messages in a variety of forms – from print to video to the internet. Media literacy builds an understanding of the role of media in society as well as essential skills of inquiry and self-expression necessary for citizens of a democracy."[31] In combating disinformation, media literacy constitutes a defense mechanism that is needed to counter information-based attempts at political manipulation.

The Finnish effort is based within the nation's democratic structure and education system, but it extends to the greater public. One Finnish government official noted that "it's everyone's task to protect the Finnish democracy," and he added, about the role of schools: "The first line of defense is the kindergarten teacher."[32]

In secondary schools, media literacy is now a core, cross-disciplinary part of the national curriculum. A report published in the *Guardian* described how different courses emphasized different aspects of this approach. In math class, students "learn how easy it is to lie with statistics. In art, they see how an image's meaning can be manipulated. In history, they analyze notable propaganda campaigns, while Finnish language teachers work with them on the many ways in which words can be used to confuse, mislead, and deceive." Kari Kivinen, a Finnish educator who is a leading pioneer in media literacy training, said: "The goal is active, responsible citizens and voters. Thinking critically, factchecking, interpreting, and evaluating all the information you receive, wherever it appears, is crucial."[33] Kivinen also told a CNN reporter, "What we want students to do is ... before they like or share in the social media they think twice – who has written this? Where has it been published? Can I find the same information from another source?"[34] One of Kivinen's students, a 16-year-old, said: "The problem is, anyone can publish anything. There's not much a government can do when they're faced with big multinationals like Google or Facebook, and if it does too much it's censorship. So yes, education is what's most effective."[35]

Other schools in other places are also taking media literacy seriously, but Finland stands out because it has moved so comprehensively and made this facet of Finnish education – including making it part of adult education programs – an element of the nation's broader security policy.

It is worth remembering that Finland began this effort soon after Russia invaded Ukraine in 2014, seeing its own electronic borders as dangerously porous in terms of defending against an invasion by information that might precede an invasion by Russian military. At about the same time, the European Union began its EUvsDisinfo project, which uses data analysis and media monitoring in 15 languages to identify, compile, and expose disinformation cases originating from pro-Kremlin media.[36]

IREX, a US-based NGO, works throughout the world on projects related to media literacy and other fields. In Ukraine, as reported by

Nina Jankowicz, IREX has focused on "increasing consumers' ability to recognize emotional manipulation" in disinformation (and other venues, including commercial advertising). The 15,000 Ukrainian participants in the IREX program shared their newly learned skills with 90,000 more persons, and soon thereafter the Ukrainian Ministry of Education officially endorsed adding media literacy to the national curriculum.[37]

An important ally for media literacy advocates is the growing community of fact-checking organizations. A roster prepared by the Duke University Reporters' Lab in April 2020 included 237 fact-checking entities in 78 countries. The number of fact-checkers reflected a 26 percent increase since June 2019.[38] Of course, the true significance of fact-checking is not the number of those doing it, but in their thoroughness and the receptivity of those who receive the information. When facts – however well documented – collide with personal biases, the facts might be dismissed.

The news media's role

News organizations have reported in considerable detail about the effects of information used as a weapon. In the United States after the 2016 presidential election and in the United Kingdom following the 2016 Brexit vote, news organizations explained – with varying levels of detail – how Russia had tampered with the political process in those countries. In Eastern and Northern Europe, where Russian information meddling is seen as a persistent threat, news organizations have become increasingly attentive to information-related efforts at political sabotage. Journalism programs at some universities have also placed greater emphasis on fact-checking skills.

But, with some exceptions, the journalism profession and journalism education remain behind the curve in terms of addressing their responsibilities concerning information warfare. Defense ministries and intelligence agencies have done a better job of adjusting their duties to include evaluating information-related threats and designing countermeasures. Their mandate, however, does not extend to directly informing the public about these matters. As the scope and menace of disinformation grow larger, the need for a better-informed public grows as well. News organizations should consider ways to significantly upgrade their abilities to cover this topic, beginning with creation of an "information beat," just as there are politics, science, business, and other specialized coverage beats assigned to reporters with expertise in those fields.

Such knowledge is important because finding sources of

disinformation often requires navigating a maze that might lead to a complex government enterprise, or it might end up at an individual with a tiny following. In 2020, Bellingcat criticized the *New York Times* for attributing far too much significance to a particular Twitter account, @TheRussophile, which had been tweeting false material about the coronavirus, alleging that it had been created by American scientists. But @TheRussophile, reported Bellingcat, is a one-person operation, an aggregator of Russian news. Its tweeting is prolific – 781,000 tweets as of May 2020 – but the account had only about 5,300 followers. It probably gained more exposure from the *Times* story than its proprietor could have dreamed of.[39] (Worth noting is that, other than the relatively minor point of overstating the significance of TheRussophile, the *Times* report, "Putin's Long War Against American Science," by William J. Broad, provides valuable analysis of the Kremlin's long-term efforts to blame the United States for the spread of AIDS, Ebola, and other deadly infectious diseases.)[40]

Journalists who cover information issues need training in forensic techniques that will help them to dig through piles of falsehood under which truth may be found. When a government at war denies it has been bombing civilian areas, evidence that can help reporters includes video and audio recordings, photographs, flight data, debris at the sites of the bombing, eyewitness testimony, and other pieces of the puzzle that can undermine the government's claims and let the public learn the truth. Just as a homicide detective in a police department must master specialized procedures to make a case against a murderer, so too must a journalist know how to find and report about the evidence needed to expose those disseminating disinformation.

Given the increasing sophistication of disinformation and the frequency with which damaging information reaches the public, there would be more than enough investigative work to justify a news organization assigning several journalists with specialized skills to this beat. This kind of emphasis has been placed by some news organizations in recent years on coverage of complex topics. One example is reporting about climate issues, with many news organizations working with Covering Climate Now, a journalism consortium that includes more than 400 news outlets with a combined audience approaching 2 billion people. Covering Climate Now works directly with newsrooms, sharing content, providing story ideas and background resources, amplifying its partners' coverage, convening climate journalism conferences, and publishing a weekly newsletter highlighting best practices.[41] This is the kind of effort needed to properly cover information issues.

Any plan for specialized information coverage would include close cooperation with other news beats – obviously with colleagues covering military matters, but also with many others. The *annus horribilis* of 2020 featured a surge of medical disinformation, some circulated out of ignorance but also a considerable amount delivered to global publics by governments and other interested parties with malign intent. Even medical issues can become political tools.

Pandemics and other medical matters

Disinformation about medical issues might not be directly related to warfare, but the techniques used to confuse and anger large numbers of information consumers are in many ways similar to those used in conflict situations. Manipulation of information about a pandemic or other health emergencies can contribute to social unrest and undermine a country's civic unity. This is closely related to other efforts, such as interfering in elections, that may subvert a nation's political system. Is it war? That could depend on the intent, intensity, and effects of the measures employed.

As the Covid-19 pandemic swept across the world in 2020, information flowed at a rate unprecedented in other medical emergencies. Some of it – about washing hands, wearing a mask, and social distancing – was valid, important, and easy to understand. It was taken seriously by much (but certainly not all) of the public. The World Health Organization (WHO), the US Centers for Disease Control (CDC), and other health agencies took advantage of social media to deliver crucial information quickly and widely. But this was not always the case.

Sometimes the online content was colored by political agendas that took precedence. In the Middle East, as the dispute continued between Qatar and some of its neighbors (discussed earlier in this chapter), Qatar's foes could not resist tactics such as producing an online video labeling Qatar Airways "the official carrier of the coronavirus."[42]

Such messaging could be dismissed as childishness were it not for the fact that the virus was killing hundreds of thousands of people. Elise Thomas wrote of this: "The all-too-real impacts and stresses of the pandemic feed into preexisting dynamics of the online information ecosystem, amplifying rumors, misinformation, conspiracies, and outright lies. For governments seeking to build trust and communicate clearly, it's a nightmare. For those looking to sow chaos and doubt, it's an opportunity."[43]

In Ukraine in February 2020, "chaos and doubt" prevailed when social media spread the contents of a letter claiming that the first cases of coronavirus had appeared in the country, and people took to the streets to protest the arrival of Ukrainian evacuees from Wuhan, China, an early center of the virus. It turned out that the letter was a forgery, created outside Ukraine, but pro-Kremlin media reported the protests as showing that Ukrainians hate each other and pose a danger to Europe.[44]

When people are frightened, they can more easily be taken advantage of. At such times, conspiracy theories and other disinformation may easily find fertile ground in which to grow. Another forgery related to the Covid-19 crisis created uncertainty in Lithuania when rumors circulated about NATO soldiers in Lithuania being infected with the virus. Then, an email purportedly sent by NATO Secretary-General Jens Stoltenberg said that NATO would withdraw its troops from the country. The email was phony, but much effort was required to debunk its content. Lithuanian military officials said that hundreds of fake news stories along similar lines were circulating, all aimed at destabilizing the nation's security.[45]

In January and February 2020, as the coronavirus began to spread outside China, the US State Department found roughly 2 million tweets pushing conspiracy theories, such as that the virus was a creation of the Gates Foundation or the US Department of Defense. The false narratives seemed to be spreading faster than the virus itself.[46]

When targeting the United States about Covid-19, Russia found that China and Iran were spreading similar messages. (How much coordination was involved is not known.) For a while, according to a US State Department official, China allowed Russian-generated disinformation to proliferate on Chinese social media, and then China began producing its own messaging claiming that the United States was the source of the virus. Iranian officials, meanwhile, blamed the US media for spreading "lies and disinformation" and also praised China's "humanitarian moves" related to the pandemic.[47] China and Russia both used disinformation in efforts to bolster their reputations by comparing their handling of the pandemic to the allegedly less effective ways Western countries were responding. A report from the Carnegie Endowment for International Peace underscored the exacerbation of health and public safety risks these disinformation efforts created.[48]

By 2020, Russia had moved beyond the Internet Research Agency and its fake social media accounts and bots for disseminating disinformation. According to the *New York Times*, "the Russian technique is a kind of information laundering, akin to money laundering. Stories originate with Russian-backed news sites, some of them directly connected to Moscow's spy agencies ... They are then picked up by Americans on social media or in domestic news outlets, and their origins quickly become obscured."[49] During the pandemic, many members of the information audience were frightened and uncertain what reports they should believe. This made them tempting targets for disinformation produced by Russian and other sources.

Among the Kremlin's new tools was Global Research, based in Canada.[50] The US State Department reported that by August 2020 Global Research had accumulated 12.4 million page views, an average of more than 350,000 people per article published on the site. Also becoming a major player was InfoRos, which was branded as a news service (similar to TASS) but had been linked by American intelligence officials to the psychological warfare unit (Unit 54777) of the GRU, the Russian military's foreign intelligence service. Articles published by InfoRos and its ilk would be republished by other news organizations, amplifying the Russian message, sometimes unwittingly, but sometimes intentionally.[51] The Russian stories "in well-written English ... are cycled through other news sources to conceal their origin and enhance the legitimacy of the information."[52]

Antecedents of Russian disinformation about health issues date back to Soviet times, notably Operation Infektion during the 1980s, which accused the United States of creating the HIV virus at a US military facility in Maryland. The Soviet KGB spread the idea that the AIDS virus was designed to kill African Americans, and by 1987 stories based on this premise had appeared in 25 languages and 80 countries.[53] In 2005, a study conducted by RAND and Oregon State University among African Americans found that conspiracy theories had acquired sizable constituencies of believers. Nearly 27 percent of respondents agreed that AIDS was produced in a government laboratory; about 16 percent believed that AIDS was created by the government to control the black population; and about 15 percent agreed that AIDS is a form of genocide against African Americans.[54] Similarly, in 2014 when an Ebola epidemic hit West Africa, RT broadcast reports that once again the US government was behind a devastating virus. Russian disinformation creators seemed to have mastered the art of the "infodemic."[55]

More recently, disinformation has been aimed at vaccinations for children, especially vaccinations for measles. According to the CDC, 1,282 measles cases were reported in the United States in 2019, more than any year since 1992. The majority of cases occurred among people who had not been vaccinated.[56] Russian troll accounts were found to be the most frequent tweeters about vaccination issues. Here are two examples of these tweets:[57]

- #vaccines are a parent's choice. Choice of a color of a little coffin.
- Did you know there was a secret government database of #vaccine-damaged children?

Other tweets, found to have originated in St. Petersburg, Russia, claimed that the CDC had silenced a whistle-blower who had found evidence that vaccines cause autism, especially among African American infants.[58]

Writing in *Foreign Policy*, Katherine Kirk noted that "the existence of a Russian disinformation campaign that could make Americans hesitant to vaccinate their children highlights something important about the Kremlin's information war on the United States." Moscow's goal, Kirk wrote, is "the exacerbation of Americans' distrust of one another and, in turn, the erosion of their confidence in society and the U.S. government."[59]

Adversaries of the United States must have been pleased with the situation in America in mid-2020. The coronavirus had killed more than 170,000 Americans, and many US cities were ripped asunder in the aftermath of the killing of George Floyd in Minneapolis and by anger about the killing of other African Americans. These responses cannot be attributed directly to information attacks, but the backbone of the country had been weakened by doubt rooted partly in malign information from foreign and domestic sources. The distrust of one another and the diminished confidence in the resilience of American society were plain to see and were symptoms of a weakened nation.

7

Where We've Been, Where We're Going

Earlier in this book are stories of individuals who shaped the way that information about war has been delivered to and received by various publics. In the ninth century BCE, Homer – an author perhaps as mythic as his stories – spoke in person to audiences sometimes consisting of just dozens at a time. By the mid twentieth century, Edward R. Murrow broadcast his word pictures of London aflame across the Atlantic to several million Americans. As that century drew to a close, the likes of CNN's Christiane Amanpour and the BBC's Martin Bell could be seen reporting in real time from war zones by global audiences. And today, you who are reading this book, assuming you have internet access, possess the tools to hear from and reach millions (or even billions) instantly, receiving and disseminating information about war or any topic of your choosing.

Progress? Perhaps.

The size of the reachable audience and the speed with which information can reach it have grown phenomenally, as has the breadth of information available to most of the planet with just a tap or a click. But information per se has limited value. Its *accuracy* and its *effects* are what matter. That is certainly the case with information related to war.

If information took months or even longer to travel from one place to another, its impact might be determined by this slow transit. For instance, during the War of 1812 in the United States, when General Andrew Jackson defeated British forces at the Battle of New Orleans, word of the Treaty of Ghent, which had ended the war several weeks earlier, was still making its way to the opposing armies. More than 2,000 soldiers died in that battle, which presumably would not have been fought had the information about the peace treaty moved at modern speed.

When Marshall McLuhan pondered the concept of the "global village," he envisioned ways that communicating information could shrink time and space. In a village, all was physically proximate: neighbors, shops, and the like. They were familiar and we cared about them. Beyond the village boundaries lay a different, less-known world. The farther one went, the more likely one was to encounter, in Neville Chamberlain's words, "people of whom we know nothing" – people whom we need not care about, much less aid when they are in distress.

This is how it was before information processes expanded. Eventually they became globalized and boundaries of knowledge and concern began to dissolve. Village borders stretched farther and farther; enlightened and energized by torrents of information, our village became global.

The Churn

That is where we are today, with the information torrents continuing to gather strength while we try to figure out how to wade through them, make sense of their content, and decide what we should do with what we learn. We cannot scrutinize everything, so we must be selective if we are to make sense of "the churn" of information. A former senior official of the Central Intelligence Agency described how she evaluated the churn during the first stages of the Covid-19 pandemic in early 2020. She studied news reports coming out of China, which were not particularly revealing, but then also picked up open source information about reactions from Taiwan and Hong Kong, which indicated that their governments saw a serious problem coming their way that would require a significant response. This led the intelligence official to be more selective, looking beyond the Beijing government as a source and paying closer attention to bits and pieces of possibly relevant information as they surfaced around the world.

Making sense of the churn is like assembling a complex jigsaw puzzle, and it is an important task for those who work with information at war. This is a sizable constituency; it includes not just the military and the intelligence community, but also universities, think tanks, private corporations, news organizations, and the many other entities that monitor security-related matters throughout the world. Their task is complicated because the churn must be analyzed for information about tactics not necessarily as blatant as Russia's 2007 cyberattack on Estonia or its interference with the 2016 US presidential election. The Russian initiative "Secondary Infektion" (a descendant of the Russian "Operation Infektion" that during the 1980s sought to blame the United States for creating the AIDS virus) aimed to weaken links between countries. Lily Hay Newman wrote that Secondary Infektion, which apparently began in early 2014, involved "stoking tension between the U.S. and the United Kingdom, trying to ignite controversy between Poland and Germany, or pushing anti-American sentiment among Germans."[1] Pieces of evidence of such attempts at disruption may be found by those closely watching the churn.

Most of Secondary Infektion's content failed to gain traction; this kind of disinformation was still unrefined and, as a result, was not as convincing as more recent efforts have been. But in the disinformation field, expertise develops quickly and even an unsuccessful project can lay groundwork for a later version that has significant effect. The Secondary Infektion case also underscored some inherent weaknesses of certain information platforms. According to a 2019 Atlantic Council report, it

> exploited the vulnerabilities of online forums to plant and amplify forgeries, fake stories, and divisive content. Its activity on Facebook and Twitter – the social networks at the center of public scrutiny over their abuse by disinformation campaigns – paled beside its use of online platforms such as Medium, Reddit, the German homment.com, the Spanish globedia.com, and San Francisco-based site indybay.org to seed its toxic content. Such platforms, with their minimal or nonexistent user transparency requirements, represent the soft underbelly of the internet. It remains disturbingly simple for malicious actors to create false profiles on these platforms and use them as a launch pad for disinformation.[2]

Soft targets for dissemination, such as platforms with little oversight, can serve as feeders for more broadly viewed venues. See something on indybay that appeals to you? Post it on Twitter and you may quickly reach a vastly larger audience.

For those studying the churn, it can be difficult to distinguish between legitimate information and material designed to deceive. Looking ahead, military and intelligence analysts – as well as journalists and the general public – will need to devise new ways to evaluate information that appears online and elsewhere. One path toward this skill takes us to artificial intelligence (AI), which is discussed in chapter 6. AI can be programmed to identify factors such as similarities in vocabulary and other reference points within vast quantities of information, and it can do so quickly. It will then remain for humans to decide what to do with what they learn.

Social Media Culture and Information at War

Lessons from the past are useful, but they should be considered in the light of an important difference in the 21st-century information environment: the expansion of public conversation and participation in the information domain enabled by social media.

In some ways, this involvement supplements traditional information flow, and in other instances it replaces – or at least reduces the importance of – traditional information suppliers such as major news organizations. The Kremlin recognized this when it set out to influence American political conversation during 2016 through efforts of the Internet Research Agency, which found Facebook, Twitter, and other online venues so useful. This followed Russia's conflict-related information manipulation and disruption related to its 2014 invasion of Ukraine and in its interference in the politics and security affairs of the Baltic States and elsewhere. These cases are examined in chapter 5, and in general terms they reflect some of the ways that internet-based tools can spotlight vulnerabilities that may become targets for information at war.

Another factor in growing public reliance on social media is the widening breach of trust between citizens and their governments, as well as between the public and many long-relied-upon information sources. This distancing is mostly a gradual process, with ups and downs, and is sometimes triggered by collective unhappiness about the broader state of society. The result may be a years-long search for alternative providers of information – those perceived as not beholden to either the government or big media organizations. In the United States, among those who prospered from such a search was conservative radio host Rush Limbaugh, who built a huge audience while specializing in name-calling and diatribes that contributed to expanding political polarization. The voices of Limbaugh and others of his ilk became increasingly common during the early 1990s. Then, in 1996, Fox News Channel was born, and within a few years it found a large and profitable conservative viewership to call its own as it relied on a kind of journalism that was unabashedly partisan. With post-9/11 America preparing to invade both Afghanistan and

Iraq, the slick jingoism of Fox News and some other news outlets provided much useful support to the George W. Bush administration's war efforts.[3]

A few years later, during Donald Trump's presidency, Fox News (and others of its ilk) and vast amounts of online activity nurtured polarization. One example of online political information activism is Breitbart.com, which traffics in far-right political rumors and conspiracy theories. It claims to have 25 million unique monthly website visitors and to be the most engaged political Instagram page in the United States.[4] Breitbart is just one participant in the flourishing online hubbub of dubious information sources that are unaccountable but globally accessible.

The temptation to dismiss content such as Breitbart's "news" as inconsequential is dangerous. As was seen in Russia's efforts in the United States in 2016, and elsewhere over a number of years, those intent on waging information warfare can amplify even an obscure website's rumors and damage the integrity of a targeted country's political processes.[5] In such ways, online probing is likely to be increasingly used to "soften up" adversaries, whether just to roil their civic life or to make them more susceptible to military action.

Changes in the social media environment have not escaped the attention of Russian disinformation specialists, including those at the Internet Research Agency (IRA). As the United States prepared for its 2020 presidential election, the IRA adopted a new tactic. Instead of relying on its Russia-based team to generate tweets and other online content, the IRA created a new website, PeaceData.net, which hired Americans to write for it. A theme of PeaceData postings was that Democratic nominee Joe Biden was not liberal enough and so was not worthy of the votes of left-leaning Democrats.[6] In 2016, much IRA messaging was designed to suppress the turnout of Hillary Clinton voters, and this effort replicated that approach with regard to Biden.

As an apparently independent website with identifiable writers, PeaceData's content spread through social media via Twitter, Facebook, and other platforms. By mid-2020, PeaceData had attracted the attention of US law enforcement and intelligence agencies, as well as managers at the social media giants, who removed its content from their pages. In early September 2020, Peacedata – stripped of its "journalistic" identity – posted a notice on its website: "Today we decided to shut down PeaceData … . Some corrupt forces (FBI, NSA, CNN, Facebook, the New York Times, The Washington Post, and many others) attacked us in an attempt to silence free speech."[7]

Given that reliance on social media is particularly dominant among younger audiences, there exists a significant risk that these social-media-dependent information consumers will be vulnerable to the superficial or malign content that can be created and disseminated so easily. This problem will remain particularly acute until media literacy education, which is discussed in chapter 6, is taken more seriously and pursued more comprehensively.

Even when media content is subject to regulatory oversight, social media sometimes provide options to avoid controls and deliver the information to a wide audience. Theoretically, this is valuable – a way to evade censorship and ensure that the public can access diverse information sources. This assumes, however, that policing of content is never appropriate. In the United Kingdom in April 2020, Britain's communications regulator, Ofcom, censured a small television channel for endangering public health by broadcasting part of an interview with a conspiracy theorist who argued that the ongoing pandemic was a hoax. By the time of Ofcom's ruling, only 80,000 viewers had seen this excerpt on the television channel, but 6 million had seen the full interview on YouTube (which is not within Ofcom's jurisdiction).[8] Thus, we face a dilemma: give up on regulation because social media provide detours around it, or expand regulation to cover more media venues. Some countries, such as China, may prefer the latter, but if unrestricted media openness (with a few exceptions such as banning child pornography and other criminal content) is regarded as essential to freedom, intensified regulation may be both undesirable and unenforceable.

It is easy to become hypnotized by the latest technology. It is always newer, faster, farther-reaching – delivering information in nice, shiny packaging. From radio to television to internet to …? Sometimes, technology may seem to be an end in itself, not just a means to reach a higher level of information accuracy and usefulness. A case can be made that in television war reporting – to cite one example – the quality and value of the information being provided diminished when real-time transmission of events became possible. During the Vietnam War, limitations on satellite access meant that "breaking news" was rarely a factor for television correspondents, so their reporting was often more thorough and analytical than the high-speed, live dispatches the public received decades later during the Iraq War, when journalists reported breathlessly from their embedded billets with the troops.

Embedding journalists largely worked advantageously for both the military and journalists, and, at least at first, it enthralled the public. Presenting war with the vividness of a sporting event may be audience-pleasing, but is the intellectual value of information debased when content of this kind owes more to military public relations efforts than to journalistic standards of accuracy and insight?

For those who are waging war, responses to such questions are significant because they can affect the political foundation on which armed conflict is built, especially when undertaken by a government with some concern for public opinion. Around the world, governments and their militaries have recognized that they can use social media – YouTube, Instagram, Twitter, and the like – to reach domestic and foreign publics without their content being filtered by the news media. This process continues to develop slowly; the competition for audience attention is fierce and requires skillsets unlike those most often associated with military and government bureaucracies. (This is, presumably, one reason behind Russia's creating an information corps within its army.) In essence, information – regardless of the topic – is fundamentally a consumer product, although the sophistication and expectations of the consumers vary greatly. Drawing attention to it is in many ways similar to the demands advertising professionals face in making their work stand out amidst a crowded array of competitors.

Those pondering the future of such matters might consider what gives information its value. Is it the flashy technology we use to access it? Is it the imprimatur that accompanies wisdom from popular or "official" sources? Is it the fervor with which partisans deliver their message? Or is the true worth of information determined by the next step – what we do with it?

Sometimes we ignore information that we receive – there is just too much of it. But sometimes it changes our lives. Information is intellectual protein; at its best, it heals and nourishes. At its worst, however, it can wreak havoc.

Next Steps for Information in the Battle Space

American General Richard D. Clarke, commander of the US Special Operations Command (SOCOM), stated in mid-2020 that "great power competition is about influence," and therefore reliance on Military Information Support Operations (MISO) will increase.[9] MISO's stated objective is "to convince enemy, neutral, and friendly nations and forces to take actions favorable to the United States and its allies." SOCOM considers information operations to be "force multipliers that use nonviolent means in often violent environments. Persuading rather than compelling physically, they rely on logic, fear, desire, or other mental factors to promote specific emotions, attitudes, or behaviors."[10]

That mission seems much like a soft-power task being assigned to a quintessentially hard-power entity. It also seems to echo some of the Russian observations (cited in chapter 5) about a strategic shift away from kinetic force and toward information/propaganda.

Walter Pincus wrote that a MISO WebOps Center, planned to be fully operational by the end of fiscal year 2025, will include "regional experts and linguists who understand political, cultural, ethnic, and religious subtleties with abilities to use persuasion to influence perceptions and encourage desired behavior." This center will also incorporate Social Media Analysis Cells as part of the effort to embrace up-to-date messaging techniques and to upgrade influence operations.[11] These messaging techniques will, presumably, rely in part on what is gained by *listening* to the foreign publics, which is a key element of public diplomacy and can also be invaluable in MISO work.

Meanwhile, other parts of the US defense bureaucracy were also working to institutionalize responses to foreign influence efforts. The 2020 National Defense Authorization Act called for creation of a Social Media Data and Threat Analysis Center. Among its tasks would be to maintain an overview of content on various platforms, a necessity because objectionable content found and removed on one site might be left standing on other sites.[12]

While the United States moves forward with updating its information operations, another superpower has been pursuing its own path toward mastering information at war.

China

Waiting until this late in the book to address China's information-related strategies is purposeful. The author is convinced that China is *the* power that will exercise determinative influence on the nature of information at war during the coming decade and beyond. Former US Secretary of Defense and CIA Director Robert Gates wrote that "no other country, including the United States, comes close to China's comprehensive and far-reaching communications strategy and apparatus for shaping perceptions about it and advancing its interests."[13]

Russia's information operations have deservedly received much attention. They are a vital part of the Kremlin's hopes to resurrect the Soviet era's map of Europe and its attempts to keep the United

States politically off-balance. Russia is formidable; it is willing to use its military forces (and mercenary add-ons), and it possesses a large arsenal of nuclear weapons, second in size only to that of the United States. As described in chapter 5, the Kremlin possesses ways to cause considerable damage through its information vehicles such as RT, Sputnik, the Internet Research Agency, and other less visible mechanisms. The combined information and kinetic attacks on Ukraine served notice that Russia will dial up the rheostat of conflict when it believes it has the upper hand. This was a warning that the Baltic States, Finland, and others took seriously. Russia's economic fragility leaves it vulnerable to countermeasures, but if allowed to act unchecked it will become a far more serious threat.

China is a very different kind of adversary.

Why China matters

In June 2020, NATO Secretary-General Jens Stoltenberg said, "The rise of China is fundamentally shifting the global balance of power. Heating up the race for economic and technological supremacy. Multiplying the threats to open societies and individual freedoms. And increasing the competition over our values and our way of life." Stoltenberg noted that China would soon have the world's largest economy, and it already had the world's second-largest defense budget. Because China's progress affects Western Europe as well as Asia, NATO has been forging stronger relationships with partner nations in the Pacific.[14]

That is an overview of China's significance. Narrowing the focus to matters related more closely to information issues, Graham Allison wrote:

> War for Chinese strategists is primarily psychological and political; military campaigns are a secondary concern. In Chinese thinking, an opponent's perception of facts on the ground may be just as important as the facts themselves. Creating and sustaining the image of a civilization so superior that it is the "center of the universe," for example, deters enemies from challenging Chinese dominance.[15]

Writing in a 2020 Carnegie Endowment for International Peace report, James Pamment noted that many experts

> view China as Russia's superior in terms of its potential capabilities and intent to spread disinformation and develop influence campaigns, as well as to coordinate them with broader forms of soft power. Not

all its disinformation activities appear particularly sophisticated at present, but experts express much interest in how it might develop and test techniques at home before expanding their reach abroad.[16]

China benefits from a growing imbalance in nations' attention to information issues. In language matters, for example, the Chinese government places heavy emphasis on young people learning English. In the United States, on the other hand, a significant portion of Chinese-language instruction is provided by Confucius Institutes at dozens of college campuses, and the content of that instruction is supervised by the Chinese Communist Party. Further, *Cankao Xiaoxi,* the Chinese newspaper with the largest domestic circulation, offers a compilation of foreign-language news articles translated into Chinese. In the United States and much of the West, there is no major publication with anything comparable. Journalist John Pomfret observed that "the Chinese language is the first level of encryption."[17]

China's "Three Warfares"

Russia's notoriety related to information at war is due in part to its minimal efforts to disguise the links between its information tactics and conventional warfare. Pro-forma denials by the Kremlin of its sponsorship of information assaults convince few. Disdaining to mask the Russian origins and the implicit menace of its Baltic information attacks and deploying "little green men" to invade Ukraine are hardly subtle. So far, the Kremlin has paid a price only in sanctions that hurt, but not to the point of being an effective deterrent. It continues to build on the Putin–Gerasimov vision of redefining the Russian approach to conflict, making information a more prominent ingredient.

China, meanwhile, has modernized its approach to information at war in ways that do not attract as much hostile attention. It has adopted an information-centric strategy that fits within its broader goal, as articulated by President Xi Jinping, of his "great modern socialist country" becoming the world's dominant power by 2049, the centennial of the birth of the People's Republic of China. Rob Joyce of the US National Security Agency defined the difference between the Russian and Chinese approaches to information warfare this way: "Russia is the hurricane. It comes in fast and hard. China, on the other hand, is climate change: long, slow, pervasive."[18]

Whatever label is attached to the two nations' information efforts, they have begun to move along similar paths to create a perfect storm of content that is hostile toward the United States and its allies.

In December 2019, Russian broadcaster RT aired a documentary accusing the United States of funding pro-democracy protests in Hong Kong, and the network also echoed Beijing's views on the Chinese government's treatment of Uighur Muslims and the trade war between China and the United States. Russian media giants, such as Sputnik, and Chinese news outlets have shared content and exchanged personnel. Both countries' information output has increasingly been directed not at Western audiences but instead at public opinion in the Middle East and Africa, where anti-American information is likely to often find receptive audiences.[19]

Two former US Department of Defense analysts, Andrew Krepinevich and Barry Watts, wrote in 2015 that Chinese military officials "have concluded that 'informationalized' war is a new type of war dominated by 'informationized' forces" that can prevail in local wars and against "an opponent such as the United States that is stronger in most other respects."[20]

As a key element of its overall national security strategy, the Chinese leadership has embraced the "Three Warfares" doctrine. The US Defense Department, in a 2019 report to Congress, defined Three Warfares as comprising psychological, public opinion, and legal forms of warfare:

> Psychological warfare uses propaganda, deception, threats, and coercion to affect the adversary's decision-making capability. Public opinion warfare disseminates information for public consumption to guide and influence public opinion and gain support from domestic and international audiences. Legal warfare uses international and domestic laws to gain international support, manage political reper-cussions, and sway target audiences ... The PLA [People's Liberation Army] likely seeks to use online influence activities to support its overall Three Warfares strategy and to undermine an adversary's resolve in a contingency or conflict.[21]

The Department of Defense appraisal also noted that "China's foreign influence activities are predominantly focused on establishing and maintaining power brokers within a foreign government to promote policies that China believes will facilitate China's rise."[22] Targets of Chinese information operations include members of the global Chinese diaspora who might exert influence within the countries where they now are living. Chinese information tacti-cians also are attentive to think tanks and academic institutions. A Confucius Institute on a foreign university's campus, for example, can be a useful vehicle for propounding the Chinese government's views about matters such as Tibet and the Dalai Lama.

The coherence of China's international presence is based on overall policy guidance from the Chinese Communist Party Propaganda Department, which is overseen by the Party's Central Committee's Leading Group for Propaganda and Ideology. A 2019 report from Reporters Without Borders listed parts of China's worldwide information apparatus. Among them are these:[23]

- China Global Television Network (CGTN), launched in 2016, broadcasts in five languages and can be seen in more than 140 countries. Its online content has more than 150 million followers worldwide.
- China International Broadcasting Network includes more than 70 foreign radio stations, from which China Radio International broadcasts in 65 languages.
- United Front Work Department oversees financial transfers to foreign media (including Chinese-language media) to buy advertising and acquire ownership shares.
- China Watch is an offshoot of the English-language *China Daily* and appears as an advertorial supplement in newspapers such as the *Wall Street Journal*, *Daily Telegraph*, *Le Figaro*, and *Manichi Shimbun*.
- Some prominent Chinese diaspora media, such as New Zealand's *Chinese Herald* and Australia's *Pacific Times*, which had long been independent and critical of China's government, are now controlled by Beijing, as are growing numbers of other national/ local news media around the world.
- Social media messaging app WeChat, created by Chinese conglomerate TenCent, reported reaching 1 billion regular users in 2018, 100 million of whom are outside China. Data collected by WeChat are not encrypted and are managed by servers in China, making the data a useful resource for the government's censorship, influence, and surveillance efforts.

In addition, the Chinese government can call upon hundreds of thousands of internet trolls in the "50-cent army" (so named because of the amount the trolls were supposedly paid, although today they are apparently not paid at all). Much of this "army's" work entails cheerleading for the Communist Party; the trolls posted an estimated 500 million pro-Party comments in 2017.[24] The political edge of the trolls' comments has grown sharper, with increasing criticism of Taiwan and democracy supporters in Hong Kong.

Twitter, along with Facebook and Instagram, is blocked in China, but in 2020, as the coronavirus spread across the world, tens of thousands of Twitter accounts disseminated messages painting a favorable picture of the Chinese government's response to the pandemic. In June 2020, Twitter suspended more than 170,000 of these accounts, alleging that they were spreading deceptive information about the virus.[25] Despite Twitter's closing these accounts, Beijing is well aware that hundreds of millions of Chinese can be galvanized to quickly generate a massive volume of online content as a facet of the "information dominance" that is an important part of the Three Warfares concept.

It is worth noting that the role of China's military, specifically the PLA, is very different from that of the armed forces of countries such as the United States and the United Kingdom. As Peter Mattis has written, the PLA is a political institution; it is the Communist Party's army, not the Chinese state's, and, as Mao Zedong proclaimed, "the Chinese Red Army is an armed body for carrying out the political tasks of the revolution ... to help the masses establish revolutionary political power." Mattis stated that the purpose of influence operations is creating political power, which is what the Three Warfares concept is designed for.[26] Chinese policymakers, like their Russian counterparts, recognize the value of targeting domestic as well as foreign audiences when they design and manage information initiatives.

An example of how Three Warfares has been put to use can be seen in the dispute over China's claims to territory in the South China Sea (SCS). Since 2013, China has engaged in land reclamation and fortification on islands in the SCS. Some countries in the region – including Vietnam, the Philippines, Brunei, and Malaysia – have their own claims to SCS territory and so oppose China's moves, as do some of the nations – including major powers such as the United States – that use the South China Sea's maritime commerce routes. Addressing Chinese strategy in the SCS, Doug Livermore wrote:

> The PRC has pursued a textbook application of the Three Warfares doctrine to advance its interests without triggering a conventional conflict. The brazen construction of the fortified islands and the staging of advanced military equipment (integrated air defense systems, coastal defense cruise missiles, airborne surveillance drones, and modern jet fighters) demonstrates the PRC's effort to undermine the psychological ability of the other claimants to oppose its *fait accompli*. Additionally, the PRC deploys maritime militia throughout the region to reinforce its claim, sowing confusion as the opposing naval forces are uncertain of how exactly to respond. To reinforce the psychological impact of the PRC's aggressive posture in the SCS, China has also pursued robust media messaging through news outlets and other mediums to promote

narratives reinforcing the historicity of its claim and warning others to refrain from antagonism. The UNCLOS [United Nations Convention on the Law of the Sea] arbitration did not fall in the PRC's favor, though the very process itself provided ample opportunity for China to continue pursuing its island-building campaign. Throughout this crisis, the PRC has successfully prevented other regional and international powers from effectively responding to its non-kinetic provocations of military posturing, propaganda overmatch, and legal obfuscation. Continued application of the Three Warfares in the SCS buys the PRC additional time to strengthen its position in the region, which alone will serve as an ever-greater deterrent to other claimants who will see their comparative ability to resist China's claim dwindle.[27]

As Livermore points out, the SCS case illustrates China's ability to coordinate the elements of Three Warfares – psychological, public opinion, and legal warfare – in ways that advance its objectives while keeping its opponents off-balance. When there have been military confrontations about the SCS with countries such as Japan and the Philippines, China has responded primarily with economic pressure that has required challengers to back off, although sometimes it has flexed its military muscle.

China's approach can serve as a capstone for consideration of information at war as it stands today ... but only today. It is a dynamic part of the security–technology–media continuum and is almost constantly evolving in one way or another. Expanding technological capabilities require expanding analysis of information at war. At the root of that is deciding what information providers and content we should believe.

Information at War

From Homer to Edward R. Murrow to Vladimir Putin and Xi Jinping. A long and twisting trail.

These people have one thing in common: an understanding that war and information are inseparable, whether in terms of memorializing fabled battles, describing a city's brave survival as bombs rained down upon it, undermining a nation's unity to try to make it ripe for conquest, or finding a way to win global supremacy without gore and destruction.

Because war is a matter of politics as well as combat, the battlefield is not the only place where information is important. Information helps to shape opinion: let's go to war; let's not go to war; let's escalate and win an existing war; let's disengage from that war. Within the past 100 years, the information on which people rely to develop and sustain those opinions has been transformed by technology – from print and telegraph, to radio, to television, to internet – with speed of delivery and vividness of content changing from one step to the next.

Technology is just part of the story of how information at war has evolved. A "journalism of attachment," once shunned as unprofessional within the news profession, has become more a part of the journalistic mainstream, bringing moral issues to greater prominence in wartime storytelling. Stories also have begun to be told by noncombatants whose fates had been dismissed as "collateral damage," and by women whose voices had for too long not been heard.

The arrival of social media further democratized the production and dissemination of information at war by enabling anyone with a computer or cellphone to use the internet to reach out to and hear from a potentially vast public. The plethora of information venues means that the the gatekeeper function of media professionals has diminished, or at least become more scattered. An important battle now rages about "freedom of information," with some governments creating firewalls to control what information their citizens can receive. Some of those citizens devote much effort to finding ways to scale those firewalls.

In 2011, US Secretary of State Hillary Rodham Clinton spoke about internet freedom, asserting that "we need to have a serious conversation about the principles that will guide us, what rules should exist and not exist and why, what behaviors should be encouraged or discouraged and how … . The freedoms to assemble and associate also apply in cyberspace."[28]

With individuals increasingly thus empowered, governments soon learned that the new information tools could be used as weapons in different stages of warfare. Russia has been the most aggressive in this process, disrupting the political processes of adversaries and using information as well as force of arms to achieve its goals.

Russia is far from alone. The United States and other countries have combined information and cyber techniques as military tactics. Non-state actors, such as Islamic State, also have found ways to use information to enhance their prospects, however nefarious they might be. And China has created a plan, as described above, to use information-based strategy to help reach its goal of becoming the dominant superpower.

Much of this maneuvering implicitly reflects low regard for the public; it is based on an assumption that people can be manipulated because most of them lack the mental energy to be skeptical about what they see on social media or hear from sources of disguised or unknown reputation. Critical thinking is in distressingly short supply, and as long as that is the case those who use information to wield influence will face too few challenges.

Intellectual nonchalance is dangerous, undermining fundamental concepts of citizenship and honesty. That is why media literacy is so important. If there is one thing to be learned from the issues addressed in this book it is that information – regardless of where it comes from – should be challenged: sources authenticated, facts corroborated, details verified.

Journalists as well as governments should be involved in developing systemic responses to the information crisis. As noted earlier, covering "information" as a news subject is important and will require expertise that, as of now, too many news organizations lack. Partnerships between the news media and educators should be part of this process. Governments' primary focus in this field should mainly address information-related threats from foreign states and malevolent non-state actors. As for the governments that seek to control information and block their publics' access ... they may succeed for a while, but eventually advances in information technology are likely to outpace these governments' efforts. You cannot drown information; it is too buoyant.

War, like cancer, is capable of metastasizing – changing and spreading and becoming more virulent. A goal of modern war is not always physical destruction, but rather the destruction of societal infrastructure such as a nation's political processes. In this version of war, battalions of words can take the place of battalions of soldiers, but deployment of words – of information – may still constitute an act of war. For those under this kind of attack, the best way to respond is to overwhelm information rooted in hatred and falsity with a deluge of truth.

War in its various forms will, unfortunately, always be with us, and information will be part of that. But the negative effects of information at war can be mitigated if honest information is widely available to offset the false and to spur action by those with the ability to respond. As a first step, the power of information at war must be recognized and its workings understood. Only then might we see the progress – and perhaps peace – in our information-dependent world.

Notes

Introduction

1 Homer, *The Iliad*, translated by Robert Fagles (London: Penguin, 1998), 77.
2 *Journalism, "Fake News," and Disinformation: A Handbook for Journalism Education and Training*, UNESCO, 2020, https://en.unesco.org/node/295873.
3 Committee to Protect Journalists, https://cpj.org/data/imprisoned/2019/?status=Imprisoned&start_year=2019&end_year=2019&group_by=location.
4 See Stanley Cloud and Lynne Olson, *The Murrow Boys* (Boston: Houghton Mifflin, 1996).
5 Melissa A. Wall, "Blogs over Baghdad: A New Genre of War Reporting," in Ralph D. Berenger (ed.), *Cybermedia Go to War* (Spokane, WA: Marquette Books, 2006), 297–8.
6 Henry Kissinger, *Does America Need a Foreign Policy? Toward a Diplomacy for the 21st Century* (New York: Simon & Schuster, 2001), 284.
7 See Peter Braestrup, *Big Story* (abridged version: Novato, CA: Presidio Press, 1994).
8 Dominique Moisi, "The Clash of Emotions," *Foreign Affairs* 86, no. 1 (January–February 2007), 8.
9 Kate Bulkley, "The Rise of Citizen Journalism," *Guardian*, June 10, 2012.
10 Philip Seib, *Headline Diplomacy: How News Coverage Affects Foreign Policy* (Westport, CT: Praeger, 1997), 1–13.
11 See Laura J. Ahlstrom and Franklin G. Mixon, Jr. (eds.), *War Movies and Economics: Lessons from Hollywood's Adaptations of Military Conflict* (London: Routledge, 2020).

12 Fiona Macdonald, "Mrs. Miniver: The Film that Goebbels Feared," BBC, February 9, 2015, www.bbc.com/culture/article/2150209-the-film-that-goebbels-feared.

13 Marvin Kalb, *Imperial Gamble: Putin, Ukraine, and the New Cold War* (Washington: Brookings Institution, 2015), 236.

14 www.medialit.org/media-literacy-definition-and-more.

15 https://americancentury.omeka.wlu.edu/files/original/60e94905a0e020 50a5b78f10b1b02b07.jpg.

16 See William Prochnau, *Once Upon a Distant War* (New York: Times Books, 1995).

17 Philip Knightley, "The Falklands: How Britannia Ruled the News," *Columbia Journalism Review*, September/October 1982, 52.

18 Bob Woodward, *The Commanders* (New York: Pocket Books, 1992), 364.

19 See Philip Seib, *Beyond the Front Lines: How the News Media Cover a World Shaped by War* (New York: Palgrave Macmillan, 2004), 69–86.

20 Julie Salamon, "New Tools Make Coverage More Instant but Coverage No Simpler," *New York Times*, April 6, 2003.

21 Seib, *Beyond the Front Lines*, 58.

22 Seib, *Beyond the Front Lines*, 78–9. Mark Jurkowitz, "Americans Want Facts and Flags," *Boston Globe*, July 14, 2003, http://forums.lukpac.org/viewtopic.php?t=230.

23 www.bbc.co.uk/send/u16904890.

24 Lilie Chouliaraki, "Citizen Voice in War and Conflict Reporting," in Piers Robinson, Philip Seib, and Romy Froehlich (eds.), *Routledge Handbook of Media, Conflict and Security* (London: Routledge, 2017), 174–5.

25 See Martin Bell, *In Harm's Way* (London: Penguin, 1996).

26 See Abdel Bari Atwan, *Islamic State: The Digital Caliphate* (Oakland: University of California Press, 2015).

27 www.pewresearch.org/internet/2018/11/16/algorithms-in-action-the-content-people-see-on-social-media.

28 See Henry Hemming, *Agents of Influence: A British Campaign, a Canadian Spy, and the Secret Plot to Bring America into World War II* (New York: PublicAffairs, 2019).

29 See Thomas Rid, *Active Measures: The Secret History of Disinformation and Political Warfare* (New York: Farrar, Straus and Giroux, 2020).

30 Lawrence Freedman, *Ukraine and the Art of Strategy* (New York: Oxford University Press, 2019), 140.

31 Julian E. Barnes, "Cyber Command Operation Took Down Russian Troll Farm for Midterm Elections," *New York Times*, February 26, 2019.

32 Jens Stoltenberg, "NATO Will Defend Itself," NATO, August 29, 2019, www.nato.int/cps/en/natohq/news_168435.htm?selectedLocale=en.

33 Adam Nicolson, *Why Homer Matters* (New York: Henry Holt, 2014), 181.

1 Living-Room Wars

1 For additional material about wartime information's effects, see (among others) Stuart Allan and Barbie Zelizer, *Reporting War: Journalism in Wartime* (London: Routledge, 2004).
2 See Ronald D. Asmus, "Power, War, and Public Opinion," *Hoover Institution Policy Review*, February/March 2004, www.hoover.org/research/power-war-and-public-opinion; Philip Seib (ed.), *War and Conflict Communication* (London: Routledge, 2010), 171–305.
3 Philip Seib, *The Global Journalist: News and Conscience in a World of Conflict* (Lanham, MD: Rowman and Littlefield, 2002), 121.
4 Quoted in Piers Brandon, *The Dark Valley* (New York: Knopf, 2000), 624.
5 Philip Ziegler, *London at War, 1939–1945* (London: Pimlico, 2002), 126, 154.
6 Edward R. Murrow, *This Is London* (New York: Simon & Schuster, 1941), 161, 163. See also Philip Seib, *Broadcasts from the Blitz: How Edward R. Murrow Helped Lead America into War* (Dulles, VA: Potomac Books, 2006).
7 Murrow, *This Is London*, 163.
8 Murrow, *This Is London*, 167, 169–70.
9 Murrow, *This Is London*, 172, 173, 178.
10 Murrow, *This Is London*, 180, 182.
11 Robert E. Sherwood, *Roosevelt and Hopkins* (New York: Enigma, 2001), 170.
12 Susan Dunn, *A Blueprint for War: FDR and the Hundred Days that Mobilized America* (New Haven: Yale University Press, 2018), 8–9.
13 Cloud and Olson, *The Murrow Boys*, 97.
14 Robert Dallek, *Franklin D. Roosevelt and American Foreign Policy 1932–1945* (New York: Oxford University Press, 1979), 250.
15 Hadley Cantril, "Public Opinion in Flux," *Annals of the American Academy of Political and Social Science* 220 (March 1942), 138, 146.
16 Cantril, "Public Opinion in Flux," 144, 145.
17 Cantril, "Public Opinion in Flux," 141, 147, 150.
18 Cantril, "Public Opinion in Flux," 138.
19 A. M. Sperber, *Murrow: His Life and Times* (New York: Freundlich Books, 1986), 174.
20 Jon Meacham, *Franklin and Winston* (New York: Random House, 2003), 52.
21 Nicholas John Cull, *Selling War: The British Propaganda Campaign against American "Neutrality" in World War II* (New York: Oxford University Press, 1995), 157–8.
22 Meacham, *Franklin and Winston*, 75.
23 Paul W. White, *News on the Air* (New York: Harcourt Brace, 1947), 31.
24 See Eytan Gilboa, "The CNN Effect: The Search for a Communication

Theory of International Relations," *Political Communication* 22 (2005), 27–44.

25 www.fdrlibrary.marist.edu/_resources/images/msf/msf01403.

26 Eric Sevareid, *Not So Wild a Dream* (New York: Atheneum, 1976), 178.

27 Murrow, *This Is London*, 150, 152, 158–9.

28 Edward R. Murrow, "A Report to America," in "In Honor of a Man and an Ideal: Three Talks on Freedom," CBS, December 2, 1941, 31.

29 Archibald MacLeish, "A Superstition Is Destroyed," in "In Honor of a Man and an Ideal: Three Talks on Freedom," CBS, December 2, 1941, 6, 7.

30 Stanley Karnow, *Vietnam: A History* (New York: Penguin, 1991), 526–7.

31 Clark Clifford, *Counsel to the President* (New York: Random House, 1991), 474.

32 Turner Catledge, *My Life and The Times* (New York: Harper & Row, 1971), 264. See also Seib, *Headline Diplomacy*, 74.

33 Max Frankel, *High Noon in the Cold War: Kennedy, Khrushchev, and the Cuban Missile Crisis* (New York: Presidio Press, 2004), 105.

34 www.archives.gov/publications/prologue/2002/fall/cuban-missiles.html.

35 Graham Allison, "The Cuban Missile Crisis at 50," *Foreign Affairs* 91, no. 4 (July/August 2012), 16.

36 Quoted in Prochnau, *Once Upon a Distant War*, 220.

37 Prochnau, *Once Upon a Distant War*, 143.

38 Prochnau, *Once Upon a Distant War*, 378.

39 See Prochnau, *Once Upon a Distant War.*

40 Quoted in Richard Reeves, *President Kennedy: Profile of Power* (New York: Simon & Schuster, 1993), 636–7.

41 Prochnau, *Once Upon a Distant War*, 454.

42 Quoted in Prochnau, *Once Upon a Distant War*, 405.

43 Richard Harwood and Haynes Johnson, *Lyndon* (New York: Praeger, 1973), 122–3.

44 Reeves, *President Kennedy*, 282.

45 Benjamin C. Bradlee, *Conversations with Kennedy* (New York: W. W. Norton, 1975), 58.

46 www.americanwarlibrary.com/vietnam/vwatl.htm.

47 www.vvmf.org/wall-facts.

48 See Guenter Lewy, *America in Vietnam* (New York: Oxford University Press, 1978), 442–53.

49 Michael J. Arlen, *Living-Room War* (New York: Viking, 1969), 7.

50 Arlen, *Living-Room War*, 83.

51 Arlen, *Living-Room War*, 81–2.

52 James H. Willbanks, *The Tet Offensive* (New York: Columbia University Press, 2007), 30.

53 Clifford, *Counsel to the President*, 479.

54 Peter Arnett, *Live from the Battlefield* (New York: Simon & Schuster, 1994), 256.

55 Herbert Y. Schandler, *The Unmaking of a President* (Princeton University Press, 1977), 81.
56 Arnett, *Live from the Battlefield*, 257.
57 Daniel Hallin, *The "Uncensored War": The Media and Vietnam* (Berkeley: University of California Press, 1989), 173.
58 Hallin, *The "Uncensored War,"* 53.
59 Don Oberdorfer, *Tet* (New York: Avon, 1971), 264.
60 www.npr.org/templates/story/story.php?storyId=106775685.
61 Quoted in Townsend Hoopes, *The Limits of Intervention* (New York: David McKay Co., 1969), 140.
62 Hoopes, *The Limits of Intervention*, 156.
63 www.pewresearch.org/fact-tank/2013/11/22/50-years-ago-america-turned-on-the-television.
64 Quoted in Austin Ranney, *Channels of Power* (New York: Basic Books, 1983), 134.
65 Quoted in Schandler, *The Unmaking of a President*, 198.
66 Braestrup, *Big Story*, 508.
67 Braestrup, *Big Story*, 468.
68 Quoted in John Lewis Gaddis, *George F. Kennan: An American Life* (New York: Penguin, 2011), 593.

2 Competing for Information Control

1 Jeffrey Gottfried, Galen Stocking, and Elizabeth Grieco, "Partisans Remain Sharply Divided in Their Attitudes About the News Media," Pew Research Center, September 25, 2018, www.journalism.org/2018/09/25/partisans-remain-sharply-divided-in-their-attitudes-about-the-news-media.
2 Amy Mitchell, Katerina Eva Matsa, Elisa Shearer, et al., "In Western Europe, Public Attitudes Toward News Media More Divided by Populist Views Than Left–Right Ideology," Pew Research Center, May 14, 2018, www.journalism.org/2018/05/14/in-western-europe-public-attitudes-toward-news-media-more-divided-by-populist-views-than-left-right-ideology.
3 Marvin Kalb, "A View from the Press," in W. Lance Bennett and David L. Paletz, *Taken by Storm: The Media, Public Opinion, and Foreign Policy in the Gulf War* (University of Chicago Press, 1994), 4.
4 A. J. H. Bouwmeester, "Showtime: Embedded News Media During Operation Iraqi Freedom," *Militaire Spectator*, www.militairespectator.nl/sites/default/files/uitgaven/inhoudsopgave/MS%206-2006%20Bouwmeester%20Embedded%20news%20media%20during%20Operation%20Iraqi%20Freedom.pdf.
5 Seib, *Headline Diplomacy*, 60–7.
6 Robert Harris, *Gotcha! The Media, the Government, and the Falklands Crisis* (London: Faber and Faber, 1983), 62.
7 Quoted in Derrik Mercer, Geoff Mungham, and Kevin Williams, *The Fog of War* (London: Heinemann, 1987), 23.

8   Quoted in Leonard Downie, Jr., "How Britain Managed the News," *Washington Post*, August 20, 1982.

9   Harris, *Gotcha!* 56.

10 Mercer, Mungham, and Williams, *The Fog of War*, 156.

11 Quoted in Michael Cockerell, *Live from Number 10* (London: Faber and Faber, 1988), 270.

12 Glasgow University Media Group, *War and Peace News* (Milton Keynes: Open University Press, 1985), 9.

13 Cockerell, *Live from Number 10*, 274.

14 Quoted in Simon Jenkins, "When Soldiers Play Journalist and Journalists Play at Soldiers," *The Times*, May 10, 1982.

15 Quoted in Harris, *Gotcha!* 50.

16 Denis Healey, *The Time of My Life* (New York: W. W. Norton, 1990), 495.

17 Peter Jenkins, *Mrs. Thatcher's Revolution* (Cambridge, MA: Harvard University Press, 1988), 163.

18 Quoted in Downie, "How Britain Managed the News."

19 Quoted in Cockerell, *Live from Number 10*, 275.

20 John Meacham, *Destiny and Power: The American Odyssey of George Herbert Walker Bush* (New York: Random House, 2015), 417.

21 Jean Edward Smith, *George Bush's War* (New York: Henry Holt, 1992), 103.

22 Lawrence Grossman, "A Television Plan for the Next War," *Nieman Reports* (Summer 1991), 28.

23 John Martin, "The Plan to Sell the War," *ABC News 20/20*, January 17, 1992.

24 Woodward, *The Commanders*, 130.

25 Everette E. Dennis (ed.), *The Media at War* (New York: Gannett Foundation Media Center, 1991), 1.

26 Daniel C. Hallin and Todd Gitlin, "The Gulf War as Popular Culture and Television Drama," in Bennett and Paletz (eds.), *Taken by Storm*, 154.

27 Jason DeParle, "Long Series of Military Decisions Led to Gulf War News Censorship," *New York Times*, May 5, 1991.

28 Dennis, *The Media at War*, 68.

29 DeParle, "Long Series of Military Decisions."

30 DeParle, "Long Series of Military Decisions."

31 Dennis, *The Media at War*, 70.

32 Johanna Neuman, *Lights, Camera, War* (New York: St. Martin's, 1996), 215.

33 Marcy Darnovsky, "The Media Environment after Desert Storm," in Marcy Darnovsky, Barbara Epstein, and Richard Flacks (eds.), *Cultural Politics* (Philadelphia: Temple University Press, 1995), 223.

34 Murrow, "A Report to America," 21.

35 Martin Walker and David Fairhall, "Iraqi Missiles Strike Israel," *Guardian*, January 18, 1991.

36   Elisabeth Bumiller, "U.S. Lifts Photo Ban on Military Coffins," *New York Times*, December 7, 2009.
37   www.cnn.com/2016/01/19/middleeast/operation-desert-storm-25-years-later/index.html.
38   Douglas Kellner, "The Persian Gulf TV War Revisited," in Allan and Zelizer (eds.), *Reporting War*, 144.
39   www.ncbi.nlm.nih.gov/pubmed/8071721.
40   www.pbs.org/wgbh/pages/frontline/gulf.html.
41   Judge Leonard B. Sand, "Excerpts from the Court Opinion," in Hedrick Smith (ed.), *The Media and the Gulf War* (Washington: Seven Locks Press, 1992), 415.
42   John Van, "Satellites Signal New Era in News Coverage, Viewing," *Chicago Tribune*, March 22, 2003.
43   Patrick O'Heffernan, "A Mutual Exploitation Model of Media Influence in Foreign Policy," in Bennett and Paletz (eds.), *Taken by Storm*, 241.
44   Richard N. Haass, *War of Necessity, War of Choice* (New York: Simon & Schuster, 2010), 5–6.
45   Howard Kurtz, "The *Post* on WMDs: An Inside Story," *Washington Post*, August 12, 2004.
46   Kurtz, "The *Post* on WMDs."
47   Kurtz, "The *Post* on WMDs."
48   Daniel Okrent, "Weapons of Mass Destruction? Or Mass Distraction?" *New York Times*, May 30, 2004.
49   Seib, *Beyond the Front Lines*, 32.
50   John Pilger, "Why Are Wars Not Being Reported Honestly?" *Guardian*, December 10, 2010.
51   Barry Sussman, "The Press Gets a Low Grade for Pre-Iraq War Reporting," *Nieman Watchdog*, September 29, 2008.
52   Paul Krugman, "Behind the Great Divide," *New York Times*, February 18, 2003.
53   United States Department of Defense, "Public Affairs Guidance on Embedding Media During Possible Future Operations/Deployments in the U.S. Central Command's Area of Responsibility," www.defenselink.mil/news/Feb2003/d20030228pag, 1–2.
54   Howard Kurtz, "The Ups and Downs of Unembedded Reporters," *Washington Post*, April 3, 2003.
55   John Laurence, "Embedding: A Military View," *Columbia Journalism Review*, March/April 2003, www.cjr.org/year/03/02/webspecial. Cited in Seib, *Beyond the Front Lines*, 53.
56   Pew Research Center for the People and the Press, "War Coverage Praised, But Public Hungry for Other News," April 9, 2003, www.pewresearch.org/politics/2003/04/09/war-coverage-praised-but-public-hungry-for-other-news.
57   Jacqueline E. Sharkey, "The Television War," *American Journalism Review* 25, no. 4 (May 2003), 20.
58   https://watson.brown.edu/costsofwar/costs/human/civilians/iraqi.
59   https://watson.brown.edu/costsofwar/costs/human/military.

60 https://en.wikipedia.org/wiki/Casualties_of_the_Iraq_War.

61 W. Lance Bennett, Regina G. Lawrence, and Steven Livingston, *When the Press Fails: Political Power and the News Media from Iraq to Katrina* (University of Chicago Press, 2007), 106–7.

62 Haass, *War of Necessity*, xx–xxii.

63 Seib, *Beyond the Front Lines*, 93.

64 Howard Kurtz, "'Webloggers' Signing On as War Correspondents," *Washington Post*, March 23, 2003.

65 James Dao, "Pentagon Keeps Wary Watch as Troops Blog," *New York Times*, September 8, 2009.

66 John Hockenberry, "The Blogs of War," *Wired*, August 1, 2005, www.wired.com/2005/08/milblogs.

67 Jeffrey Ghannam, "Social Media in the Arab World: Leading Up to the Uprisings of 2011," Center for International Media Assistance, National Endowment for Democracy, February 3, 2011, 30.

68 Quoted in Frank Rich, "Wallflowers at the Revolution," *New York Times*, February 5, 2011.

69 Philip Seib, *Real-Time Diplomacy: Politics and Power in the Social Media Era* (New York: Palgrave Macmillan, 2012), 33.

70 Clay Shirky, "From Innovation to Revolution: Do Social Media Make Protests Possible?" *Foreign Affairs* 90, no. 2 (March/April 2011), 154.

71 www.statista.com/statistics/274774/forecast-of-mobile-phone-users-worldwide.

72 Colombia, India, Jordan, Kenya, Lebanon, Mexico, Philippines, South Africa, Tunisia, Venezuela, and Vietnam.

73 Aaron Smith, Laura Silver, Courtney Johnson, Kyle Taylor, and Jingjing Jaing, "Publics in Emerging Economies Worry Social Media Sow Division, Even As They Offer New Chances for Political Engagement," Pew Research Center, May 13, 2019, www.pewinternet.org/2019/05/13/publics-in-emerging-economies-worry-social-media-sow-division-even-as-they-offer-new-chances-for-political-engagement.

74 Megan Specia, "How Syria's Death Toll Is Lost in the Fog of War," *New York Times*, April 13, 2018.

75 www.unhcr.org/en-us/syria-emergency.html.

76 http://worldpopulationreview.com/countries/syria-population.

77 Sahar Khamis, Paul H. Gold, and Katherine Vaughn, "Beyond Egypt's 'Facebook Revolution' and Syria's 'YouTube Uprising': Comparing Political Contexts, Actors, and Communication Strategies," *Arab Media & Society* 15 (Spring 2012), www.arabmediasociety.com/index.php?article=791&p=0.

3 War Information Expands

1 https://reason.com/2009/01/07/the-death-of-one-man-is-a-trag.

2 www.un.org/en/genocideprevention/genocide.shtml.

3 Bill Clinton, "Remarks by the President to Genocide Survivors, Assistance Workers, and U.S. and Rwandan Government Officials," Kigali,

Rwanda, March 25, 1998, www.whitehouse.gov/Africa/19980325-1872.html.

4   Kofi Annan, "Transcript of Press Conference in Gigiri, Kenya," United Nations press release SG/SM/6547, May 4, 1998.

5   Romeo Dallaire, "The Media and the Rwanda Genocide," in Allan Thompson (ed.), *Media and Mass Atrocity: The Rwanda Genocide and Beyond* (Waterloo, ON: Center for International Governance Innovation, 2019), 25.

6   Dallaire, "The Media and the Rwanda Genocide," 18.

7   www.ohchr.org/EN/NewsEvents/Pages/Racismignitesconflictanditmust bechallengedatalllevels.aspx.

8   For further information about Rwanda and genocide, see Samantha Power, *"A Problem from Hell": America and the Age of Genocide* (New York: Basic Books, 2002), 329–89, and Thompson (ed.), *Media and Mass Atrocity.*

9   Charlayne Hunter-Gault, *New News Out of Africa: Uncovering Africa's Renaissance* (New York: Oxford University Press, 2008), 117.

10 Peter Maass, *Love Thy Neighbor* (New York: Knopf, 1996), 76.

11 Maass, *Love Thy Neighbor*, 104.

12 Harry Kreisler, "Witness to Genocide: Conversation with Roy Gutman," Institute of International Studies, University of California at Berkeley, globetrotter.berkeley.edu/conversations/Gutman.

13 David Rieff, "Murder in the Neighborhood," in Nicolaus Mills and Kira Brunner (eds.), *The New Killing Fields: Massacre and the Politics of Intervention* (New York: Basic Books, 2002), 66.

14 Nadda Osman, "Egypt Censors Media from Reporting on Libya, Sinai, Renaissance Dam and Covid-19," *Middle East Eye*, June 19, 2020, www.middleeasteye.net/news/egypt-media-censors-libya-sinai-renaissance-dam-covid.

15 Bell, *In Harm's Way*, 129.

16 David Rieff, *Slaughterhouse: Bosnia and the Failure of the West* (New York: Simon & Schuster, 1995), 216.

17 Walter Goodman, "Horror and Despair in the Balkans," *New York Times,* July 25, 1995.

18 Roy Gutman, *A Witness to Genocide* (New York: Macmillan, 1993), vii.

19 Bell, *In Harm's Way*, 108.

20 Philip Seib, *The Global Journalist: News and Conscience in a World of Conflict* (Lanham, MD: Rowman and Littlefield, 2002), 55.

21 See also, *re* Bosnia: Power, *"A Problem from Hell,"* 247–327, 391–441.

22 "Myanmar Rohingya: What You Need To Know about the Crisis," BBC, January 23, 2020, www.bbc.com/news/world-asia-41566561.

23 United Nations Office for the Coordination of Humanitarian Affairs (UNOCHA), www.unocha.org/rohingya-refugee-crisis.

24 Hannah Ellis-Petersen, "Myanmar Frees Reuters Journalists Jailed for Reporting on Rohingya Crisis," *Guardian*, May 7, 2019.

25 Nicholas Kristof, "I Saw a Genocide in Slow Motion," *New York Times*, March 2, 2018.

26 www.cia.gov/library/publications/the-world-factbook/geos/bm.html.

27 Hong Tien Vu and Nyan Lynn, "When the News Takes Sides: Automated Framing Analysis of News Coverage of the Rohingya Crisis by the Elite Press from Three Countries," *Journalism Studies* 21, no. 9 (2020), 1284–1304.

28 Lisa Brooten and Yola Verbruggen, "The Problems of Reporting on the Rohingya Crisis," East Asia Forum, December 16, 2017, www.eastasiaforum.org/2017/12/16/the-problems-of-reporting-on-the-rohingya-crisis.

29 Ralph Rinalli, "The 'Next Rwanda' Will Look Different," Harvard Kennedy School, www.hks.harvard.edu/faculty-research/policy-topics/human-rights-justice/samantha-power-reflects-what-weve-learned-and.

30 www.un.org/en/genocideprevention/about-responsibility-to-protect.shtml.

31 Eleanor Albert and Lindsay Maizland, "The Rohingya Crisis," Council on Foreign Relations, January 23, 2020, www.cfr.org/backgrounder/rohingya-crisis.

32 Katy Long, "Are Humanitarians Making the Rohingya Crisis Worse?" *Washington Post*, December 4, 2017.

33 Howard Rosenberg, "What We Continue to Miss in Bosnia," *Los Angeles Times*, June 7, 1995.

34 Bell, *In Harm's Way*, 127–8.

35 Bell, *In Harm's Way*, 134.

36 Martin Bell, *War and the Death of News* (London: Oneworld, 2017), 87–8.

37 Bell, *War and the Death of News*, 88.

38 Christiane Amanpour, "Television's Role in Foreign Policy," *Quill*, April 1996, 17.

39 Nik Gowing, "Real-Time Television Coverage of Armed Conflicts and Diplomatic Crises: Does It Pressure or Distort Foreign Policy Decisions?" Working Paper 94-1, Joan Shorenstein Barone Center, John F. Kennedy School of Government, Harvard University, June 1994, 85.

40 William J. Burns, *The Back Channel: A Memoir of American Diplomacy and the Case for Its Renewal* (New York: Random House, 2019), 394.

41 www.canon-europe.com/pro/stories/james-nachtwey-memoria-interview.

42 Luis Carballo, "James Nachtwey: We Must Think Deeply Before People Commit to War," Euronews, October 21, 2016, www.euronews.com/2016/10/21/james-nachtwey-we-must-think-deeply-before-people-commit-to-war.

43 *War Photographer* (film), Christian Frei Filmproduction, 2001.

44 Torin Douglas, "Shaping the Media with Mobiles," BBC, August 4, 2005, http://news.bbc.co.uk/2/hi/uk_news/4745767.stm.

45 Gwilym Mumford, "*City of Ghosts* director Matthew Heineman:

'Imagine Seeing People Crucified – Every Day,'" *Guardian*, July 21, 2017.

46 Matthew Heineman (writer, producer, director), *City of Ghosts* (film), Amazon Studios, 2017.

47 Lindsey Hilsum, "The Smartphone War," *New York Review of Books*, April 19, 2018.

48 Daniel Green and Jacob Granger, "Mobile Journalism Training Helps Sudanese Citizen Journalists Tell Their Own Stories," journalism.co.uk, April 29, 2019, www.journalism.co.uk/news/report-mobile-journalism-training-helps-sudanese-citizen-journalists-tell-their-own-stories/s2/a737902.

49 Matthew Daniels, "The Forgotten Toll of Terrorism in Nigeria," *Washington Times*, May 15, 2019.

50 www.bellingcat.com.

51 Jacob Beeders, "What Happened at Kulbiyow, Somalia: An Open Source Investigation," Bellingcat, March 21, 2017, www.bellingcat.com/news/africa/2017/03/21/happened-kulbiyow-somalia-open-source-investigation.

52 "Yemen Project Release: Attacks Causing Grave Civilian Harm," Bellingcat, September 2, 2019, www.bellingcat.com/news/mena/2019/09/02/attacks-causing-grave-civilian-harm.

53 Christiaan Triebert, Evan Hill, Malachy Browne, Whitney Hurst, and Dmitriy Khavin, "Proving Russia Bombed Hospitals," *New York Times*, October 13, 2019.

54 See Caroline Alexander, *The War that Killed Achilles* (New York: Viking, 2009), 217–18.

55 Joyce Hoffman, *On Their Own: Women Journalists and the American Experience in Vietnam* (Cambridge, MA: Da Capo Press, 2008), 1, 3, 12.

56 Hoffman, *On Their Own*, 170.

57 Hoffman, *On Their Own*, 268.

58 "Public Affairs Guidance on Embedding Media During Possible Future Operations/Deployments in the U.S. Central Command's Area of Responsibility," US Department of Defense, www.defenselink.mil/news/Feb2003/d20030228pag.

59 Hannah Allam, "The Woman Question," in Zahra Hankir (ed.), *Our Women on the Ground: Essays by Arab Women Reporting from the Arab World* (New York: Penguin, 2019), 1–2.

60 Jane Arraf, "Maps of Iraq," in Hankir (ed.), *Our Women on the Ground*, 62.

61 Zaina Erhaim, "Hurma," in Hankir (ed.), *Our Women on the Ground*, 215.

62 Romy Froehlich, "Women, the Media, and War," in Josef Seethaler, Matthias Karmasin, Gabriele Melischek, and Romy Wohlert (eds.), *Selling War: The Role of the Mass Media in Hostile Conflicts* (Chicago: Intellect, 2013), 164, 174.

63 "YPJ: Women's Protection Units," https://thekurdishproject.org/history-and-culture/kurdish-women/ypj.
64 www.unhcr.org/figures-at-a-glance.html.
65 Matthew Brunwasser, "A 21st-Century Migrant's Essentials: Food, Shelter, Smartphone," *New York Times*, August 26, 2015.
66 Ivy Kaplan, "How Smartphones and Social Media Have Revolutionized Refugee Migration," UNHCR Blogs, October 26, 2018, www.unhcr.org/blogs/smartphones-revolutionized-refugee-migration.
67 "Phones Are Now Indispensable for Refugees," *Economist*, February 11, 2017, www.economist.com/international/2017/02/11/phones-are-now-indispensable-for-refugees.
68 "Phones Are Now Indispensable for Refugees."
69 www.infomigrants.net/en/about.
70 www.refugee.info/greece/welcome/welcome-to-refugee-info?language=en.
71 www.signpost.ngo.
72 www.etcluster.org/about-etc.

4 Social Media Go to War

1 "World Internet Users and 2020 Population Statistics," https://internet-worldstats.com/stats.htm.
2 www.washingtonpost.com/graphics/2019/investigations/afghanistan-papers/documents-database.
3 www.statista.com/statistics/218984/number-of-global-mobile-users-since-2010.
4 Barbie Zelizer, "When War Is Reduced to a Photograph," in Allan and Zelizer (eds.), *Reporting War*, 115.
5 Andrew Hoskins and Ben O'Loughlin, *War and Media: The Emergence of Diffused War* (Cambridge: Polity, 2010), 23.
6 Susan Sontag, *On Photography* (New York: Picador, 1990), 5.
7 Gary S. Messinger, *The Battle for the Mind: War and Peace in the Era of Mass Communication* (Amherst: University of Massachusetts Press, 2011), 8.
8 Sontag, *On Photography*, 18.
9 Evelyn Theiss, "The Photographer Who Showed the World What Really Happened at My Lai," *Time*, March 15, 2018, https://time.com/longform/my-lai-massacre-ron-haeberle-photographs.
10 Torie Rose DeGhett, "The War Photo No One Would Publish," *Atlantic*, August 8, 2014, www.theatlantic.com/international/archive/2014/08/the-war-photo-no-one-would-publish/375762.
11 DeGhett, "The War Photo No One Would Publish."
12 Harold Evans, "Facing a Grim Reality," *American Photo*, July–August 1991, 48.
13 DeGhett, "The War Photo No One Would Publish."

14 Donald Matheson and Stuart Allan, *Digital War Reporting* (Cambridge: Polity, 2009), 146.
15 Philip Kennicott, "A Wretched New Picture of America," *Washington Post*, May 5, 2004.
16 www.omnicoreagency.com/instagram-statistics.
17 Lynsey Addario, *It's What I Do: A Photographer's Life of Love and War* (New York: Penguin, 2015), 191.
18 Quoted in Sontag, *On Photography*, 186.
19 Donald R. Winslow, "Reuters Apologizes over Altered Lebanon War Photographs," *NPPA News*, August 7, 2006, nppa.org/news/2156.
20 www.cnn.com/2016/08/15/health/september-11-cancer-diagnoses/index.html.
21 Joseph Nye, *Do Morals Matter?* (New York: Oxford University Press, 2020), 156.
22 Charlie Winter, "ISIS Is Using the Media Against Itself," *Atlantic*, March 23, 2016, www.theatlantic.com/international/archive/2016/03/isis-propaganda-brussels/475002.
23 Counter Extremism Project, "Terrorists on Telegram," www.counterextremism.com/terrorists-on-telegram.
24 Charlie Winter, "Redefining 'Propaganda': The Media Strategy of the Islamic State," *RUSI Journal*, January 2020, 3.
25 Philip Seib, *As Terrorism Evolves: Media, Religion, and Governance* (Cambridge University Press, 2017), 113.
26 Steve Coll and Susan B. Glasser, "Terrorists Move Operations to Cyberspace," *Washington Post*, August 7, 2005.
27 Nadya Labi, "Jihad 2.0," *Atlantic Monthly*, July–August 2006, 102.
28 Seib, *As Terrorism Evolves*, 117.
29 Jesse Morton, "I Invented the Jihadist Journal," *Wall Street Journal*, June 3, 2019.
30 Graham Macklin, "The Christchurch Attacks: Livestream Terror in the Viral Video Age," *CTC Sentinel* (Combating Terrorism Center at West Point) 12, no. 6, July 2019.
31 Elizabeth Dwoskin and Craig Timberg, "Inside YouTube's Struggles to Shut Down Video of the New Zealand Shooting – and the Humans Who Outsmarted Its Systems," *Washington Post*, March 18, 2019.
32 Tiffany Hsu, "2,200 Viewed Germany Shooting Before Twitch Removed Post," *New York Times*, October 9, 2019.
33 Emily Bell, "Terrorism Bred Online Requires Anticipatory, Not Reactionary Coverage," *Columbia Journalism Review*, March 21, 2019, www.cjr.org/tow_center/facebook-twitter-christchurch-emily-bell-terrorism.php.
34 Paul Chadwick, "How to Report Terrorism: Name, But Don't Amplify," *Guardian*, March 24, 2019.
35 www.cia.gov/library/publications/the-world-factbook/geos/gz.html.
36 P. W. Singer and Emerson T. Brooking, *Like War: The Weaponization of Social Media* (New York: Houghton Mifflin Harcourt, 2018), 197.
37 Nikolaj Krak, "When Bombs Receive Applause," *Kristeligt Dagblad*,

July 11, 2014, www.kristeligt-dagblad.dk/2014-07-11/when-bombs-receive-applause.

38 David Patrikarakos, *War in 140 Characters* (New York: Basic Books, 2017), 47.

39 Ian Burrell, "Israel–Gaza Conflict: Social Media Becomes the Latest Battleground in Middle East Aggression – But Beware of Propaganda and Misinformation," *Independent*, July 14, 2014, www.independent.co.uk/news/world/middle-east/israel-gaza-conflict-social-media-becomes-the-latest-battleground-in-middle-east-aggression-but-9605952.html.

40 William Merrin, *Digital War: A Critical Introduction* (London: Routledge, 2019), 201.

41 Patrikarakos, *War in 140 Characters*, 63.

42 Thomas Zeitzoff, "Does Social Media Influence Conflict? Evidence from the 2012 Gaza Conflict," *Journal of Conflict Resolution* 62, no. 1, January 2018, 29.

43 Merrin, *Digital War*, 199.

44 Michele Bos and Jan Melissen, "Rebel Diplomacy and Digital Communication: Public Diplomacy in the Sahel," *International Affairs* 95, no. 6 (November 2019), 1331, 1339.

45 Bos and Melissen, "Rebel Diplomacy and Digital Communication," 1343, 1346.

46 Bos and Melissen, "Rebel Diplomacy and Digital Communication," 1347.

47 Matthew Wallin, "Military Public Diplomacy: How the Military Influences Foreign Audiences," American Security Project White Paper, February 2015, 5, www.americansecurityproject.org/wp-content/uploads/2015/02/Ref-0185-Military-Public-Diplomacy.pdf.

48 Wallin, "Military Public Diplomacy," 26.

49 Wallin, "Military Public Diplomacy," 35.

50 Wallin, "Military Public Diplomacy," 21.

51 Marc Grossman, "Diplomacy Before and After Conflict," *Prism* (National Defense University) 1, no. 4 (September 2010), 12.

5 Russia and New Dimensions of Information at War

1 Hemming, *Agents of Influence*, 165.
2 Hemming, *Agents of Influence*, 166.
3 Hemming, *Agents of Influence*, 167.
4 Hemming, *Agents of Influence*, 261.
5 Cull, *Selling War*, 158.
6 John Lewis Gaddis, *The Cold War: A New History* (New York: Penguin, 2005), 84.
7 Allen Dulles, *The Craft of Intelligence* (New York: Signet Books, 1965), 212–13.
8 Frances Stonor Saunders, *The Cultural Cold War: The CIA and the World of Arts and Letters* (New York: New Press, 1999), 1.

9   Stonor Saunders, *The Cultural Cold War*, 85.
10 Gregory M. Tomlin, *Murrow's Cold War: Public Diplomacy for the Kennedy Administration* (Dulles, VA: Potomac Books, 2016), 44.
11 Tomlin, *Murrow's Cold War*, 29, 40.
12 Tomlin, *Murrow's Cold War*, 98.
13 Esko Salminem, *The Silenced Media: The Propaganda War Between Russia and the West in Northern Europe* (London: Macmillan, 1999), 2–3.
14 Seth G. Jones, *A Covert Action: Reagan, the CIA, and the Cold War Struggle in Poland* (New York: W. W. Norton, 2020), 240.
15 Jones, *A Covert Action*, 248.
16 Jones, *A Covert Action*, 303.
17 Frederick C. Barghoorn, *Soviet Foreign Propaganda* (Princeton University Press, 1964), 7.
18 https://tass.com/history.
19 https://ria.ru.
20 "Georgia 'Started Unjustified War,'" BBC, September 30, 2009, http://news.bbc.co.uk/2/hi/europe/8281990.stm.
21 Julia Ioffe, "What Is Russia Today?" *Columbia Journalism Review*, September/October 2010, https://archives.cjr.org/feature/what_is_russia_today.php.
22 Amanda Erickson, "If Russia Today Is Moscow's Propaganda Arm, It's Not Very Good at Its Job," *Washington Post*, January 12, 2017.
23 Jim Rutenberg, "RT, Sputnik and Russia's New Theory of War," *New York Times Magazine*, September 13, 2017.
24 Rutenberg, "RT, Sputnik."
25 Neil MacFarquhar, "Playing on Kansas City Radio: Russian Propaganda," *New York Times*, February 13, 2020.
26 Mark Galeotti, "The 'Gerasimov Doctrine' and Russian Non-Linear War," In Moscow's Shadows, June 7, 2014, https://inmoscowsshadows.wordpress.com/2014/07/06/the-gerasimov-doctrine-and-russian-non-linear-war.
27 Quoted in Galeotti, "The 'Gerasimov Doctrine.'"
28 Andrew E. Kramer, "Russian General Pitches 'Information' Operations as a Form of War," *New York Times*, March 2, 2019.
29 Vladimir Isachenkov, "Russia Military Acknowledges New Branch: Info Warfare Troops," *Military Times*, February 22, 2017, www.militarytimes.com/news/pentagon-congress/2017/02/22/russia-military-acknowledges-new-branch-info-warfare-troops.
30 Keir Giles, *The Next Phase of Russian Information Warfare* (Riga, Latvia: NATO Strategic Communications Centre of Excellence, 2016), 3.
31 Rand Waltzman, "The Weaponization of Information," Testimony before the Committee on Armed Services, Subcommittee on Cybersecurity, United States Senate, April 27, 2017, 6, www.rand.org/pubs/testimonies/CT473.html.
32 Quoted in Ofer Fridman, "'Information War' as the Russian

Conceptualisation of Strategic Communications," *RUSI Journal* 165, no. 1 (March 2020), 4.

33   Cited in Oscar Jonsson, *A Russian Understanding of War: Blurring the Lines Between War and Peace* (Washington: Georgetown University Press, 2019), 118.

34   Giorgio Bertolin, "Conceptualizing Russian Information Operations: Info-War and Infiltration in the Context of Hybrid War," *IO Sphere*, Summer 2015, 10 (cited in Christopher Paul and Miriam Matthews, *The Russian "Firehose of Falsehood" Propaganda Model* [Santa Monica, CA: RAND, 2016], 1).

35   "Manoeuvring into the Future of Information Manoeuvre," www. army.mod.uk/news-and-events/news/2020/03/manoeuvring-into-the-future-of-information-manoeuvre.

36   www.army.mod.uk/who-we-are/formations-divisions-brigades/6th-united-kingdom-division/77-brigade.

37   Paul and Matthews, *The Russian "Firehose of Falsehood" Propaganda Model*, 2–4, 6–7.

38   www.npr.org/sections/alltechconsidered/2016/07/24/486941582/the-reason-your-feed-became-an-echo-chamber-and-what-to-do-about-it.

39   Amol Rajan, "Do Digital Echo Chambers Exist?" BBC, March 4, 2019, www.bbc.com/news/entertainment-arts-47447633.

40   Singer and Brooking, *Like War*, 111.

41   Singer and Brooking, *Like War*, 111–12.

42   Adrian Chen, "The Agency," *New York Times Magazine*, June 7, 2015.

43   Singer and Brooking, *Like War*, 113.

44   David E. Sanger, *The Perfect Weapon* (New York: Broadway Books, 2019), 183.

45   *The Mueller Report* (New York: Scribner, 2019), 14.

46   *The Mueller Report*, 74.

47   *The Mueller Report*, 75.

48   *The Mueller Report*, 93.

49   *The Mueller Report*, 551.

50   *The Mueller Report*, 563, 564.

51   *The Mueller Report*, 568.

52   www.nytimes.com/elections/2016/results/president.

53   Devlin Barrett, Sari Horwitz, and Rosalind S. Heiderman, "Russian Troll Farm, 13 Suspects Indicted in 2016 Election Interference," *Washington Post*, February 16, 2018.

54   Ellen Nakashima, "U.S. Cyber Command Operation Disrupted Internet Access of Russian Troll Factory on Day of 2018 Midterms," *Washington Post*, February 27, 2019.

55   David Ignatius, "The U.S. Military Is Quietly Launching Efforts to Deter Russian Meddling," *Washington Post*, February 7, 2019.

56   "An Interview with Paul M. Nakasone," *Joint Force Quarterly* no. 92 (January 2019), 4.

57   "An Interview with Paul M. Nakasone," 6–7.

58   Ignatius, "The U.S. Military Is Quietly Launching."

59 Nakashima, "U.S. Cyber Command Operation Disrupted Internet."

60 Erica D. Borghard, "What a U.S. Operation Against Russian Trolls Predicts About Escalation in Cyberspace," *War on the Rocks*, March 22, 2019, https://warontherocks.com/2019/03/what-a-u-s-operation-against-russian-trolls-predicts-about-escalation-in-cyberspace.

61 http://likumi.lv/ta/en/lv/starptautiskie-ligumi/id/997.

62 www.stratcomcoe.org/about-us.

63 "The Art of Info-war," *The Economist*, March 16, 2019.

64 Sanger, *The Perfect Weapon*, 159.

65 Vitaly Shevchenko, "'Little Green Men' or 'Russian Invaders?'" BBC, March 11, 2014, www.bbc.com/news/world-europe-26532154.

66 www.cia.gov/library/publications/the-world-factbook/geos/up.html.

67 Justin Lynch, "StopFake Braces for 'Bombardment' of Russian Propaganda in Ukraine Election," *Columbia Journalism Review*, April 9, 2019, www.cjr.org/watchdog/stopfake-russian-propaganda-ukraine-election.php.

68 Lynch, "StopFake Braces."

69 John Vandiver, "SACEUR: Allies Must Prepare for Russia 'Hybrid War,'" *Stars and Stripes*, September 4, 2014, www.stripes.com/news/saceur-allies-must-prepare-for-russia-hybrid-war-1.301464.

70 Patrikarakos, *War in 140 Characters*, 3.

71 Anna Nemtsova, "There's No Evidence the Ukrainian Army Crucified a Child in Slovyansk," *Daily Beast*, July 15, 2014, www.thedailybeast.com/theres-no-evidence-the-ukrainian-army-crucified-a-child-in-slovyansk?ref=scroll.

72 Rid, *Active Measures*, 353.

73 Chen, "The Agency."

74 Shane Harris, "Hack Attack," *Foreign Policy*, March 3, 2014, https://foreignpolicy.com/2014/03/03/hack-attack.

75 Julia Summers, "Countering Disinformation: Russia's Infowar in Ukraine," Henry M. Jackson School of International Studies, University of Washington, October 25, 2017, https://jsis.washington.edu/news/russia-disinformation-ukraine.

76 Alan Yuhas, "Russian Propaganda over Crimea and the Ukraine: How Does It Work?" *Guardian*, March 17, 2014.

77 www.rferl.org/a/death-toll-up-to-13-000-in-ukraine-conflict-says-un-rights-office/29791647.html.

78 "Ukraine Is Attacked Again. And Again. Repetitive Kremlin Disinformation. Again," *DisInfo Review* no. 168, October 17, 2019, https://euvsdisinfo.eu/ukraine-attacked-again-and-again-repetitive-kremlin-disinformation-again.

79 Freedman, *Ukraine and the Art of Strategy*, 146–7.

80 Vandiver, "SACEUR: Allies Must Prepare."

81 www.cia.gov/library/publications/the-world-factbook.

82 Freedman, *Ukraine and the Art of Strategy*, 136–7.

83 Aija Krutaine, "The Parallel Universes," *Re-Baltica*, November 23, 2015, https://en.rebaltica.lv/2015/11/the-parallel-universes.

84 https://en.wikipedia.org/wiki/ETV%2B.
85 Krutaine, "The Parallel Universes."
86 Krutaine, "The Parallel Universes."
87 Krutaine, "The Parallel Universes."
88 "The Enemy Within," *The Economist*, August 3, 2019, 43.
89 Andy Greenberg, "Hackers Broke Into Real News Sites to Plant Fake Stories," *Wired*, July 29, 2020, www.wired.com/story/hackers-broke-into-real-news-sites-to-plant-fake-stories-anti-nato.
90 Benas Gerdziunas, "Baltics Battle Russia in Online Disinformation War," Deutsche Welle, October 8, 2017, www.dw.com/en/baltics-battle-russia-in-online-disinformation-war/a-40828834.
91 Damien McGuinness, "How a Cyberattack Transformed Estonia," BBC, April 27, 2017, www.bbc.com/news/39655415.
92 Gerdziunas, "Baltics Battle Russia."
93 NATO StratCom Centre of Excellence, "Executive Summary: Internet Trolling as a Tool of Hybrid Warfare: Case of Latvia," July 29, 2015, www.stratcomcoe.org/internet-trolling-hybrid-warfare-tool-case-latvia-0.
94 NATO StratCom, "Internet Trolling."
95 NATO StratCom, "Internet Trolling."
96 "Lithuanians Are Using Software to Fight Back Against Fake News," *The Economist*, October 24, 2019.
97 Benas Gerdziunas, "Lithuania Hits Back at Russian Disinformation," Deutsche Welle, September 27, 2018, www.dw.com/lithuania-hits-back-at-russian-disinformation/a-45644080.
98 Gerdziunas, "Lithuania Hits Back."
99 McGuinness, "How a Cyberattack Transformed Estonia."
100 Andrea Shalal, "Massive Cyber Attack Could Trigger NATO Response: Stoltenberg," Reuters, June 15, 2016, www.reuters.com/article/us-cyber-nato/massive-cyber-attack-could-trigger-nato-response-stoltenberg-idUSKCN0Z12NE.
101 "NATO's Response to Hybrid Threats," www.nato.int/cps/en/natohq/topics_156338.htm.
102 Martin Kragh and Sebastian Asberg, "Russia's Strategy for Influence Through Public Diplomacy and Active Measures: the Swedish Case," *Journal of Strategic Studies* 40, no. 6 (2017), 789, 808.
103 Jon Henley, "Russia Waging Information War Against Sweden, Study Finds," *Guardian*, January 11, 2017.
104 Neil MacFarquhar, "A Powerful Russian Weapon: The Spread of False Stories," *New York Times*, August 28, 2016.
105 Fredrik Lojdquist, "An Ambassador for Countering Hybrid Threats," Royal United Services Institute, September 6, 2019, https://rusi.org/commentary/ambassador-countering-hybrid-threats.
106 Lojdquist, "An Ambassador."
107 https://yle.fi/uutiset/osasto/news/poll_59_of_finns_opposed_to_joining_nato/9917418.
108 Reid Standish, "Why Is Finland Able to Fend Off Putin's Information

War?" *Foreign Policy*, March 1, 2017, https://foreignpolicy.com/2017/03/01/why-is-finland-able-to-fend-off-putins-information-war.

109 Andrew Higgins, "Three Internet Trolls Convicted of Systematic Defamation Against Journalist in Finland," *New York Times*, October 19, 2018.

110 "Naked Untruth," *The Economist*, November 9, 2019, 47.

111 Jessikka Aro, "This Is What Pro-Russia Internet Propaganda Feels Like – Finns Have Been Tricked into Believing in Lies," Yle Kioski, June 24, 2015, https://kioski.yle.fi/omat/this-is-what-pro-russia-internet-propaganda-feels-like.

112 Katherine Costello, "Russia's Use of Media and Information Operations in Turkey," *RAND Perspective* (2018), 4, www.rand.org/content/dam/rand/pubs/perspectives/PE200/PE278/RAND_PE278.pdf.

113 "In Sputnik's Orbit," *The Economist*, March 2, 2019, 43.

114 https://twitter.com/sputnik_TR?ref_src=twsrc%5Egoogle%7Ctwcamp%5Eserp%7Ctwgr%5Eauthor.

115 "In Sputnik's Orbit," 43.

116 Costello, "Russia's Use," 6.

117 Costello, "Russia's Use," 13.

118 "In Sputnik's Orbit," 43.

119 Celine Sui, "China Daily, CGTN Fight for Influence in Africa vs BBC, CNN," *Quartz*, October 29, 2019, https://qz.com/africa/1736534/china-daily-cgtn-fight-for-influence-in-africa-vs-bbc-cnn.

120 Shelby Grossman, Daniel Bush, and Renee DiResta, "Evidence of Russia-Linked Influence Operations in Africa," Stanford Internet Observatory, October 29, 2019, 53, https://fsi-live.s3.us-west-1.amazonaws.com/s3fs-public/29oct2019_sio_-_russia_linked_influence_operations_in_africa.final_.pdf.

121 Grossman, Bush, and DiResta, "Evidence of Russia-Linked Influence," 53; "Russian Disinformation Campaigns Target Africa: An Interview with Dr. Shelby Grossman," Africa Center for Strategic Studies, February 18, 2020, https://africacenter.org/spotlight/russian-disinformation-campaigns-target-africa-interview-shelby-grossman.

122 "Russian Disinformation Campaigns Target Africa: An Interview with Dr. Shelby Grossman."

123 Grossman, Bush, and DiResta, "Evidence of Russia-Linked Influence," 53–4.

6 From Media Manipulation to Media Literacy

1 Owen Pinnell, "The Online War Between Qatar and Saudi Arabia," BBC News, June 3, 2018, www.bbc.com/news/blogs-trending-44294826.

2 Peter Kenyon, "Qatar's Crisis with Saudi Arabia and Gulf Neighbors Has Decades-Long Roots," NPR News, June 17, 2017, www.npr.org/sections/parallels/2017/06/17/533054129/qatars-crisis-with-saudi-arabia-and-gulf-neighbors-has-decades-long-roots.

3 Alex Emmons, "Saudi Arabia Planned to Invade Qatar Last Summer. Rex Tillerson's Efforts to Stop It May Have Cost Him His Job," *Intercept*, August 1, 2018, https://theintercept.com/2018/08/01/rex-tillerson-qatar-saudi-uae.

4 Josh Wood, "How a Diplomatic Crisis Among Gulf Nations Led to a Fake News Campaign in the United States," *Global Post*, July 24, 2018, www.pri.org/stories/2018-07-24/how-diplomatic-crisis-among-gulf-nations-led-fake-news-campaign-united-states.

5 Mujib Mashal and Fahim Abed, "As Afghanistan Seeks Peace, Social Media Raise Fear of Reprisals," *New York Times*, September 4, 2019.

6 Mashal and Abed, "As Afghanistan Seeks Peace."

7 Mashal and Abed, "As Afghanistan Seeks Peace."

8 Samuel Ramani, "Russia Is Winning the Information War in Afghanistan," *Foreign Policy*, August 5, 2020, https://foreignpolicy.com/2020/08/05/russia-is-winning-the-information-war-in-afghanistan.

9 Katherine A. Brown, *Your Country, Our War: The Press and Diplomacy in Afghanistan* (New York: Oxford University Press, 2019), 126.

10 Quoted in Lyse Doucet, "Syria and the CNN Effect: What Role Does the Media Play in Policymaking?" *Daedalus* 147, no. 1 (Winter 2018), 141–2.

11 Doucet, "Syria and the CNN Effect," 146.

12 Quoted in Doucet, "Syria and the CNN Effect," 147.

13 Quoted in Uri Friedman, "The 'CNN Effect' Dies in Syria," *Atlantic*, March 1, 2018, www.theatlantic.com/international/archive/2018/03/cnn-effect-syria/554387.

14 Will Bardenwerper, "War Stories: Can Better Journalism Make Americans Care More about the Battles Fought on Their Behalf?" *Princeton Alumni Weekly*, January 8, 2020, 41.

15 Bardenwerper, "War Stories," 43.

16 www.statista.com/statistics/802690/worldwide-connected-devices-by-access-technology/#statisticContainer.

17 Christian Brose, *The Kill Chain: Defending America in the Future of High-Tech Warfare* (New York: Hachette, 2020), 151.

18 Lori Cameron, "Internet of Things Meets the Military and Battlefield," *Computing Edge*, www.computer.org/publications/tech-news/research/internet-of-military-battlefield-things-iomt-iobt.

19 Chris Telley, "Info Ops Officer Offers Artificial Intelligence Roadmap," *Breaking Defense*, July 11, 2017, https://breakingdefense.com/2017/07/info-ops-officer-offers-artificial-intelligence-roadmap.

20 "Autonomy in Weapons Systems," Department of Defense Directive 3000.09, May 8, 2017, www.esd.whs.mil/Portals/54/Documents/DD/issuances/dodd/300009p.pdf.

21 Sebastien Roblin, "The Pentagon Plans to Deploy an Arsenal of Hypersonic Weapons in the 2020s," *Forbes*, April 30, 2020, www.forbes.com/sites/sebastienroblin/2020/04/30/the-pentagons-plans-to-deploy-an-arsenal-of-hypersonic-weapons-in-the-2020s/#5cec12023a5d.

22   P. W. Singer, *Wired for War: The Robotics Revolution and Conflict in the 21st Century* (New York: Penguin, 2009), 128.

23   Brose, *The Kill Chain*, 113.

24   Walter Pincus, "A General's View of Future Information Wars," *Cipher Brief*, May 19, 2020, www.thecipherbrief.com/column_article/a-generals-view-of-future-information-wars.

25   Soroush Vosoughi, Deb Roy, and Sinan Aral, "The Spread of True and False News Online," *Science* 359, no. 6380 (March 9, 2018), 1146, https://science.sciencemag.org/content/359/6380/1146.

26   "How Young People Consume News and the Implications for Mainstream Media," Reuters Institute for the Study of Journalism, 2019, https://reutersinstitute.politics.ox.ac.uk/our-research/how-young-people-consume-news-and-implications-mainstream-media.

27   Shira Ovide, "Let's Clean Up the Toxic Internet," *New York Times*, May 11, 2020.

28   Elisa Shearer, "Social Media Outpaces Print Newspapers in the U.S. as a News Source," Pew Research Center, December 10, 2018, www.pewresearch.org/fact-tank/2018/12/10/social-media-outpaces-print-newspapers-in-the-u-s-as-a-news-source.

29   "Seize the Memes," *The Economist*, December 21, 2019, 85.

30   Eliza Mackintosh, "Finland Is Winning the War on Fake News," CNN, May 2019, https://edition.cnn.com/interactive/2019/05/europe/finland-fake-news-intl.

31   www.medialit.org/media-literacy-definition-and-more.

32   Mackintosh, "Finland Is Winning the War on Fake News."

33   Jon Henley, "How Finland Starts Its Fight Against Fake News in Primary Schools," *Guardian*, January 29, 2020.

34   Mackintosh, "Finland Is Winning the War on Fake News."

35   Henley, "How Finland Starts."

36   https://euvsdisinfo.eu/about.

37   Nina Jankowicz, *How to Lose the Information War: Russia, Fake News, and the Future of Conflict* (London: I. B. Tauris, 2020), 216–17.

38   https://reporterslab.org/tag/fact-checking-database.

39   www.nytimes.com/2020/04/13/science/putin-russia-disinformation-health-coronavirus.html and https://twitter.com/therussophile/with_replies.

40   William J. Broad, "Putin's Long War Against American Science," *New York Times*, April 13, 2020.

41   www.coveringclimatenow.org/about.

42   Nabih Bulos, "Virus Joins Mideast Misinformation Wars," *Los Angeles Times*, https://enewspaper.latimes.com/infinity/article_share.aspx?guid=3a0d7a1b-90df-4789-9e9d-f2e048578801.

43   Elise Thomas, "As the Coronavirus Spreads, Conspiracy Theories Are Going Viral Too," *Foreign Policy*, April 14, 2020, https://foreignpolicy.com/2020/04/14/as-the-coronavirus-spreads-conspiracy-theories-are-going-viral-too.

44 "Consequences of Disinformation," EUvsDisinfo, February 27, 2020, https://euvsdisinfo.eu/consequences-of-disinformation.

45 Elizabeth Schumacher, "'Malign Actor' Poses as NATO Chief, Emails Lithuania Saying Troops Are Pulling Out," Deutsche Welle, April 22, 2020, www.dw.com/en/malign-actor-poses-as-nato-chief-emails-lithuania-saying-troops-are-pulling-out/a-53209653.

46 Tony Romm, "Millions of Tweets Peddled Conspiracy Theories about Coronavirus in Other Countries, an Unpublished U.S. Report Says," *Washington Post*, February 29, 2020.

47 Betsy Woodruff Swan, "State Report: Russian, Chinese, and Iranian Disinformation Narratives Echo One Another," *Politico*, April 21, 2020, www.politico.com/news/2020/04/21/russia-china-iran-disinformation-coronavirus-state-department-193107.

48 James Pamment, "The EU's Role in Fighting Disinformation: Taking Back the Initiative," Carnegie Endowment for International Peace, July 15, 2020, https://carnegieendowment.org/2020/07/15/eu-s-role-in-fighting-disinformation-taking-back-initiative-pub-82286.

49 Matthew Rosenberg and Julian E. Barnes, "A Bible Burning, a Russian News Agency, and a Story Too Good to Check Out," *New York Times*, August 11, 2020.

50 Globalresearch.ca, www.globalresearch.ca.

51 Julian E. Barnes and David E. Sanger, "Russian Intelligence Agencies Push Disinformation on Pandemic," *New York Times*, July 28, 2020.

52 Associated Press, "U.S. Officials: Russia Behind Spread of Virus Disinformation," July 28, 2020, https://apnews.com/3acb089e6a333e0 51dbc4a465cb68ee1.

53 Broad, "Putin's Long War."

54 "Study by RAND and Oregon State University Finds Conspiracy Beliefs among African Americans Deter Condom Use," RAND Office of Media Relations, January 25, 2005, www.rand.org/news/press/2005/01/25.html.

55 Broad, "Putin's Long War."

56 "Measles Cases and Outbreaks," Centers for Disease Control and Prevention, www.cdc.gov/measles/cases-outbreaks.html.

57 Katherine Kirk, "How Russia Sows Confusion in the U.S. Vaccine Debate," *Foreign Policy*, April 9, 2019, https://foreignpolicy.com/2019/04/09/in-the-united-states-russian-trolls-are-peddling-measles-disinformation-on-twitter.

58 Broad, "Putin's Long War."

59 Kirk, "How Russia Sows Confusion."

7 Where We've Been, Where We're Going

1 Lily Hay Newman, "The Russian Disinfo Operation You Never Heard About," *Wired*, June 16, 2020, www.wired.com/story/russia-secondary-infektion-disinformation.

2 Atlantic Council DFRLab, "Operation Secondary Infektion," www. atlanticcouncil.org/wp-content/uploads/2019/08/Operation-Secondary-Infektion_English.pdf.

3 Bennett, Lawrence, and Livingston (eds.), *When the Press Fails*, 43; Paul Farhi, "For Broadcast Media, Patriotism Pays," *Washington Post*, March 28, 2003.

4 https://media.breitbart.com/media/2019/11/about-breitbart-news.pdf.

5 See Kathleen Hall Jamieson, *Cyberwar: How Russian Hackers and Trolls Helped Elect a President* (New York: Oxford University Press, 2018).

6 Sheera Frenkel and Julian E. Barnes, "Russians Again Targeting Americans with Disinformation, Facebook and Twitter Say," *New York Times*, September 1, 2020.

7 https://peacedata.net.

8 "Return of the Paranoid Style," *The Economist*, June 6, 2020, 49.

9 Pincus, "A General's View."

10 "4th Military Information Support Operations Group," www.military.com/special-operations/4th-military-information-support-operations-group.html.

11 Pincus, "A General's View."

12 Steven Bradley, "Securing the United States from Online Disinformation – A Whole-of-Society Approach," Carnegie Endowment for International Peace, August 24, 2020, https://carnegieendowment.org/2020/08/24/securing-united-states-from-online-disinformation-whole-of-society-approach-pub-82549.

13 Robert M. Gates, *Exercise of Power: American Failures, Successes, and a New Path Forward in the Post-Cold War World* (New York: Knopf, 2020), 375–6.

14 Jens Stoltenberg, "Remarks: Strengthening the Alliance in an Increasingly Competitive World," June 8, 2020, www.nato.int/cps/en/natohq/opinions_176197.htm.

15 Graham Allison, *Destined for War: Can America and China Escape Thucydides's Trap?* (New York: Houghton Mifflin Harcourt / Mariner, 2018), 149.

16 Pamment, "The EU's Role in Fighting Disinformation."

17 Jude Blanchette and Seth G. Jones, "The U.S. Is Losing the Information War with China," *Wall Street Journal*, June 16, 2020.

18 Quoted in Jean-Baptiste Jeangene Vilmer and Paul Charon, "Russia as a Hurricane, China as Climate Change: Different Ways of Information Warfare," *War on the Rocks*, January 21, 2020, https://warontherocks.com/2020/01/russia-as-a-hurricane-china-as-climate-change-different-ways-of-information-warfare.

19 Thomas Grove, "Russia Gives China a Leg Up in Foreign Broadcasting," *Wall Street Journal*, January 14, 2020.

20 Andrew Krepinevich and Barry Watts, *The Last Warrior: Andrew Marshall and the Shaping of Modern American Defense Strategy* (New York: Basic Books, 2015), 240.

21 Office of the Secretary of Defense, *Annual Report to Congress: Military and Security Developments Involving the People's Republic of China 2019*, 112, https://media.defense.gov/2019/May/02/2002127082/-1/-1/1/2019_CHINA_MILITARY_POWER_REPORT.pdf.
22 Office of the Secretary of Defense, *Annual Report*, 113.
23 Reporters Without Borders, *China's Pursuit of a New World Media Order*, March 2019, https://rsf.org/sites/default/files/en_rapport_chine_web_final.pdf.
24 Vilmer and Charon, "Russia as a Hurricane, China as Climate Change."
25 Katie Paul and Pei Li, "Twitter Takes Down Beijing-Backed Influence Operation Pushing Coronavirus Messages," *New York Times*, June 11, 2020.
26 Peter Mattis, "China's 'Three Warfares' in Perspective," *War on the Rocks*, January 30, 2018, https://warontherocks.com/2018/01/chinas-three-warfares-perspective.
27 Doug Livermore, "China's 'Three Warfares' in Theory and Practice in the South China Sea," *Georgetown Security Studies Review*, March 25, 2018, https://georgetownsecuritystudiesreview.org/2018/03/25/chinas-three-warfares-in-theory-and-practice-in-the-south-china-sea.
28 Hillary Rodham Clinton, "Internet Rights and Wrongs: Choices and Challenges in a Networked World," speech at The George Washington University, February 15, 2011, www.state.gov/secretary/rm/2011/02/156619.htm#.

Selected Bibliography

Addario, Lynsey. *It's What I Do: A Photographer's Life of Love and War*. New York: Penguin, 2015.

Allan, Stuart, and Barbie Zelizer. *Reporting War: Journalism in Wartime*. London: Routledge, 2004.

Arlen, Michael J. *Living-Room War*. New York: Viking, 1969.

Arnett, Peter. *Live from the Battlefield*. New York: Simon & Schuster, 1994.

Bell, Martin. *In Harm's Way*. London: Penguin, 1996.

Bennett, W. Lance, Regina G. Lawrence, and Steven Livingston. *When the Press Fails: Political Power and the News Media from Iraq to Katrina*. University of Chicago Press, 2007.

Bennett, W. Lance, and David L. Paletz. *Taken by Storm: The Media, Public Opinion, and Foreign Policy in the Gulf War*. University of Chicago Press, 1994.

Braestrup, Peter. *Big Story*. Abridged version: Novato, CA: Presidio Press, 1994.

Brose, Christian. *The Kill Chain: Defending America in the Future of High-Tech Warfare*. New York: Hachette, 2020.

Brown, Katherine A. *Your Country, Our War: The Press and Diplomacy in Afghanistan*. New York: Oxford University Press, 2019.

Cull, Nicholas John. *Selling War: The British Propaganda Campaign against American "Neutrality" in World War II*. New York: Oxford University Press, 1995.

Dennis, Everette E. (ed.). *The Media at War*. New York: Gannett Foundation Media Center, 1991.

Freedman, Lawrence. *Ukraine and the Art of Strategy*. New York: Oxford University Press, 2019.

Giles, Keir. *The Next Phase of Russian Information Warfare*. Riga, Latvia: NATO Strategic Communications Centre of Excellence, 2016.

Gutman, Roy. *A Witness to Genocide*. New York: Macmillan, 1993.

Hallin, Daniel. *The "Uncensored War": The Media and Vietnam*. Berkeley: University of California Press, 1989.

Hankir, Zahra (ed.). *Our Women on the Ground: Essays by Arab Women Reporting from the Arab World*. New York: Penguin, 2019.

Harris, Robert. *Gotcha! The Media, the Government, and the Falklands Crisis*. London: Faber and Faber, 1983.

Hemming, Henry. *Agents of Influence: A British Campaign, a Canadian Spy, and the Secret Plot to Bring America into World War II*. New York: PublicAffairs, 2019.

Hoffman, Joyce. *On Their Own: Women Journalists and the American Experience in Vietnam*. Cambridge, MA: Da Capo Press, 2008.

Jamieson, Kathleen Hall. *Cyberwar: How Russian Hackers and Trolls Helped Elect a President*. New York: Oxford University Press, 2018.

Jankowicz, Nina. *How To Lose the Information War: Russia, Fake News, and the Future of Conflict*. London: I. B. Tauris, 2020.

Jones, Seth G. *A Covert Action: Reagan, the CIA, and the Cold War Struggle in Poland*. New York: W. W. Norton, 2020.

Kalb, Marvin. *Imperial Gamble: Putin, Ukraine, and the New Cold War*. Washington: Brookings Institution, 2015.

Karnow, Stanley. *Vietnam: A History*. New York: Penguin, 1991.

Matheson, Donald, and Stuart Allan. *Digital War Reporting*. Cambridge: Polity, 2009.

Merrin, William. *Digital War: A Critical Introduction*. London: Routledge, 2019.

Murrow, Edward R. *This Is London*. New York: Simon & Schuster, 1941.

Oberdorfer, Don. *Tet*. New York: Avon, 1971.

Patrikarakos, David. *War in 140 Characters*. New York: Basic Books, 2017.

Power, Samantha. *"A Problem from Hell": America and the Age of Genocide*. New York: Basic Books, 2002.

Prochnau, William. *Once Upon a Distant War*. New York: Times Books, 1995.

Rid, Thomas. *Active Measures: The Secret History of Disinformation and Political Warfare*. New York: Farrar, Straus and Giroux, 2020.

Rieff, David. *Slaughterhouse: Bosnia and the Failure of the West*. New York: Simon & Schuster, 1995.

Robinson, Piers, Philip Seib, and Romy Froehlich (eds.). *Routledge Handbook of Media, Conflict and Security*. London: Routledge, 2017.

Saunders, Frances Stonor. *The Cultural Cold War: The CIA and the World of Arts and Letters*. New York: New Press, 1999.

Seib, Philip. *As Terrorism Evolves: Media, Religion, and Governance*. Cambridge University Press, 2017.

Beyond the Front Lines: How the News Media Cover a World Shaped by War. New York: Palgrave Macmillan, 2004.

The Global Journalist: News and Conscience in a World of Conflict. Lanham, MD: Rowman and Littlefield, 2002.

Headline Diplomacy: How News Coverage Affects Foreign Policy. Westport, CT: Praeger, 1997.

Singer, P. W., and Emerson T. Brooking. *Like War: The Weaponization of Social Media.* New York: Houghton Mifflin Harcourt, 2018.

Sontag, Susan. *On Photography.* New York: Picador, 1990.

Stengel, Richard. *Information Wars: How We Lost the Global Battle against Disinformation.* New York: Atlantic Monthly Press, 2019.

Thompson, Allan (ed.). *Media and Mass Atrocity: The Rwanda Genocide and Beyond.* Waterloo, ON: Center for International Governance Innovation (CIGI), 2019.

Tomlin, Gregory M. *Murrow's Cold War: Public Diplomacy for the Kennedy Administration.* Dulles, VA: Potomac Books, 2016.

Index

ABC News 33
Abkhazia 122
Abu Ghraib prison 60, 62, 101–2
"active measures" 130
Adams, Eddie 36, 99
Addario, Lynsey 102
Adie, Kate 89
Afghanistan 58, 61, 154-5, 161
  Afghan National Army 154
  cellphone use 154
  foreign news coverage of 155
  internet access 154
  reconstruction 155
  social media influence 154
  US invasion of 54, 56
  US role 154
Afghanistan Papers project 96
age and media usage 163, 164
  Arab world 164
  India 164
  United Kingdom 164
AIDS 174
Alaoui, Leila 89
Al Arabiya 64, 152
algorithms 13
Alhamza, Abdelaziz 84

Al Jazeera 58, 63, 65, 152
"Al Jazeera effect" 64
Allam, Hannah 90
Allan, Stuart 101
Allison, Graham 28, 180
Al Qaeda 3, 12, 56, 61, 103–5, 154
  Global Islamic Media Front 104
  see also September 11 terrorist
    attacks
Al Shabaab 12, 86–7
Alsop, Joseph 31
Alter, Jonathan 49
Al Udeid air base 152
Amanpour, Christiane 80, 82, 172
Amaq News Agency (Islamic State)
  104
American Civil War 99, 111
Amnesty International 87
Annan, Kofi 70
Ansar Dine 112–13
Arab uprisings (2011) 63–5
  results 65
  social media 63
  television 63
Ardern, Jacinda 106
Argentina 44-5

Arlen, Michael 34-5
Arnett, Peter 36
Aro, Jessika 146–7
Arraf, Jane 90
artificial intelligence (AI) 13, 106,
    158–60, 175
Asberg, Sebastian 144
al-Assad, Bashar 11, 63, 65, 156
Associated Press 100
asymmetric warfare 159
Atlantic Council 174
autonomous weapon systems 159,
    160

Bahrain 152
Baltic States 138–44, 180
    as NATO members 138–9, 143–4
    population statistics 139
Bardenwerper, Will 157
Barghoorn, Frederick C. 121
Battle of New Orleans 172–3
Bay of Pigs 26–7
BBC News 45, 64, 83
Bell, Emily 106
Bell, Martin 73, 75, 79–80, 82, 172
Bellingcat 86–7, 167
Berg, Nicholas 105
bias 86
Biden, Joseph 176
Big Story 40
biometric data 159
blockade of Qatar 152–3
blogging 61–2
Boko Haram 12, 86
Borghard, Erica 133
Bos, Michele 112–13
Bosnia War 72–5, 77, 79, 80
    Muslims 74, 75
    public opinion 73, 74
    Serbs 74
Boston Marathon terrorist attack
    (2013) 105
Bots 152

defined 2
Bracken, Brendan 22–3, 116
Bradlee, Benjamin 32
Brady, Mathew 99
Braestrup, Peter 40
Breedlove, Philip 136, 139
Breitbart.com 176
Brinkley, David 33
British Army 126–7
Broad, William J. 167
Brooking, Emerson 129, 130
Brose, Christian 158, 160
Brown, Katherine 155
Brussels terrorist attack (2016) 104
Bundy, McGeorge 28
Burma *see* Myanmar
Burns, William J. 81
Bush, George H. W. 46–53, 76
Bush, George W. 54–60, 176

Cameron, Lori 159
Cankao Xiaoxi newspaper 181
Cantril, Hadley 21–2
car bombings 90
Carnegie Endowment for
    International Peace 169, 180
Caro, Robert 41
Carr, David 101
Castro, Fidel 26
Catledge, Turner 26–7
CBS News 33, 37, 161
cellphones 10, 65
    user statistics 97
censorship 5, 9, 44–5, 49, 50–1
Center for Media Literacy 164
Centers for Disease Control and
    Prevention (CDC) 168, 170
Central African Republic 93
Central Intelligence Agency (CIA)
    30–1, 114, 173
    covert operations in Poland 121
    Propaganda Assets Inventory 119
Chadwick, Paul 107

Chamberlain, Neville 17, 173
Cheney, Dick 47
China 12, 78, 149, 173, 179–85
  Chinese Communist Party (CCP)
    181
Confucius Institutes 181, 182
differences from Russian information
    strategy 181
  economy 180
  English-language training 181
  media venues 183
  pandemic disinformation 169,
    183–4
  People's Liberation Army (PLA)
    182, 184
  South China Sea strategy 184–5
  "Three Warfares" strategy 15,
    181–5
    defined 182
  trade war with United States 182
  Xi Jinping 181
China Global Television Network
    (CGTN) 183
China International Broadcast
    Network 183
China Radio International 183
China Watch 183
Chinese diaspora 182, 183
Christchurch (NZ) terrorist attack
    (2019) 105
Churchill, Winston 22–3, 116, 118
"churn" 173, 174
citizen journalists 6, 11, 83–6
Citizens for a Free Kuwait 47
City of Ghosts 84–5
civilian casualties 11
Clarke, Richard D. 160, 178
Clifford, Clark 26, 36, 37
climate issues 167
Clinton, Bill 69–70, 77
Clinton, Hillary 131–2, 176, 186
Clooney Foundation for Justice 92
CNN 48, 51–2, 64, 72

Cold War 118–22
Cole, Jonathan 126
"collateral damage" 6, 68, 186
Colvin, Marie 89
Confucius Institutes 181, 182
conspiracy theories 128, 177
  AIDS 170
  ebola 170
Costello, Katherine 147
counterinsurgency 113
Covering Climate Now project 167
Covid-19 pandemic 14, 168, 169,
    173
Cox's Bazar (Bangladesh) 75
credibility 6, 8, 39–40, 61, 175
Crimean War 44, 99
Cronkite, Walter 33, 37–8, 161
crowd-sourcing 86
Cuban Missile Crisis 27–9
CuentaNos 92
cyberattacks 14
Czechoslovakia 17

Daily Telegraph 89
Dallaire, Romeo 70
Dao, James 62
Darnovsky, Marcy 50
deepfakes 6
  defined 2–3
DeGhett, Torie Rose 100
Department of Defense (US) 48–9,
    51, 52, 53, 114
  evaluation of China 182
  Iraq War news coverage policies
    57–9, 61–2
  Special Operations Command
    (SOCOM) 160, 178
  use of autonomous weapon systems
    159, 160
Department of Justice (US) 130
Department of State (US) 97, 114
  tracking pandemic disinformation
    169

Deutsche Welle 140
DeYoung, Karen 55
Di Giovanni, Janine 89
disinformation 14–15, 130, 143, 151–3
 countermeasures 161–71
 defined 2
 medical issues 168–71
Donovan, Bill 117
Doucet, Lyse 89
Douma (Syria) chemical attack 86
Dover (Delaware) US Air Force Base 50–1
drones 87, 159
Duke University Reporters' Lab 166
Dulles, Allen 119
Dryfoos, Orville 27
Dunkirk 5

East Asia Forum 77
echo chamber 128
The Economist 134, 147
Egypt 63, 64, 152
"elves" 142–3
embedding journalists 9–10, 57–9, 89, 177–8
Emergency Telecommunications Cluster (ETC) 92–3
Engel, Richard 63–4, 156
Erdogan, Recep Tayyip 147
Erhaim, Zaina 90
Estonia 138–41
 cyberattack from Russia (2007) 141, 143, 174
Estonian Public Broadcasting 140
similarities to Ukraine case 141
Ethiopia 76
European Union (EU) 135, 138
 EU Stratcom Task Force 137–8
 EUvsDisinfo reports 137, 165
Evans, Harold 100–1
"expeditionary diplomats" 114

Faas, Horst 89
Facebook 6, 63, 88, 165, 183
 Afghanistan use 155
 "friends'" influence 128
 Russian influence on African content 149
fact-checking 166
"fake news" 3
Falklands War 9, 43–6
 British public opinion 45, 46
 television news coverage 45
Female Engagement Teams 114
Finland 120–1, 146–7, 164–5, 180
 online attacks on journalist Jessika Aro 146–7
opposition to joining NATO 146
 population statistics 146
 public broadcasting (YLE) 146
 relationship with Russia 146
 trolls' attacks 146–7
"Finlandization" 121
Floyd, George 171
forensic journalism 167
Fox News 56, 175–6
Freedman, Lawrence 138, 139
Froelich, Romy 90
Fuller, Jack 59

Gaddis, John Lewis 118
Galeotti, Mark 124
Gallup Poll 21, 37
Gannett Foundation 48
gatekeepers 4–5, 12–13, 28–9, 154, 186
 social media as alternatives 162
Gates, Robert M. 179
Gaza 11–12, 108–11
Gellhorn, Martha 89
gender issues 113–14, 147, 154
genocide defined 69
Georgia 122
Gerasimov, Valery 124, 161
 "Gerasimov doctrine" 124, 126

rules of war 124
Germany 17, 174
Gillespie, Marie 92
Glavset *see* Internet Research Agency
globalization 173
Global Positioning System (GPS) 92
Global Research 170
"global village" 173
globedia.com 174
Goebbels, Joseph 5
Goldwater, Barry 39
Google 165
Google Earth Pro 87–8
Gowan, Richard 156
Gowing, Nik 156
Graham, Philip 27
"Grand Theft Auto" 84
Grenada 53
Grossman, Lawrence 47
Grossman, Marc 114
Grossman, Shelby 149
GRU *see* Russia, Main Intelligence
    Directorate
Guardian 106–7, 165
Gulf War (1990–1) 9, 46–53
    Arab public opinion 52
casualties 50–1, 53, 100
news photographs 100–1
television news coverage 47–8, 50,
    51–2
        local television stations 48–9
    US public opinion 47
Gutman, Roy 72, 74

Haass, Richard 61
Haeberle, Ron 99
Haftar, Khalifa 150
Hajj, Adnan 102
Halberstam, David 8, 29–31, 59
Halle, Germany terrorist attack
    (2019) 106
Hallin, Daniel 36–7
Hamas 11–12

Hamas–Israel Wars 108–11
    casualties 109, 110
    narratives 111
    social media strategies 109, 110
    Twitter use 109, 110, 111
Harris, Robert 44
Healey, Denis 45
Heineman, Matthew 84
Hemming, Henry 116–17
Herodotus 91
Hersh, Seymour 99
Hezbollah 85
Higgins, Marguerite 31
Hill and Knowlton 47
Hilsum, Lindsey 85
Hoffman, Joyce 89
Hollingworth, Clare 89
Holocaust 143
Homer 1–2, 15, 91, 172
homment.com 174
Hong Kong 173, 182, 183
Hoopes, Townsend 38
Hoskins, Andrew 98
Hotel Rwanda 78
Hull, Peggy 89
Hultqvist, Peter 145
Hunter-Gault, Charlayne 71
Huntley, Chet 33
Hurd, Douglas 80–1
Hussein, Saddam 46, 51–2, 54, 58
hybrid warfare 14, 139, 144
hypersonic weapons 160

Ignatius, David 133
Iliad 1–2, 88
indybay.org 174
InfoMigrants 92
"information beat" coverage 166,
    168
information freedom 186, 187
"information hegemony" 5
information laundering 169–70
information value 178

InfoRos 170
In Harm's Way 79
Instagram 102, 183
insurgencies 65
International Crisis Group 156
International Rescue Committee 92
internet freedom 186
internet monitoring 66
Internet of Things (IoT) 158–60
Internet Research Agency (IRA)
     129–33, 137, 142, 162, 175
  employees' tasks 129
  Facebook accounts 131
  false news stories 129–30
  stolen American identities 131
  targeted by US Cyber Command
     (2018) 132–3
  Twitter accounts 131
  US presidential election (2016)
     130–2, 176
  US presidential election (2020) 176
internet use statistics 94–5
Ioffe, Julia 122–3
Iran 66, 152
  pandemic disinformation 169
Iraq 46, 90
Iraq War (2003–) 9, 54–62, 111, 177
  casualties 60
  embedded journalists 9–10, 57–9,
     89, 177–8
  global public opinion 54, 58, 59–60
  news coverage flaws 54–5
  photography 101–2
  social media 61
  "unilateral" journalists 58
  US public opinion 54, 57, 59
  weapons of mass destruction
     (WMDs) 55, 60
IREX 165–6
  Ukraine program 165–6
Islamic State (IS) 12, 14, 84, 85, 91,
     114, 147, 153
  in Afghanistan 154–5

media use 105
  recruiting 107–8
  territory 103
Islas Malvinas *see* Falklands War
Israel 50
  see also Hamas–Israel Wars
Israel Defense Forces (IDF) 11–12, 91
Israel–Hezbollah War (2006) 102
Iwo Jima 99
Izvestia 122

Jackson, Andrew 172
Jankowicz, Nina 166
Japan 185
Jarecke, Kenneth 100
Jenkins, Peter 46
Jennings, Peter 74
Jihad Recollections 105
Johnson, Lyndon B. 26, 33–5, 47
Jones, Seth G. 121
Jordan 92
"journalism of attachment" 11, 78–9,
     186
journalism education 166
journalists' ethics 3, 4, 25
  see also objectivity
Joyce, Rob 181

Kafr Nabl Surgical Hospital 88
Kartapolov, Andrei 126
Kellner, Douglas 52
Kennan, George 41
Kennedy, John F. 27–8, 30–3, 38, 120
Kennedy, Joseph P. 22
Kennicott, Philip 101
Kenya 86
KGB *see* Russia, Federal Security
     Service (FSB)
Khabrona 92
Khrushchev, Nikita 28
Kirk, Katherine 171
Kissinger, Henry 4
Kivinem, Kari 165

Knight Ridder / McClatchy 56
Koppel, Ted 49
Kragh, Martin 144
Krepinevich, Andrew 182
Kristof, Nicholas 76
Krugman, Paul 56
Krutaine, Aija 140
Kurtz, Howard 61
Kuwait 43

language skills 142, 149
Latvia 134, 138–40, 142, 143
Lenin, V. I. 121–2
Lerner, Peter 110, 111
Libération (France) 100
Libya 93, 149–50
Life magazine 99
Limbaugh, Rush 175
Lindbergh, Charles 22
listening 179
Lithuania 138–43, 169
  banning Russian TV channels 140
  Demaskuok software 142
  micro-information tracking 141
  news media hacked 141
Livermore, Doug 184, 185
Lojdquist, Fredrik 145–6
London Blitz 18–25, 50
  American response 18–19
  casualties and damage 18
  effect on 1940 US presidential
    campaign 20
London terrorist bombings (2005) 83
Los Angeles Times 49

Maass, Peter 72
MacFarquhar, Neil 123
MacLeish, Archibald 25
Malaysia Airlines flight MH 17 86
Mali 112–13
mal-information 2
Massachusetts Institute of Technology
  162

Matheson, Donald 101
Matthews, Miriam 127
Mattis, Jim 152
Mattis, Peter 184
McKinley, William 5
McLuhan, Marshall 173
McNamara, Robert 26
media literacy 14, 151, 164–6, 177
  defined 164
  in school curricula 165
medical issues 168
Medium 174
Meldrum, Andrew 56
Melissen, Jan 112–13
Mercy Corps 92
Meyer, Eugene 23
MI6 (UK) 116
Ministry of Defence (UK) 44
Ministry of Information (UK) 22, 116
misinformation 2
MISO (Military Information Support
    Operations) 113, 178
  WebOps Center 179
Missick, Chris 62
Mrs. Miniver 5
Mubarak, Hosni 64
Mueller, Robert S., III 130
Mueller Report 131
  indictments cited 131
Murrow, Edward R. 3, 7, 50, 52,
    116, 172
  broadcasts from London 18–25
  supporting truthful propaganda
    120
  United States Information Agency
    (USIA) director 119–20
Muslim Brotherhood 152
Myanmar 75–8
  ethnic cleansing 76
  Facebook role 76
  public opinion 76
  refugees 75
  religions 76, 77

Myanmar (*cont.*)
 Rohingya 75, 77, 78
My Lai massacre 99–100

Nachtwey, James 81–2
Nakashima, Ellen 133
Nakasone, Paul M. 132–3
narratives 111
 Cold War narratives 118
National Association of Broadcasters 39
National Defense Authorization Act 2020 (US) 179
National Movement for Liberation of Azawad (MNLA) 112–13
"national security" 29, 42
National Security Agency (US) 132
NATO 14, 135, 143, 169
 Article 5 provisions 138, 143
 updated 143–4
 China 180
 report on Russian strategy (2016) 125
 Strategic Communications Centre of Excellence 134–5, 142
NBC News 33, 41
Neuman, Johanna 50
Newman, Lily Hay 174
"news" defined 163
Newsweek magazine 49
New Yorker magazine 34
New York Times 30, 55–6, 76, 96, 167
 Bay of Pigs coverage 26–7
 Cuban Missile Crisis coverage 27–8
 Syria hospital bombing investigation 87–8
Ngo Dinh Diem 30
Ngo Dinh Nhu 30
Nguyen Nao Loan 36
Nguyen Van Lem 36
Nicolson, Adam 15
Nigeria 86

Ninisto, Sauli 164
Nixon, Richard 26
noncombatants 186
non-governmental organizations (NGOs) 67, 92
nuclear weapons 180
Nye, Joseph 104

Obama, Barack 3, 81, 156
objectivity 72, 80
O'Brien, Tim 157
Observer newspaper (UK) 100–1
Ofcom (UK) 177
O'Loughlin, Ben 98
Operation Cast Lead (2008–9) *see* Hamas–Israel Wars
Operation Infektion 170, 174
Operation Pillar of Defense (2012) *see* Hamas–Israel Wars
Operation Protective Edge (2014) *see* Hamas–Israel Wars
optics 8
O'Reilly, Mary Boyle 89
Overseas News Agency (ONA) 117
Ovide, Shira 163

Palestinian Legislative Council 208
Pamment, James 180
Panama 53
pandemics 168
Panorama 80
paparazzi 2
Patrikarakos, David 110–11, 136
patriotism 4, 56–7, 59
Paul, Christopher 127
PeaceData.net 176
Pearl Harbor attack (1941) 117
Pentagon *see* Department of Defense
Pentagon Papers 96
Pew Research Center 43, 59, 163
Philippines 185
photography 81–2, 87, 98–103
 distortion 102–3

history 99
  social media dissemination 102–3
  soldiers' photographs 101–2
  Vietnam War 99–100
Pincus, Walter 55, 179
Platoon 157
Poland 121
politicized journalism 161
Pomfret, John 181
popular culture 5, 78, 117, 157
Poroshenko, Petro 136, 137
Powell, Colin 47
Power, Samantha 77
Pravda 122
Prigozhin, Yevgeniy 131, 149
Prochnau, William 29
propaganda 52–3, 117–18, 123, 140
  as percentage of war 126
  cultural propaganda 118
PSYOPS (psychological operations)
    113
  see also MISO
public diplomacy 112–14, 118, 124
Putin, Vladimir 116, 122, 123, 181
  Ukraine 135, 137
Pym, Francis 44

Qaddafi, Saif al-Islam 150
Qatar 151–3
"Qatar Insider" 153
Qatar News Agency 151–3

racism 71
radio 20, 22
  US audience 23, 25
Radio Free Europe 121
Radio Télévision Libre des Mille
    Collines (Rwanda) 70–1
Rafi, Habibullah 154
Raqqa (Syria) 84
"Raqqa Is Being Slaughtered Silently"
    (RBSS) 84
Rather, Dan 56

Reagan, Ronald 47, 121
"rebel diplomacy" 112–13
Reddit 174
Reeves, Richard 32
Refugee.info 92
refugees 13
  defined 91
  escape techniques 92
  statistics 91
  use of cellphones 91
regulation 177
Reporters Without Borders 183
"responsibility to protect" 77
Reston, James 27–8
Restrepo 157
retweets 152
Reuters 102
Reuters Institute for the Study of
    Journalism 163
Revere, Paul 83
RIA Novosti 122
Rid, Thomas 137
Riefenstahl, Leni 5
Rieff, David 72, 73
"right to know" 42
robots on battlefield 160
Rohingya *see* Myanmar
Roosevelt, Eleanor 22
Roosevelt, Franklin D. 7, 20, 21
  aiding British 116–18
  fireside chats 23–4
Rosenberg, Howard 78
Rosenman, Sam 20
Rostow, Walt 39
Royal Navy (UK) 44
RT 95, 122, 123, 128
  audience 123
  China-related content 182
  coverage of Russia–Georgia War
    (2008) 122–3
Rumsfeld, Donald 96
Russia 6, 13–14, 66, 85, 88, 114,
    116, 166, 179–80, 186

Russia (*cont.*)
  differences from Chinese
    information strategy 181
  Federal Security Service (FSB) 137
  in Afghanistan 154–5
  information warfare troops 124,
    129, 178
  interference in US presidential
    election (2016) 130–2, 175
  Main Intelligence Directorate of
    the General Staff (GRU) 133,
    136–7, 170
  pandemic disinformation 169–70,
    174
  relations with Baltic States
    138–44
  Ukraine invaded by 135, 165
  see also Soviet Union
Russian "Firehose of Falsehood"
  Information Model (RAND
  report) 127
Russian Ministry of Defense 125
  definition of "information war"
    125–6
Russia Today 122
  see also RT
Rutenberg, Jim 123
Rwanda 69–71
Ryan, Paul 132

Sahel 112–13
Salman, Mohammed bin 152
Salminem, Esko 121
Sanger, David 130, 135
satellite dishes 66
satellite telephones 51–2
satellite transmission 9, 54
Saudi Arabia 152–3
Saunders, Francis Stonor 119
Schandler, Herbert 36
Secondary Infektion 174
Second Intifada (2000) 64
Second World War 5, 7, 18–25

British information operations
    116–18
  news photography 99
  Tokyo and Dresden firebombings
    98
US public opinion 21–2
secrecy 96–7
September 11 terrorist attacks (2001)
    10, 54, 60, 103
  NATO Treaty Article 5 138–9
Sevareid, Eric 3, 21, 24
Sherwood, Robert 20
Shirer, William L. 3
Shirky, Clay 64
Shoigu, Sergei 124–5
Siarurusevicius, Audrius 140
Signpost 92
Singer, P. W. 129, 130, 160
Skirpal, Sergei 86
Sky News Arabia 152
social media 94–7
  as news provider 163
  as organizing tool 63, 96
  venues' creation dates 95
Social Media Data and Threat
    Analysis Center 179
sockpuppets 128
Solidarity movement 121
Somalia 76, 86, 113
Sontag, Susan 98–9
South China Sea 95, 184–5
South Ossetia 122
South Park 105
South Sudan 93
Soviet Union 27–9, 118–22
  dissolution of 143
  in Afghanistan 154
  troops in Baltic States 143
  see also Russia
Spanish–American War 5
Special Operations Command
    (SOCOM) 178
Sperber, A. M. 22

Sputnik News 123, 128, 145
  Dari content 155
  Turkish-language content 148
Stalin, Joseph 68
Stephenson, William 116, 117
Stoltenberg, Jens 144, 169, 180
Sudan 85–6
Sudan Media Capacity-Building
    Project 85
Sulzberger, Arthur O. 31
Summers, Julia 137
Sun newspaper (UK) 45
Sweden 144–6
  relationship with NATO 144
    disinformation about NATO 145
  Russian interference in 144–5
Syria 63
Syrian War 3, 11, 65–6
  casualties 66
  citizen journalism 84
  global public opinion 66, 156
  refugees 66

Taiwan 173, 183
Taliban 58, 154
TASS 122, 128
Telegram 88, 104, 112
television news 34–5, 38, 98, 123,
    139–40
  centrist influence 128
"Tennessee GOP" 131
terrorism 103–8
  defined 104
  media use 103–8
  recruiting 107–8
  responses to 106–7
  targeting tourists 107
  video of attacks and executions 105
  see also Al Qaeda; Islamic State
Tet offensive 4, 35–9
Al-Thani, Tamim bin Hamad 151
Thatcher, Margaret 44–5
Theiss, Evelyn 99–100

TheRussophile 167
The Things They Carried 157
Thomas, Elise 168
Thomson Foundation 85
Tillerson, Rex 152
Time 100, 148
Tomlin, Gregory M. 120
torture 60, 101–2
Treaty of Ghent 172
Trethowan, Ian 46
Triumph of the Will 5
Trojan War 1–2
trolls 13, 129, 141–2
  Chinese 183
  defined 2
  hybrid trolls 142
Trotta, Liz 89
Trump, Donald 3, 79, 130, 131, 152
  impeachment (2019) 131
  use of Twitter 162
  Trump campaign (2016) 131, 132
  Russian involvement 132
  vote results 132
Tunisia 63
Turkey 2, 84, 147–9, 152
  public opinion about Russia and
      United States 148
relationship with NATO 148
  relationship with Russia 148
Twitch 106
Twitter 4, 6, 12, 63, 128
  China-related content 183–4
  relied on as information source 163
  rumors on 162–3

Uighur Muslims 182
Ukraine 6, 13, 114, 131, 135–8, 139,
    180
  Crimea 135, 137
  cyberattacks on 135, 137
  disinformation 136, 138
  Donbas 135, 138
  Euromaidan movement 135

Ukraine (*cont.*)
  Facebook 136
  media literacy programs 165–6
  pandemic rumors 168–9
  population statistics 136
  television 136
  Twitter 136
  war with Russia (2014–) 135
    casualties 135
UNESCO 2
Unian News (Ukraine) 95
United Arab Emirates 152–3
United Front Work Department
  (China) 183
United Kingdom 7, 43–6, 85, 126
  Brexit referendum (2016) 13, 166
  see also British Army
United Nations 69, 77–8, 92
  High Commissioner for Refugees
    91
  Security Council 77–8
United States Cyber Command 132–3
United States Information Agency
  (USIA) 120
Ut, Nick 99

vaccinations 14, 171
"Vietnam syndrome" 39–40, 44, 59
Vietnam War 4, 7–8, 10, 25–41, 43,
  49, 53
  casualties 33
  public opinion 25–6, 37
  television news coverage 34–5, 177
  US troop numbers 33
Viner, Katherine 106–7
Vkontakte 136, 137
Voice of America 121, 140

Wagner Group 150
Wallin, Matthew 113
Waltzman, Rand 125

War and the Death of News 79
war defined 115–16, 138
War of 1812 17, 172
"war on terror" 60
War Photographer 82
Warsaw Pact 121
Warsaw Uprising (1944) 83
Washington Post 40, 55, 96
Watson Institute (Brown University)
  60
Watts, Barry 182
weaponization of information 5
WeChat 183
Westmoreland, William 36
Weston, Edward 102
WhatsApp 85
Wheeler, Earle 36
Whitman, Bryan 58
WikiLeaks 96, 97
Willkie, Wendell 20, 21
Winter, Charlie 104
Wintour, Charles 46
women
  women combatants 91
women war correspondents 89–90
  women war victims 89, 90
Women's Protection Units (Kurds) 91
World Health Organization (WHO)
  168
Wuhan, China 169

Yanukovych, Viktor 135
Yemen 87
YouTube 6, 65, 105–6
Yuhas, Alan 137

al-Zarqawi, Abu Musab 105
Zedong, Mao 184
Zeitzoff, Thomas 111
Zelensky, Volodymyr 136
Zelizer, Barbie 98